Campaign 2001

Campaign 2001

Nicholas Jones

First published in Great Britain 2001
Politico's Publishing
8 Artillery Row
Westminster
London
SW1P 1RZ

www.politicospublishing.co.uk

A catalogue record for this book is available from the British Library.

ISBN 1 902301 78 1

Printed and bound by Creative Print and Design

Contents

Preface

A suggestion from my publisher that I write an account of the 2001 general election campaign was irresistible. Preparing my books on the 1992 and 1997 elections was a source of great personal satisfaction, and I relished the chance to compile what I hope will be seen as a fair and faithful record of the highs and lows of a third campaign. I have found writing political books highly rewarding – but also a time-consuming and costly self-indulgence. My books have all been written during holidays or unpaid leave, and while I have no complaint whatsoever about criticism of my work or my ideas, I do wish the Labour Party's spin doctors would check their facts. Alastair Campbell, the Prime Minister's newly appointed director of communications and strategy, has made no secret of what he considers is the unfairness of a BBC political correspondent being 'subsidised' by the licence-payer to write books which are critical of Blair's government. Charlie Whelan, a former press adviser to the Chancellor, Gordon Brown, suggests that I have taken to boasting about being a well-paid author. After a contribution I made for a BBC Radio Four programme, *Why I Hate . . . Spin Doctors*, Whelan asserted with confidence that '[Jones] admits he has made a tidy income out of his series of alarmist book on spin doctors.' So, just for the record, the media monitors at Millbank Tower might like to know what happened when I departed on six weeks' unpaid leave to write *Campaign 2001*. Even before I managed finally to escape the office and start writing, I was told that the six weeks' salary which I was about to give up had already been reallocated and was going to be spent by the BBC paying for the installation of a permanent feed point for television cameras and radio microphones outside Conservative Central Office, ready for use in live broadcasts during the Tory leadership election contest. So not only do I hope readers might find my account of the 2001 general election of interest; they will know that by writing it, I contributed indirectly to one small advance in the democratic process and ensured the even faster reporting of the twists and turns in the contest to choose William Hague's successor.

Introduction

Despite the best efforts of politicians, reporters and broadcasters, the 2001 general election became notorious for entirely the wrong reason. Almost five million fewer voters went to the polling stations than in 1997 and the turnout of 59.4 per cent, down by 12 per cent in four years, was the lowest for any general election since 1918, an outcome which shocked MPs and should lead to some soul-searching in the news media. Many reasons have been advanced for the massive drop in participation: the seeming inevitability of the result; a healthy economy; a general feeling of well-being in the country at large; and a growing sense of disenchantment with the whole political process. However, if some of the voters weren't interested, the media certainly were: our editorial input as journalists was as large as, if not larger than ever before, to feed a massive expansion in the total output of news and comment, both in print and in the electronic media. There were even more rolling news channels covering a general election for the first time, and numerous websites helped provide an unprecedented degree of access and a further quantum leap in the amount of information available to the public.

I found the 2001 campaign like no other I had previously reported. On the one hand a Labour victory seemed all but certain; on the other hand, there were unsettling factors suggesting an unpredictable outcome. Because of a crippling outbreak of foot and mouth disease that had beset the country since February, Tony Blair had to disappoint the Labour Party and abandon his preferred polling date of Thursday 3 May. When he postponed the election until Thursday 7 June, many of his MPs feared that history was about to repeat itself and that Blair had taken a step which could prove as dangerous as the ill-fated decision of Labour's last Prime Minister, Jim Callaghan, who delayed polling day until May 1979 and lost, when most of the Labour movement believed he might have won if he had gone to the country in October 1978 as they had recommended. Blair's decision to wait until June led to a month-long phoney election which again threw up fresh uncertainties. Once the campaign was finally under way, we saw Labour fight a largely defensive campaign aimed at securing a second and historic full term in office, while William Hague led a vigorous offensive which took the Conservatives back to the hard-line positions of the Thatcher years. Charles Kennedy's objective for the Liberal Democrats was to build on Paddy Ashdown's historic breakthrough in 1997.

My diary opens in early April, as Blair struggles to reach a decision on the timing of the election, and closes in late July, shortly before the start of the Conservatives' first ever ballot by one member one vote to elect a new party leader.

1   The Loneliest Decision

An announcement by the Prime Minister in Downing Street usually runs like clockwork. Television crews and photographers invariably start assembling well before the allotted time, anxious to secure the most favourable positions behind the barriers erected on the opposite side of this narrow street. The first sign of action is the arrival of a civil service broadcasting engineer whose job it is to place a microphone on a stand a few paces away from the front door of No. 10. 'Testing . . . one, two, three . . . testing . . . one, two, three . . . ' Checking the Prime Minister's microphone is an essential precaution because government publicity staff from the Central Office of Information are responsible for supplying the sound feed to the competing radio and television outlets – a function over which Downing Street insists on taking control in order to ensure a clean picture of the Prime Minister standing in front of No. 10, without the clutter of the dozen or so separate microphones, sometimes bearing logos promoting rival radio and television networks, which would otherwise have to be placed in the street in front of him.

This morning, when I arrived at 10.30 a.m. the microphone was in place and the announcement was said to be imminent. There was hardly any room left; the crush behind the barriers was such that it was almost impossible to move. At 10.50 a.m. we were told the Prime Minister would be out within five minutes – but the minutes ticked by, and still he failed to emerge. It was clear there had been a serious hitch.

The statement we had been waiting for had been well trailed in advance: Tony Blair was about to confirm there would have to be a month's postponement in the 2001 council elections, which were to be delayed from Thursday 3 May to Thursday 7 June. Britain was in the seventh week of a foot and mouth epidemic which had already led to well over 800 confirmed cases of the disease on farms up and down the country, from Cornwall to southern Scotland. The Prime Minister's announcement would put the brakes on the build-up to a general election which we had all expected him to declare for the same day as the council elections.

A call on my mobile phone from the newsroom at BBC Westminster explained the reason for the delay in Blair's statement: he had been upstaged by William Hague, who had just given an impromptu news conference on the steps of Conservative Central Office and had called for an indefinite delay in the elections. Blair had been agonising for days about whether polling should be postponed because of mounting concern over the opposition which the political parties and their candidates feared they would encounter if they tried to campaign at a time when the foot and mouth outbreak had brought normal movement to a virtual halt across vast swathes of the countryside. Hague had sensed the opportunity to gain a tactical advantage. The epidemic was so serious, he argued, that the government 'could not possibly know when the crisis will end' and would be unwise to set a new date.

Hague's timing had been spot-on. His statement was broadcast live by BBC *News 24* and *Sky News*, and he knew that in all probability his appearance was being watched by Blair and his advisers in case they felt the official announcement had to be amended in the light of any remarks by the leader of the opposition. By getting in first, and by indicating that he would oppose the rescheduled date of 7 June, Hague had put the Prime Minister on the back foot. Now Blair would be unable to avoid referring to Hague's warning; and he would also have to do more to address the view, widely held in countryside communities, that as the epidemic was so severe it was far too early for ministers to be even thinking of holding elections. For once, Downing Street's well-oiled publicity machine was not operating as smoothly as the Prime Minister would have liked.

The government had been on the defensive all weekend and was already having to counter the suspicion that Blair's official announcement was nothing more than an unwelcome afterthought. A front-page exclusive in Saturday's edition of the *Sun* – increasingly seen as Downing Street's official notice-board – had been first with the news. Under a banner headline, 'Election off', it said the poll date of 3 May had been 'aborted' as Blair 'puts country before party'. As our wait behind the barriers dragged on, there was much muttering among the assembled reporters about the pointlessness of the exercise: all we needed to do was to adjourn to the press gallery in the House of Commons and wait for Downing Street to hand out copies of tomorrow's *Sun* so that we could read what the Prime Minister's official spokesman, Alastair Campbell, had deigned to tell the paper's political editor, Trevor Kavanagh, about the reasoning behind the switch in dates. However, at that precise moment, as if on cue, the No. 10 front door opened. Out strode Campbell, who took up his usual position about a dozen paces away from the microphone, well out of shot, on camera right. He looked particularly tetchy that morning, standing grim-faced, his left hand up to his chin. Campbell's arrival was the signal the television crews and photographers had been waiting for: they knew the Prime Minister would follow him out within about thirty seconds.

Finally, at 11.15 a.m., Blair began delivering his statement. Having weighed up all the arguments, he said, he had decided that the national interest was best served by postponing the council elections to 7 June. He made no reference whatsoever to the likelihood of a general election being held on the same day, or indeed any other; but he was clearly anxious to meet Hague's point head-on, and he ruled out a prolonged postponement of local authority voting. 'We cannot, should not, and will not indefinitely suspend the democratic process. A short postponement . . . is one thing.

An indefinite delay is quite another . . . To put our democratic process on hold for a prolonged period would be damaging to the true national interest.' When asked by reporters why he had made no mention of a date when the whole country might be able to go to the polls, the Prime Minister replied that he intended 'to make no announcement' about the general election because the priority for the government was to put in place 'a massive upgrading of the practical means and resources' to control and eradicate foot and mouth disease. As the questioning continued, he did all he could to rebut Hague's call for a lengthy postponement. Each answer ruled out 'an indefinite delay', a phrase he repeated seven times.

Blair took great care to avoid giving any clue as to when he would go to the country for at least two reasons. In the first place, once he indicated the date, Parliament would have to be dissolved and the civil service would be unable to implement any further changes in government policy. Second, and perhaps more to the point, once he named the day he would lose the services of Alastair Campbell and the other politically appointed special advisers who worked in Downing Street, because they were expected to resign once the election campaign began and would not be allowed back into No. 10 unless and until Blair were re-elected.

Months of work had gone into preparing for a general election to coincide with the local elections, and although staff at the Labour Party's headquarters in Millbank Tower had been warned late the previous week about a possible postponement, public confirmation of the delay was still seen as a setback. There had been a steady build-up in the momentum towards 3 May, and it was feared a sudden gear change might have unforeseen consequences. We knew that Campbell, like Blair himself, could not risk giving a straight answer to journalists' questions, but few doubted what would happen. The general assumption was that the Prime Minister would now go to the country on 7 June, the same day as the postponed council elections; but until the official announcement was made, probably in another month's time, the uncertainty looked all set to continue.

Almost every political correspondent I spoke to was disappointed. We now faced a nine-and-a-half-week wait until polling day, and no one seemed to relish the prospect of a long-drawn-out campaign. On the completion of Blair's statement, we trooped across the road to the side entrance in Downing Street which leads to the lobby briefing room situated in the basement of No. 10. Here it rapidly became apparent that Campbell shared our irritation over the postponement. When we asked why Blair had studiously avoided all mention of the general election he was curt and to the point. 'I am not saying anything about the general election beyond what the Prime Minister has not said. There's been speculation about the date since well before the New Year. I have read some garbage about it in the last few days but you never hear me talk about it, although I know you lot are obsessed with process.' This was the response we had all expected. Whenever he had no intention of answering questions about the timing of announcements or other polit-ical arrangements being made by Downing Street, Campbell accused the lobby of having become preoccupied with the process of politics and of ignoring the government's policies and the choices which Blair was presenting to the electorate.

When Nick Robinson, chief political correspondent of *News 24*, suggested that some politicians might regard the postponement of the council elections as nothing more than 'gesture politics', Campbell paused for a moment before taking aim. 'Yes, we accept that politicians will want to talk about this and I've already seen that the leader of your former party . . . ' He was immediately stopped in mid-sentence, drowned out by a roar of protest from the assembled journalists who had no intention of letting him get away with such blatant abuse of a colleague's professional reputation. Robinson, a former national chairman of the

Young Conservatives, knew that he was an easy target whenever Blair's official spokesman was in a mood to retaliate, but the lobby had grown tired of Campbell's attempts to undermine the independence and integrity of those journalists who asked awkward questions. But despite the strength of the objections, Campbell made no apology and simply continued with his reply: ' . . . I think those politicians who were out there in advance of the PM, asking for an indefinite delay, aren't really concerned about tackling the foot and mouth outbreak . . . If the Conservatives urge delay, we'll all know it is for opportunistic reasons.' I thought there was little point asking why the Prime Minister's statement had been delayed that morning; the question had already been answered. Campbell and Blair had obviously been watching Hague's statement – hence the tetchiness with Nick Robinson and the repeated rejection of 'an indefinite delay'.

As Campbell was clearly in combative mood, the *Guardian*'s political editor, Michael White, tried another tack. Why had cabinet ministers like the culture secretary, Chris Smith, been left 'wandering around' on Saturday morning unaware of Downing Street's exclusive briefing to the *Sun* about Blair's decision to delay the general election? We all waited with interest to see how Campbell would respond when challenged over yet another flagrant example of his cavalier disregard for parliamentary conventions. His tip-off to the *Sun* had annoyed other news outlets and left ministers hurrying to catch up with the official line from No. 10; yet any correspondent who dared to suggest it was an abuse of the democratic process to give exclusive briefings to Labour-supporting newspapers about something as momentous as the timing of a general election was bound to be ridiculed by him for being obsessed with spin and the 'process of politics'.

Campbell adopted a weary tone in replying to White: 'There was no question of ministers "wandering around". When Chris Smith was inter-viewed on *Today* no decision had been announced, but that didn't mean

Blair hadn't taken views. He had spoken to everyone in the cabinet. How we do things is a matter for him.' We realised there was little to be gained in pursuing the point, and with the uncertainty over 3 May at last removed, we were in no mood for another of Campbell's tirades.

None the less, although Campbell had escaped unscathed from the lobby briefing, I knew we had been given a foretaste of what to expect during the coming weeks. News management was Downing Street's forte and there was no point in protesting about the deals that were being done with those newspapers which were lining up to support Blair. In reality, Chris Smith had only himself to blame for his embarrassment over the interview he had given the BBC the previous Saturday. He should have realised that the *Sun*'s front-page splash announcing 'Election off' had been sanctioned by Campbell. An editorial claimed the story was a 'massive political exclusive' and praised the 'real guts' of the Prime Minister. 'Tony Blair has made the loneliest decision of his political career . . . This is the action of a courageous Prime Minister.' When Smith appeared on *Today* that morning, he obviously did not believe the story and repeated the message ministers had been giving all week. 'I very much hope that the county council elections scheduled for 3 May will indeed be able to go ahead . . . We must not send a message abroad that somehow Britain is closed for business because of foot and mouth.'

Smith's naïveté in not reading between the lines and grasping what was afoot was all the more surprising in view of the paper's slavish support for Blair and its pledge to back him on polling day. The *Sun* announced its endorsement of Labour when welcoming Gordon Brown's pre-election Budget. 'It's in the bag, Tony' said the headline over a front-page editorial on Thursday 8 March. 'Tony Blair should clear the decks and call the election . . . and furthermore the *Sun* says: Blair gets our support for a second term.' Later that month, when ministers still thought they could ride out the foot and mouth crisis, the *Sun* revealed on Tuesday 20 March that Blair had resisted calls for a delay: 'Election Day: Official May 3.'

When Blair performed his U-turn ten days later, Downing Street could not afford to leave the *Sun* out of the loop and run the risk of being chastised by its most prominent cheerleader. Although two other newspapers, *The Times* and the *Mirror*, had also been taken into Campbell's confidence, the *Sun* had been the most definite about the story and had given it the greatest prominence. Shortly after Blair's Downing Street statement, Trevor Kavanagh took a relaxed line when asked by Nick Clarke on the *World At One* if he could confirm that Campbell was the source of the story. 'Yes, it was someone whom I trusted . . . I am not going to go down the road of denying any name or source . . . Yes, it was a usually reliable source.'

As the *Sun*'s story was backed up by *The Times* and the *Mirror*, Campbell was perplexed by the BBC's failure that Saturday morning to accept that the council elections had definitely been postponed. Chris Smith's denial had only added to the uncertainty and it was not until late that evening, after Campbell had spoken to the BBC's political editor, Andrew Marr, that radio and television news bulletins finally went hard with the announcement. Fiona Bruce introduced Saturday's *Ten O'Clock News*: 'Good evening. In the last half hour, the BBC has learned that Tony Blair has postponed the general election until June.' *Sky News* had been leading with the story the since the first editions of the newspapers had come out the previous evening and the station's political editor, Adam Boulton, was amused by the BBC's reluctance to accept the accuracy of the *Sun*'s exclusive. 'It was pretty obvious that Campbell had been obliged to do the *Sun* a favour and that the story was correct. He could hardly have let them down after Trevor Kavanagh had originally gone with 3 May and then Blair had changed his mind.' Boulton realised early on the previous week that Blair had begun to waver about the date. 'Downing Street started ringing round opinion formers asking whether they thought the elections should be postponed. Once they started approaching leading broadcasters and journalists, it was pretty obvious what was happening. I was sure enough about it that Tuesday evening, when Blair had his weekly audience with the Queen, to predict that the elections would be delayed. Once Campbell had given it to the papers that Friday, he thought journalists would take the postponement as definite. He still cannot understand why the rest of the media aren't prepared to accept that he uses the *Sun* as Downing Street's notice-board.'

None the less, the BBC was not alone in remaining wary of the accuracy of exclusive stories published in Rupert Murdoch's biggest-selling daily newspaper. Ben Gill, president of the National Farmers' Union, told Radio Four's *Broadcasting House* on Sunday morning that he still had his doubts as to whether Blair would announce a delay the next day. 'I've been caught out before by spin and leaks and I'm not going to comment until it's in writing.' Gill's hesitancy was understandable, because although the ministers who were fielded by the government on the Sunday morning programmes were being careful not to repeat Chris Smith's mistake of knocking down the likelihood of the elections being delayed, they were anxious to strike a note of caution, so as to ensure the right build-up for the Prime Minister's statement on Monday morning. Dr John Reid, Secretary of State for Northern Ireland, told GMTV that Blair had consulted widely and was anxious to show his understanding of the suffering being experienced by farming communities. 'We think a slight delay in the elections would be a sign of that sensitivity and the Prime Minister's instinct is to be inclusive.'

The minister who had perhaps the greatest reason to feel aggrieved by the *Sun*'s exclusive was Blair's deputy, John Prescott. He had been with the Prime Minister's official spokesman the previous Friday when they attended the funeral of Tony Bevins, a former political editor of the *Independent* and *Daily Express*. Although they spent some time together, Campbell had made no mention of the briefing he was about to give Trevor Kavanagh. When the *Daily Telegraph*'s political correspondent,

Andy McSmith, described the 'unusual' circumstances surrounding this apparent snub, Prescott complained – but did not dispute the burden of the story: he demanded a correction because McSmith said they had gone to the funeral in his ministerial car when in fact they had travelled there by train. Prescott's annoyance at having been left out of the loop was still evident on the morning of Blair's announcement. He told *Today* that he had advocated holding the elections on 3 May but realised that opinion was divided on the issue and that Blair's aim was to unite the country in support of the farming community. When pressed by Jim Naughtie to say if he had been surprised by the certainty of the *Sun*'s story, he insisted the BBC had no evidence that the paper had been informed of the decision before members of the cabinet. 'Why should I accept that this is what went on . . . ? All newspapers gamble that they get it right . . . I imagine the *Sun* had made a gamble for a particular date . . . Anyway, I suppose the *Sun* might have got this one wrong.' Naughtie snorted in disbelief. 'Well, Deputy Prime Minister, we will let that one stick to the wall.'

Prescott's irritation over the agonising which had gone on about the timing of the elections was shared by most MPs and political journalists. The general assumption at Westminster was that although Blair was anxious to show solidarity with the plight of those areas devastated by foot and mouth, he remained a hard-headed political operator who would realise the tactical advantage of sticking to the carefully laid plans for a May general election. Labour and the Conservatives had both booked poster sites for early April in order to promote their campaign themes, and vast quantities of constituency literature had been ordered from the printers. The preparations had seemed unstoppable, and the push to keep to the original date had been reinforced by dire warnings of the damage which a suspension of the democratic process would inflict on confidence in the tourist industry.

On the other hand, pressure to postpone the elections had been building up as the daily count of reported cases had begun to escalate rapidly after the initial confirmation of foot and mouth on Tuesday 20 February at an abattoir at Little Warley in Essex and the detection two days later of symptoms on pigs at a farm at Heddon-on-the-Wall in Northumberland. By mid-March the enormous scale of the epidemic, especially in Cumbria and Devon, was obvious, and the need to prepare for the mass slaughter of infected animals was beginning to overwhelm the resources of the government's veterinary service. On Monday 12 March, when the number of confirmed cases rose by a further nineteen to reach 183, the Minister of Agriculture, Nick Brown, insisted that the measures he had taken were proving effective. All livestock movements had been suspended, and ramblers and visitors had been advised to avoid walking in areas where farm animals were present. 'At the beginning, people were saying the restrictions were harsh, and that we had panicked, but it is why we can say with confidence that we have it under control. What we cannot say with confidence is what is already in the national flock and what effect this will have in prolonging the outbreak.'

Brown asked MPs and other political activists to stay away from farms until the disease was under control. In view of increasing concern about the likely impact on the timing of the elections, Alastair Campbell was anxious to cool speculation in the news media. He told the morning lobby briefing that Monday, 12 March, that there were no plans to postpone the local elections scheduled for 3 May. Blair would not be required to take a decision for at least another fortnight. As the outbreak was 'not out of control' and there was 'not an epidemic', Campbell said there was no reason why horse racing or other sporting events should not take place. There were no plans to ask the army to remove slaughtered animals or to dispose of them because infected carcasses were being rendered.

As the week progressed, the confident assertions which the Downing Street press secretary had made on the government's behalf that Monday morning looked increasingly misplaced. There were reports that half a million pregnant ewes and lambs, stranded by the movement restrictions, might have to be killed. Blair confirmed at Prime Minister's questions on Wednesday 14 March that the government was considering an intensification of the slaughter programme to include all animals which might have come into contact with infected livestock. Although *The Times* reported that morning that county council leaders in the worst affected areas were urging the government to postpone the local elections, neither William Hague nor the Liberal Democrats' leader, Charles Kennedy, raised the issue with Blair. At the lobby briefing immediately after questions, Campbell urged journalists to retain a sense of perspective. In huge parts of the country the activities which people carried on in the countryside were continuing as normal, and there were 'good reasons' for proceeding with the local elections as planned. 'There are many in the tourist industry who say it would send out an alarming signal to the world, that the situation is so serious that you have to suspend the normal democratic process . . . The countryside is not closed. Tourism is open for business . . . This is a classic example of the way you guys think.' Campbell said Blair was focusing on the problems posed by foot and mouth for 'several hours each day' and once decisions were taken, the government stood by them.

But the clamour for the elections to be postponed showed no signs of abating. Ben Gill said that many rural people had effectively been disenfranchised by the outbreak. 'I cannot conceive of how you can possibly have a general election while we have restrictions on movement in significant parts of the country.' By the end of that week there were reports that as many as a million animals would have to be slaughtered, and the front pages of the newspapers were filled with pictures of smoke billowing across the countryside from huge pyres which were being used to incinerate carcasses. A MORI opinion poll published by the *Mail on Sunday* on 18 March showed that two-thirds of those questioned wanted

Blair to postpone both the local and general elections.

The start of the fifth week of the outbreak saw the end of the cross-party consensus over the measures which the government had taken to control and attempt to eradicate the disease. The morning newspapers on Tuesday 20 March gave the first hint of the political divisions which were opening up. The *Sun*'s front-page splash, announcing that 'the *Sun* was right all along' and that Blair would hold the general election on 3 May, was reinforced by a strident editorial. It asserted that on Monday 2 April the Prime Minister would, as planned, walk out of No. 10 on his way to Buckingham Palace, and it gave its advice in characteristic fashion: 'Tony – Go! Go! Go!' But a double-page spread in the *Daily Mail* told a different story, under the banner headline: 'Hague gets tough as revolt widens'. It said the Conservative leader intended to condemn the government's handling of the crisis and would question whether the elections should go ahead. Hague wasted no time that morning in calling on the Home Secretary, Jack Straw, to bring in immediate legislation to permit the postponement of county council elections in Cumbria and Devon. Against the backdrop of a sombre image of the countryside, he told a news conference at Conservative Central Office that the country faced a 'national crisis out of control'. Although 130 service personnel had been assigned that day to assist with the command and control of local operations in Cumbria and Devon, he urged the government to make far greater use of army manpower to dig trenches and construct pyres for the disposal of carcasses. The Conservatives had suggested the previous week that military assistance was needed, and Hague now said that it should be deployed in a 'much more comprehensive and wholehearted way'. His intervention was roundly condemned by the Leader of the House, Margaret Beckett, who accused him of trying to make 'political capital' out of foot and mouth. The real problem, she insisted, was a shortage of vets, and that would not be solved 'simply by sending in troops'. Postponing the elections would send 'the worst possible signal to the outside world – namely that Britain was effectively unable to function'.

Mrs Beckett's bravado was no more than inept political point-scoring, for Hague's assumption was correct: the government had finally acknowledged that it was facing a national emergency and Blair had taken personal control of the crisis. Nick Brown and the chief veterinary officer, Jim Scudamore, went to No. 10 for an hour-long meeting with the Prime Minister, and later that day it was revealed that in future there would be a daily meeting of ministers and officials in the Cabinet Office briefing room. The committee, known in Whitehall shorthand as Cobra, had last met during the petrol shortages the previous September, and its reformation in the context of the foot and mouth crisis signalled the heightened level of co-operation across government departments which the new emergency required. By the end of the day MAFF, the Ministry of Agriculture, Fisheries and Food, had reported forty-six new cases, which was far the highest daily number so far and took the total to 395.

Prime Minister's questions next day, Wednesday 21 March, showed that the political truce had been well and truly shattered. Hague renewed his call for Blair to reconsider pushing ahead with the local elections and appealed again for far greater use of the army to tackle the 'urgent, massive and growing problem' posed by the outbreak. In the previous twenty-four hours the backlog of infected animals awaiting slaughter had increased from 64,000 to 108,000, and the backlog of animal carcasses to be disposed of had doubled to 80,000. 'No one in the countryside can understand why the government are not making use of the thousands of soldiers and heavy machinery they have at their disposal.' Blair assured MPs there were sufficient slaughtermen and contractors to deal with infected animals; the army's role was to give logistical support, and that was the best way to ensure that infected animals were identified, slaughtered and disposed of.

Hague had the better of the exchanges, and after Campbell used his afternoon lobby briefing to urge journalists to recognise the damage which news coverage of foot and mouth was inflicting on the tourist industry, Blair decided to give a series of television interviews warning that Britain should not send out a message to the world that it was 'closed for business'. The interviews were conducted one after another, with a pooled camera, and as I monitored the television pictures being fed back to BBC Westminster I could see that Blair was tense and uptight. He was sitting in the cabinet room taking an occasional drink from a mug of tea; his body language suggested he had no time for small talk. Adam Boulton from *Sky News* asked the Prime Minister how he was. 'Very busy, thanks,' came the reply – though Blair did manage a faint smile in response to a jokey aside by Elinor Goodman, political editor of *Channel Four News*. The news that evening from the agriculture ministry was bleak: another forty new cases had been reported. Blair had put on a brave front for his television appearances but he must have realised the outbreak was slipping out of control.

The next day, Thursday 22 March, turned out to be a pivotal moment in the crisis. Projections of the likely pattern of the disease prepared by Professor Roy Anderson, an epidemiologist at Imperial College, London, suggested that the outbreak was unlikely to peak until May and the disease unlikely to be eliminated until August at the earliest. Professor Anderson's report made grim reading, and after a meeting that morning between the NFU and the Prime Minister, Ben Gill sounded distraught when he spoke to reporters in Downing Street. 'My worry for my members across the country is something that just tears my guts out . . . it's quite possible that the measures will have to be very, very severe.' That afternoon Blair went to Carlisle to hear directly from people 'at the sharp end' in Cumbria. On his arrival he was heckled by protestors. One woman shouted: 'Give us some troops please. We need them now. Next week is too late.' After meeting local farmers and representatives of the tourist industry he promised to provide whatever practical resources were needed to overcome the outbreak. 'What we have to do is massively gear up to the scale of the challenge we have, and make sure there's nothing, no little piece of bureaucracy, no obstacle that stands in the way of getting the job done.' Ben Gill, who had called in at BBC Westminster to give his response to Blair's visit to Cumbria, told me after recording a series of interviews that he had already begun to detect signs of a real gear change. 'It started after we met Blair on Tuesday. We had told him last week that more had to be done and he was livid when he found out that MAFF still weren't delivering, although they kept on saying everything was under control. Blair told me personally to ring directly through to Downing Street from now on. He's definitely doing much more to take control. He has a week to throw himself at this and if it's not under control by then, I think the date of the election will weigh very heavily upon him.' Gill's assessment of the Prime Minister's thinking proved highly accurate because, by chance, Blair was overheard the very next day talking about the deadline he faced.

That Friday, 23 March, Blair was attending a European Union summit in Stockholm and a television camera picked up his conversation with the European Commission president, Romano Prodi. They were discussing how long Blair had left in which to take a decision about the general election. Prodi asked if it would be as long as a month. 'No, about ten days,' replied Blair. Prodi seemed surprised: 'You're kidding me – in ten days' time, not later?' Blair's frankness made a mockery of the briefings given that morning by Alastair Campbell and his deputy, Godric Smith. Campbell had told journalists in Stockholm that the Prime Minister's mind was not 'remotely focused on the general election'. Smith had intoned the same mantra at the morning lobby briefing at Westminster, insisting that Blair's 'entire focus was on tackling foot and mouth'. In reality, as Gill had surmised, deciding what to do about the election was starting to weigh heavily on the Prime Minister. When he addressed a news conference at the summit later that day, Blair looked strained and subdued. 'There is no disguising this is a serious picture. It is going to be a long haul.' The number of confirmed cases of foot and mouth had risen by thirty-five during the day to 515, and 480,000 animals had been either culled or earmarked for slaughter, overtaking the figure for the last major outbreak in Britain in 1967, which had lasted six months.

Film of Blair's conversation with Prodi was replayed in the *Six O'Clock News*, but by then events in Stockholm had been overshadowed by a stark warning that the number of cases could rise to seventy a day, taking the total to 4,400 by June. Unless the cull of livestock was extended and speeded up, the government's chief scientific adviser, Professor David King, feared that half the country's cattle, sheep and pigs might have to be slaughtered. He advised that all animals within two miles of an outbreak should be killed and that the cull should be completed within twenty-four hours of a case being reported. Blair made an early exit from the summit the next day, Saturday 24 March, and flew to Devon. After meeting farmers' leaders and army personnel, he agreed with Professor King that the priority must be to shorten the time between confirming the disease and slaughter.

The worsening picture which had emerged towards the end of the week provided plenty of material for some reflective coverage in the Sunday newspapers on 25 March. 'Blair's wobbly Friday' was the *Sunday Telegraph*'s headline over a day-by-day account of how the previous certainty about the date of the general election had 'suddenly evaporated'. The previous Monday, when the *Sun* was told polling day would definitely be on 3 May, ministers believed the increase in cases would level off; but, as the scientific prognosis got bleaker by the day, 'panic was spreading' at Millbank Tower and Labour Party strategists realised that their long-planned campaign to win a second term was in jeopardy. The decision to reconvene Cobra was seen by the *Independent on Sunday* as another reason why the elections might be delayed. Blair had taken direct command of the crisis because he was 'infuriated' by the failure of MAFF to gain control of the outbreak; but, by taking charge himself, the Prime Minister had made it 'much harder' for him to be seen launching an election campaign.

The Sunday newspapers made grim reading for Clive Soley, chairman of the Parliamentary Labour Party, who told *Today* on Monday 26 March that from the soundings he had taken there was still an overwhelming desire among Labour MPs to stick to the original timetable for the local and general elections. He feared that a delay could be exploited by the Conservatives, who would then be able to argue for polling to be postponed until the autumn. Soley was supported by the *Sun*, which used the splash headline 'Sorry we're closed' and a map of the British Isles surrounded by a set of padlocks to portray how the country would look to the rest of the world if the elections were cancelled. An editorial brooked no delay: 'Blair must do all he can to avoid putting up the shutters and closing Britain down.' William Hague used Blair's statement to MPs on the Stockholm summit to taunt the Prime Minister about the ten-day deadline he had mentioned to Romano Prodi. It would expire on Monday 2 April, and the Tory leader said he hoped the government had followed his advice and taken the precaution of preparing legislation to postpone the council elections. In response, Blair was anxious to tell MPs about the steps he had taken to achieve slaughter of infected animals within twenty-four hours of diagnosis. Vets were being brought in from all around Britain and well over 1,200 were at work on the outbreak. Army logistics teams were giving assistance throughout the country and the number of personnel deployed exceeded 1,000.

As was perhaps only to be expected, Downing Street would give journalists no guidance on what transpired when Blair attended his weekly audience with the Queen on Tuesday 27 March. In a speech next morning to a conference organised by the British Chamber of Commerce he said he understood the desire of the tourist industry for instant results and appealed for help in getting over the message that Britain remained open for business. 'The way this issue is being presented on television abroad, as if the whole country was out of bounds, is leading to cancellations that are wholly unnecessary . . . It is difficult when there are pictures on the news every night of sheep and cattle being destroyed . . . that is what the whole of the world sees.' There was no let-up at question time in the House of Commons that afternoon. William Hague condemned the government's continued failure to devote enough resources to tackling the outbreak. 'In every way one looks at it, the crisis is getting worse. Yesterday we had forty-seven cases, a record number of outbreaks . . . When does the Prime Minister think that this disease will truly be under control?' Blair's answers revealed the uncertainty which had gripped the government. According to revised statistics from MAFF there were 1.35 million recorded movements involving the sale or export of sheep in the first three weeks of February, prior to the detection and reporting of the outbreak. 'If the disease was incubating then, it has been far more widespread than hitherto thought . . . How can we be sure when the disease will end? The answer is that we cannot be sure at the present time . . . The key matter is to ensure that the report to slaughter time of twenty-four hours is maintained in every part of the country.' Blair's answers underlined his decision to take personal charge of the whole operation. He made no mention of the role of the Minister of Agriculture, Nick Brown, and almost every other sentence began with the word 'I' – 'I think, I agree, I can say, I would also point out' – as though he wanted to emphasise his total personal commitment to tackling the outbreak.

That evening, pictures of sheep being transported for slaughter by army personnel at a disused airfield at Great Orton, near Carlisle, dominated television news bulletins. The start of the cull inside a large tent at the former air base was witnessed by General Sir Michael Jackson, commander in chief of British land forces, who told reporters it was a very different conflict from the war in the Balkans. 'It is not one involving human beings who can't agree with each other, but one involving a very tragic disease . . . This is a national tragedy. It seems absolutely right the army does what it can to help those experts whose job it is to decide how to deal with it.' Despite such clear evidence of the efforts being made to speed up the slaughter programme, Blair's lack of confidence at question time when answering questions about the expected length and extent of the outbreak gave the Conservatives a fresh opportunity to capitalise on the continuing uncertainty over polling day. Late that evening the party's assistant head of media, Andrew Scadding, told me that Hague intended to ratchet up his demand for the elections to be postponed. He planned to spend Thursday 29 March meeting farmers in Wensleydale, Cumbria and Dumfries, and would tell them that if he were Prime Minister, he would not call a general election while the spread of foot and mouth remained out of control, as that would be 'putting party before country'.

Hague's intervention apparently made no impact at the weekly cabinet meeting that morning. Godric Smith, the deputy press secretary, told the lobby that the words 'election' or 'poll' had passed the lips of none of the ministers present. He intended to adopt the advice given the previous day by Alastair Campbell that it did not help to keep 'burbling on' about when the Prime Minister might go to the country. Blair had given an undertaking to listen carefully to the representations which were being made about the timing of the local elections, but he was 'focusing 100 per cent' on tackling foot and mouth, to the virtual exclusion of everything else. At the correspondents' afternoon briefing, Smith acknowledged that as nominations for local authority candidates were to close the following Monday a decision would have to be taken shortly, but stressed that Blair intended to put the interests of the country first. Journalists were given the same answer on Friday 30 March after *The Times* reported that the Archbishop of York, Dr David Hope, had joined other senior bishops in urging Blair to postpone the general election. Later that morning Dr Hope told a news conference that he had picked up 'a general feeling of despair and bewilderment' in rural communities and that people who were preoccupied with getting on top of the crisis could not be expected to consider serious election issues like health or education. 'This is giving voice, I believe, to what large numbers of people in the rural communities are actually saying . . . I recognise that it is an extremely difficult and precarious decision which the Prime Minister has to take.' The Archbishop of Canterbury, Dr George Carey, though he stopped short of issuing a formal call for the general election to be delayed, supported Dr Hope in saying there needed to be 'calm and careful reflection' about whether the democratic process could take place 'fully and freely' in the middle of a foot and mouth outbreak.

Blair planned to spend the weekend at Chequers, the Prime Minister's official country residence, and when asked at Friday's lobby briefing whether ministerial meetings about the election would be held there on either Saturday or Sunday, Smith said he had no intention of getting into the 'processology' of what might or might not happen. Most journalists I spoke to had ended up feeling extremely confused about which way the decision might go. I thought the signals coming from Labour MPs and party headquarters were indicating that a May general election would go ahead. A MORI opinion poll published the previous day in *The Times* had shown that Labour retained a commanding lead over the Conservatives despite criticism of the way the outbreak had been handled. Labour had the support of 50 per cent of those questioned, the Conservatives were up one point at 31 per cent and the Liberal Democrats were scoring 14 per cent. Nevertheless, Blair had given the impression that although he had no intention of discussing his election options in public, he was happy for there to be a debate on the issue and he had been anxious to listen to the argument, almost as though he had wanted to be seen agonising in public about what to do. He had spent time that morning giving interviews to American television networks insisting that Britain was 'entirely open' for business, an upbeat message that was in danger of backfiring if he then cancelled the elections, although most viewers in the United States would probably have been unaware of the peculiarities of the Westminster parliamentary system which has no fixed term and allows a British Prime Minister complete freedom in deciding when to go to the country. For what turned out to be the abiding image of the day, the Prime Minister donned yellow protective clothing in order to visit a mass burial pit for animal carcasses which had been excavated at Birkshaw Forest, near Lockerbie in Dumfries. The concerned look on Blair's face as he was escorted round the site by army officers suggested that he knew all too well that the spectacle of the mass slaughter of farm livestock was far too gruesome to provide the backdrop for the launch of an election campaign. On the other hand, if he was opting for a postponement, why hadn't he announced it earlier in the week – and denied Hague the opportunity to give his statesmanlike pledge that the Conservatives would definitely put 'country before party'?

When the first editions of the newspapers began appearing just before 10 p.m. I realised that I had misread some of the signals Blair had given. *The Times* and the *Mirror* were nowhere near as categoric as the *Sun* in announcing that local and general elections had been postponed, but it was obvious there had been a ring-round from Downing Street. Philip Webster, political editor of *The Times*, told me the day after the official announcement that he was still dictating his story straight to the sub-editors at 8.20 that Friday evening. 'It was a very late story but the subs told me it was the splash. I was worried they were going so hard but the office rang back and said, "You're not alone, it's front page in the *Sun*" and I knew the election was definitely off.' Alastair Campbell told journalists who felt aggrieved at not having got the story that they could have worked it out for themselves: Blair had made his mind up mid-week and once his deputy, Godric Smith, started briefing the lobby that the Prime Minister was 'focusing 100 per cent' on tackling foot and mouth,

Downing Street expected political correspondents to take on board the implications of what was being said. Campbell said the problem had been that most journalists were 'too stupid' to get the message. I wrote a mental note to myself: must try harder next time and spend even longer trying to decode Downing Street's 'processology.'

2 The Phoney Election

Tony Blair and Alastair Campbell vied with each other for the top spot in the morning press. Every national newspaper carried a photograph of the Prime Minister standing in front of 10 Downing Street as he announced his decision the previous day to postpone the 2001 council elections until Thursday 7 June. However, some newspapers published an even larger picture of his official spokesman. Campbell had been standing to one side, glowering at the photographers, television crews and journalists who were crowding behind the barriers which had been erected on the other side of the road. His defiant, grim-faced pose had caught the eyes of the cameramen and their picture editors. The *Daily Telegraph*'s front page highlighted the contrast in the demeanour of the two men. The photograph of Campbell was three times the size of that of Blair, and the headline reinforced the message which these images conveyed: 'PM puts a gloss on election delay but spin doctor's face says it all'. The caption to the main picture rammed home the point: 'Black looks: Alastair Campbell reflects the reluctance to put the campaign off because of foot and mouth'.

Blair's announcement of a month's delay in the local elections made no mention of the date for the general election, but the newspapers took it for granted that the Prime Minister would go to the country on 7 June. Press opinion was sharply divided about the wisdom of interrupting the electoral cycle for the first time since the Second World War. Unexpected support was given by the *Daily Mail*, often one of the Labour Party's sternest critics. Blair had made the right decision and put himself on the side of the public by showing that he was sensitive to the countryside's plight. 'To have gone to the country in the present circumstances would have been shamefully opportunistic and cynical.' By contrast, the *Independent*, which usually gave encouragement to the aims and objectives of New Labour, said Blair should have obeyed his instincts and stuck to 3 May. The decision to delay was 'a laughably cosmetic affair' which sent an unhelpful signal to the world and would have 'disastrous and costly implications' for the livestock and tourist industries. 'Clearly, Blair wanted to be seen to have "done something", to have empathised with the plight of farmers, however ineffective and irrelevant delaying the election is . . . As it is, Blair looks cowed, muddled and manipulative.' Leader writers and columnists were united on one point: they were all appalled at the prospect of nine and a half weeks of electioneering. Although Blair had made no mention of the date when he would hold the general election, thus leaving the official campaign undeclared, there was a widespread recognition that the shadow boxing between the politicians, which had already being going on for weeks, was bound to continue unabated. 'The country is not itching for a pre-election contest,' declared *The Times*, which admitted that it would be difficult to persuade senior officials at Labour or Conservative headquarters to hold their fire.

In order to monitor the 'spurious stunts' which the parties were bound to inflict on the public during the longest campaign in British political history, *The Times* launched a column headed 'The Phoney Election' in which it promised to publish a daily round-up of 'who goes where and what they say'. The cynicism which was felt by newspaper commentators was summed up by Hugo Young of the *Guardian*. He said Blair's 'childish coyness' and 'tired old political game-playing' had prevented him from telling the nation in an adult way that he did intend to seek a fresh mandate in just under ten weeks' time. Young predicted that within a month foot and mouth would have ceased to be a major concern for the public and that Labour would win 'handsomely' on 7 June.

Despite the strictures of the columnists about sham electioneering,

William Hague was determined to demonstrate that there was no pretence about the Conservatives' demand that the government should do more to assist the farming community by speeding up the slaughter and disposal of infected livestock. Alongside the *Daily Telegraph*'s front-page picture of Alastair Campbell was the headline, 'Put army in charge of crisis, says Hague', above a story which said the leader of the opposition wanted the army to 'take full control of the drive to eradicate foot and mouth'. For once the *Daily Telegraph* had done the Tory leader a disservice with its exclusive story, because the statement which was issued on his behalf later that morning, when he visited farmers in the Forest of Dean, was rather more specific than the headline suggested. Hague was asking the government to allow the army to take command of field operations, such as the slaughter, transport, burial and incineration of carcasses. A brigadier from each of the three divisional areas of the United Kingdom should be required to report back to a new cabinet committee chaired by the Prime Minister. To back up their case, the Conservatives published a list of the occasions when shadow cabinet members had asked for the army to be deployed. Tim Yeo, the Tories' agriculture spokesman, made the first request for military help on Sunday 11 March, but it was only on Tuesday 20 March that the army was given a limited logistical role and not until Tuesday 27 March that the deployment reached the strength of 800 soldiers. In the three weeks that had elapsed since Yeo's first request there had been a tenfold increase in the backlog of animals waiting to be slaughtered, which had risen from 30,000 to nearly 350,000.

Even though the general election had been delayed, ministers had no intention of relaxing their expertise in the art of rapid rebuttal, and the full firepower of the government's media machine was wheeled out first to ridicule, and then to destroy, Hague's attempt to seize the political initiative. After the Ministry of Defence issued a statement saying the army did not have the expertise to take charge of the operation to bring foot and mouth under control, the military took the unexpected step, given the context of pre-election skirmishing, of putting up serving officers to respond to the Conservatives. Brigadier Alex Birtwistle, the army commander in Cumbria, had no hesitation in rejecting Hague's idea. 'To be frank, I don't want to lead this operation. It would be too difficult with the resources I have. We can add command and control.' He was backed up by Major David Holt, who said service personnel had not been trained to track down foot and mouth. 'It's MAFF which has the expertise in the enemy. They understand the disease. They have the veterinary experts, the epidemiologists and the people to predict what they believe the disease is going to do so we can react. The situation here, where we are in support of MAFF, is perfectly workable.' Tim Yeo told BBC *News 24* that the government should not have asked army officers to score political points against the Conservatives. 'It was wholly inappropriate to have used the military in this way. A minister should have given the government's response.' The Ministry of Defence press office in London put the blame on television reporters, who should not have got 'an officer nearing retirement' involved in political controversy. James Gaskin, the army's press officer in Cumbria, told me that Brigadier Birtwistle answered reporters' questions because he wanted to be gallant and show his support for the lead civil servant, Jane Brown, who had been sent there by MAFF.

Tony Blair, who was in Wales, on his seventh visit to an infected area within twelve days, said he understood the army's reluctance to take on overall control but insisted there were no constraints on military assistance; in a statement that morning, Downing Street announced that another 300 soldiers were to be deployed, taking the total number of service personnel assigned to the outbreak to 1,700. This included twenty army vets and thirty trained slaughtermen from the Royal Logistical Corps. The extra deployment was of little comfort to the Conservatives and Hague was mocked by Labour MPs for having over-reached himself.

Iain Duncan Smith, the shadow defence secretary, insisted that the army
had been consulted and did want a greater operational role in order to
'cut through the chaos and confusion' which officers were having to
contend with in the worst-affected areas. None the less, despite their
contention that Hague had not asked for the army to take on the task of
detecting and eradicating foot and mouth, the damage had been done,
and Downing Street was anxious to play up the Conservatives' discomfort while diverting attention from the government's attempt to beat a
hasty retreat after the minister for the environment, Michael Meacher,
promised a wide-ranging public inquiry into the outbreak.

Meacher, who had been appointed head of the government's rural task
force, told a news conference in London that people would want to know
how the disease had managed to get such a firm hold in large areas of the
country. Public inquiries had been established after the 1952 and 1967
outbreaks and 'unquestionably, there will be one this time' to ascertain
what should be done to prevent it happening again. Meacher's certainty
about an inquiry caught No. 10 by surprise and the deputy press secretary, Godric Smith, said that although Downing Street was not denying
what the minister had said, there was no intention of making an
announcement that day about the terms of reference for a public inquiry.
Blair sounded irritated when he was stopped by reporters at Usk and
asked how long the inquiry promised by Meacher might take: 'The whole
issue of how we learn the lessons of this, that we will have to consider
another time.' Downing Street's clumsy attempt to deflect the media's
interest in probing the government's handling of the outbreak only drew
attention to the news, released at the afternoon lobby briefing, that the
Ministry of Agriculture had changed the way it was publishing figures for
the number of confirmed cases. In future the total for each day would be
released the following day, covering the previous twenty-four hours.
Journalists had complained about discrepancies in the statistics being
supplied on MAFF's website. Godric Smith read out revised figures for

the previous week, revealing that the total number of cases identified on Saturday 31 March was in fact fifty-two, one fewer than the previous highest tally of fifty-three cases on Thursday 29 March. 'In future we will be giving out figures on a 7 a.m. to 7 p.m. basis . . . It has been extremely difficult to get robust data because the first priority for the vets out in the field has been to get on with their work rather than delay themselves with form-filling.'

Because Blair had taken over the lead role in co-ordinating the government's response, Downing Street had become much more hands-on in briefing journalists, to the annoyance of those correspondents who had been keeping track of the outbreak, many of whom did not have access to the lobby briefings confined to political correspondents. The daily news conferences which had previously been given by the Minister of Agriculture, Nick Brown, had also been scrapped, depriving reporters of an opportunity to question Brown and his officials. Alastair Campbell told political correspondents on Wednesday 28 March that the press conferences had ceased because of 'a bit of fatigue' at the Ministry of Agriculture but that the government intended to be 'open and transparent' in communicating with the public. None the less there was no doubt as to the intention of the Prime Minister and his official spokesman: they were determined to exercise far greater control over the way information about the foot and mouth outbreak was being released to the media. A month's delay in the local and general elections had given Downing Street the breathing space it needed to improve public confidence in the handling of the epidemic. A MORI opinion poll published in *The Times* on Thursday 29 March showed that 69 per cent of those questioned were dissatisfied with the government's response to the foot and mouth outbreak. In mid-afternoon that day it was confirmed that the number of animals authorised for slaughter had passed the one million mark. The number still waiting to be killed was approaching 400,000, indicating a further increase in the backlog which William

Hague had complained about that morning. Godric Smith accepted that the government was still failing to slaughter infected animals within twenty-four hours, the target recommended by the government's chief scientific adviser, Professor David King, on Friday 23 March. 'We are striving constantly to meet that target and there is now a hotline open to No. 10. The PM is saying to the military and the NFU, "If there are problems, ring me, I can sort them out. We can deal with problems more quickly in No. 10 than they have been dealt with in the past."

The clear-sighted pursuit of defined objectives by Blair's staff in Downing Street could not be replicated so easily across Westminster at Millbank Tower, where Labour Party strategists were having to pick up the pieces and start all over again in preparing a timetable for the election campaign. There was concern that the enthusiasm of local activists might wane during the month's delay; and ways would also have to be found to boost the morale of the extra staff hired to help at party headquarters in the expectation of a May general election.

Friday 6 April

After delaying the general election, and thus depriving himself of the opportunity to campaign on behalf of the Labour Party, Tony Blair tried his hand at promoting the tourist industry. The Easter holiday was only a week away, and the Prime Minister and two of his cabinet colleagues spent the day out of London doing what they could to get publicity for attractions which had been hit by a catastrophic slump in visitors and bookings since the start of the foot and mouth outbreak. Tony and Cherie Blair mingled with tourists at York, where they were greeted outside the Jorvik Centre by thirty members of a Viking re-enactment society. The Prime Minister took snaps of his wife as she posed with a group of fully clad Viking raiders. When Blair saw a Japanese man with a camera round his neck he rushed over and suggested they should have their photograph taken together. Hiroshi Yamamoto had to tell the Prime Minister that he was not a tourist but a London-based journalist for JHK, the Japanese Broadcasting Corporation. The Jorvik Centre provided a useful backdrop for the Japanese, American and French television crews which had been invited to accompany Blair as he attempted to repair the damage which had been done to Britain's standing as a tourist destination. International travel agents said the United Kingdom had become the victim of what was known in the trade as 'CNN syndrome', referring to the power of the images broadcast by the US news media giant: television news stations across the United States had been repeatedly using footage of cattle and sheep burning on huge pyres to illustrate the news from Britain, and this had put off potential holidaymakers.

When told by American reporters that all their people saw back at home was pictures of livestock going up in flames, as if in some sort of medieval plague scene, Blair said he understood the lack of knowledge about the foot and mouth outbreak. 'It's very serious for the farming communities directly affected, but it's possible to get it out of perspective. It's important for people in your country to realise that all the things they normally want to do in Britain, they can do.' During a phone-in on BBC Radio York, he said he was working 'every hour God sent' to get the disease under control. The Yorkshire Tourist Board estimated that the county had lost £60 million in tourist income in the past month; callers who enquired about possible financial assistance were told the government could not compensate everyone, but Blair did announce that a further £120 million would be made available to underwrite loans for small businesses hit by the crisis.

John Prescott chose the Norfolk Broads for the first of several photo-opportunities. Wearing an oilskin and life-jacket, he was taken out for trip in a cruiser, and afterwards he encouraged the Broads Authority to do what it could to reopen those mooring points and footpaths bordering rivers which remained out of bounds. 'Easter is coming. A lot of people have cancelled but it's still not too late to have a break. The daffodils are coming out and the message is that it's important people come to the countryside.' Dr Mo Mowlam, minister for the Cabinet Office, used her visit to Warwick Castle to remind reporters that 80 per cent of all visitor attractions were open for business.

For Blair, the only blot on the landscape was closer to home. Despite there having been no confirmed foot and mouth outbreaks in its area, Buckinghamshire County Council was refusing to reopen any of the 6,000 footpaths it controlled, including those in the Chilterns which ringed Chequers, the Prime Minister's official country residence, where he planned to spend the weekend with his family. Bill Chapple, the council's deputy leader, said the authority was following a stringent risk assessment. 'I want the tourists to come along and see the countryside as it should be, alive and kicking, and not coming along to an empty shell because we have opened it up too early . . . The Prime Minister has gone all around the country to affected areas recently and I know he's coming back to Chequers this weekend. I hope he has taken all the right precautions.'

Thursday 12 April

Nine days after seeing, to his annoyance, that pictures of himself in the morning newspapers were larger than those of Tony Blair, Alastair Campbell found yet again that he was getting a higher billing in the news media than the Prime Minister. Once more Downing Street's chief press secretary had become the story of the day – and he responded characteristically, firing off a complaint about the news media's obsession with personalities and the process of politics.

The source of the trouble was an exclusive front-page lead in the *Independent* which had a rather misleading headline: 'Campbell to quit as spin-master after the election'. It said that if Labour were re-elected, Campbell would withdraw entirely from day-to-day briefings with political journalists and would be promoted to become No. 10's director of communications. Andrew Grice, the paper's political editor, said the intention was that Campbell would spend more time devising long-term strategies to promote policies on the economy, health, education and transport. An unnamed minister was quoted as saying that Blair considered the high profile acquired by his official spokesman was continuing to fuel the suspicion that his government was 'run by spin, instead of just using spin'. Downing Street's initial response was that it was not going to comment on speculation about what might happen after the election, but more details emerged as the day progressed. Rather than quitting, Campbell was to become a super-spin-master, exercising even greater control than he had during Blair's first four years in Downing Street. Andrew Marr, the BBC's political editor, confirmed the story for the *One O'Clock News*. He told Anna Ford that if Labour were returned to power, the Prime Minister's official spokesman would be given a 'grand title' to do more of what 'he's doing already'.

Campbell complained about the coverage. He told the Press Association news agency that it was 'typical of the media's obsession with process and personality' that a newspaper story about himself featured on BBC television news ahead of 'an important speech' by the Prime Minister on the future of the country's schools. Blair's promise to the annual conference of the Association of Teachers and Lecturers, that Labour's election manifesto would make a commitment to raise the share of the national income going into education, did secure a higher position in the running orders of the later news bulletins; but there were also more reports throughout the day explaining why Campbell wanted to take a lower profile, while remaining one of Blair's closest and most senior advisers.

To make the point that Campbell's belligerent attitude when dealing with the news media had become counterproductive and was damaging

the Prime Minister, the *Six O'Clock News* included a clip from the satir-
ical Channel Four programme *Bremner, Bird and Fortune*, in which the
impressionist Rory Bremner took the part of the hesitant, stumbling
Prime Minister. At one point the domineering press secretary, played by
the actor Andrew Dunn, puts the plaintive premier in his place: 'Who has
been running the country, you or me?' The relevance of the
Bremner–Dunn routine parodying life in No. 10 was highlighted by the
very report which had preceded it, covering Blair's speech from the
teachers' conference in Torquay, for this had provided a graphic illustration of the way in which Blair could be upstaged and humiliated by his
press secretary. Julia Neal, a delegate at the conference, said many hard-
working and committed teachers had been offended by a lobby briefing
Campbell had given in February 2001 at which he declared that the development of specialist schools signalled that 'the day of the bog-standard
comprehensive school' was over. Ms Neal demanded an answer from
Blair: 'You have not dissociated yourself from this. Do you agree with
him?' The delegates shared her anger and interrupted the Prime
Minister's unconvincing reply: 'I think what's important is not to get
hung up on a phrase, and say . . . '

Campbell had also fuelled the unease of Blair's colleagues by his role
in the circumstances surrounding Peter Mandelson's second resignation
from the Cabinet in 2001. Some ministers and MPs considered Blair's
official spokesman had exceeded his authority in telling journalists after
Mandelson's enforced departure that the former Secretary of State for
Northern Ireland had been 'curiously detached' about the circum-
stances surrounding an application for a British passport by a wealthy
Indian businessman, Srichand Hinduja, who, with his brother
Gopichand, had contributed £1 million towards the faith zone in the
Millennium Dome.

Despite Downing Street's outright refusal to comment on Campbell's
likely new appointment, an explanation was provided by David Hill, who

was regarded as one of Labour most experienced spokesmen. Hill had resigned from his long-standing position as the party's director of communications in 1998 to join the celebrated lobbyist Sir Tim Bell and become a senior director of Bell Pottinger Good Relations. However, Hill had promised Blair that he would return to assist with the 2001 election campaign and he frequently appeared in news programmes defending Labour's record. He told The *World At One* that Campbell recognised he had 'become the story' and that this was a handicap. 'Alastair's concern is that if he is going to be able to ensure that his new job as head of communications for the Prime Minister is done well, it can only be done properly if he leaves the day-to-day job of talking to the press to others.'

My impression was that Campbell had reached a point of no return. He could no longer go on giving lobby briefings and expect to get away with comments like his reference to 'bog-standard' comprehensive schools or his assertion that a cabinet minister had been 'curiously detached'. He had promised before to lower his profile, announcing in June 2000 that he intended to hold fewer of the twice-daily lobby briefings and delegate more of this work to the deputy press secretary, Godric Smith, and the chief press officer, Ann Shevas. However, unable to resist the opportunity to speak to the journalists with whom he had once worked, he continued to give several briefings a week, including the first briefing of the week on Monday morning, the briefing on Wednesday afternoon following Prime Minister's questions and some of the Friday briefings held exclusively for political correspondents on the Sunday newspapers. I felt that unless Campbell pulled back, Blair would face renewed calls for lobby briefings to be curtailed or televised, because of the concern both within his own party and in Parliament as a whole over the way an unelected spokesman could speak privately to journalists without any form of accountability or apparent check on what was said.

Newsnight used another extract from *Bremner, Bird and Fortune* as a teaser to a discussion on Campbell's imminent retreat from front-line duty. When Bremner portrayed Blair's look of concern as he tried to challenge the need for yet another signed article in the *News of the World*, Dunn bridled at the criticism and delivered the press secretary's firm riposte: 'Look, the press run the country; there is nothing else.' In the discussion that followed Joe Haines, who was appointed Harold Wilson's press secretary in 1969, cited the jibes about Campbell being the 'real Deputy Prime Minister' as the real reason for his proposed withdrawal from the public eye. Haines doubted whether the new arrangement would last. 'If Alastair gets a grand title to supervise the whole of the government's public relations machine, I have a fear it will end in tears . . . Alastair would be better to cut if off now and go and run Manchester United.'

Another of *Newsnight's* guests, Donald Baer, who was President Clinton's communications director in 1995–7, tried to put the appointment into context. He said the post dated back to the days of Ronald Reagan. American presidents found they needed a media strategist who had the 'back-seat job' of looking forward, a week, a month and a year, to the 'message requirements' which the administration would need. The director had to look at all forms of communication – press, television, speeches and other ways to connect with the public. 'If you have the right division of responsibility, the press secretary deals with the press and the communications director doesn't try to run over anything he does but is co-ordinating with the different departments and co-ordinating the different means through which the President communicates with the public.' Baer's description of Campbell's likely role confirmed my belief that Blair was moving inexorably towards a presidential style of government – but without the democratic safeguards which applied in Washington, such as the televising of White House briefings.

Friday 13 April

Perhaps because of my compulsion to jot down notes after almost every conversation I have with politicians and their advisers, no matter how trivial the subject might seem, I find I rarely get invited to look behind the scenes and observe what happens when governments and political parties seek to exploit the news media. My interest in the manipulative techniques of the spin doctor has made me an unwelcome visitor. Therefore, I had no prior inkling that my Good Friday shift as the duty political correspondent at BBC Westminster would include a short tour of a fully operational war room, the inner sanctum for any lengthy political campaign.

I knew that when he took charge of the foot and mouth outbreak and called for seemingly unlimited resources to be allocated towards eradicating the disease, Tony Blair had not overlooked the importance of controlling the flow of information to the public. Much had already been made of the many reported failings of MAFF, and it had been clear to me for several weeks that the task of managing relations with the news media was one of the responsibilities which had passed to Downing Street. Whenever journalists asked at lobby briefings about the role being performed by the Minister of Agriculture, Nick Brown, and the reasons why he had apparently been sidelined by the Prime Minister, we were told by Alastair Campbell that it was the nature of the problem which had dictated the level of the government's response. The scale of the epidemic was 'beyond the expectations which had existed at the outset' and although Brown was doing 'a very good job in horrendously difficult circumstances', the government had to take policy decisions on the basis of the latest advice. Campbell's convoluted explanation meant only one thing: Brown and the officials at his department had been forced to relinquish much of the day-to-day management of the epidemic. One of the functions which had definitely outstripped MAFF's capabilities was the task of devising a media strategy which would allow the government to take the initiative and have greater influence over the way the outbreak was being reported. The aim had to be to stem the constant flow of horror stories about the plight of farmers and the appalling suffering of their livestock. If that could be achieved, the next objective was to find ways of turning the attention of journalists towards a more positive agenda.

The Downing Street press office started taking the lead in mid- to late March, and once Blair had announced on Monday 2 April that he had postponed the council elections, No. 10 stepped up its offensive. Each evening the deputy press secretary, Godric Smith, or one of his colleagues would ask to speak to the correspondent preparing news reports for the radio and television bulletins next morning. By trailing a government announcement or releasing advance information on the Prime Minister's movements or a forthcoming speech, Downing Street hoped to secure a forward-looking spin on the news. This is a well-worn technique; but occasionally it backfires, especially if there are any inaccuracies in the information or if the journalists who have been fed a line push the story further than the briefer expected or the facts allow.

One of Smith's first overnight briefings on foot and mouth came on the evening of Monday 26 March, when he gave me a preview of a state-ment to be made to the House of Commons next day. He said Nick Brown intended to announce a ban on the use of catering waste to feed pigs. 'The minister will say that the foot and mouth infection may have entered the country through illegally imported meat which ended up as catering waste and then became pigswill . . . We don't know how the meat got into the country illegally, but it wasn't through catering waste from airports or ships.' There had clearly been an extensive ring-round because numerous journalists had got hold of the story. Next morning some newspapers claimed that waste food from Chinese restaurants was responsible for the outbreak at the pig farm at Heddon-on-the-Wall in Northumberland. 'Dodgy Chinese linked to killer farm virus', was the headline in the *Daily Star*. The fullest report appeared in *The Times*, which said 'smuggled meat served in a Chinese restaurant' was being investigated as the most likely source. '*The Times* has been told that officials in the north east were alerted to possible illegal activity after a container of illegal meat, clearly labelled for a Chinese restaurant, was found concealed inside a load of household goods.' When he delivered his statement to MPs, Brown made no mention of Chinese restaurants being to blame – but by then the story had taken off, and it made the front-page splash next morning in the *Mirror* under the headline: 'Sheep and sow source'.

These stories sparked an angry reaction among the managers and staff of Chinese restaurants, culminating in a protest march through London on Sunday 8 April organised by the Chinese Civil Rights Action Group. Hundreds of banner-waving protestors massed outside the offices of the Ministry of Agriculture demanding that the government should identify the unnamed source of the story. Brown, who addressed the crowd through a loudhailer, denied that his department had pinpointed Chinese restaurant waste as the cause. He said he despised the 'racist overtones' of ill-informed and groundless speculation.

In the days leading up to my Good Friday shift, Downing Street had turned its attention to the concerted efforts which were being made to get the countryside opened up in time for the Easter weekend. One overnight briefing concerned a fresh attempt to persuade local authorities to reopen footpaths; another produced a list of measures which Brown was taking to encourage farmers to continue taking stringent precautions in order to stop the spread of the infection. We were told that there would be no let-up in Whitehall and that ministers and officials would be at work throughout the holiday weekend. In order to demonstrate that civil servants and service personnel were working round the clock, journalists were invited to a news conference at MAFF's headquarters in Smith Square, followed by a photo-opportunity that afternoon at the foot and mouth co-ordination centre in the ministry's offices in Page Street.

Because it was a holiday weekend there were fewer reporters than might otherwise have been expected at the 11 a.m. press conference, but for the specialist correspondents who had spent weeks tracking the epidemic, and who had been complaining vociferously about the inadequate and unreliable statistics being issued by the government, it was an opportunity not to be missed. On seeing that those present included Mike Granatt, head of the government information service, I sensed that this was more than a routine briefing. There were well over a dozen officials sitting along two sides of the room. They were led by Brigadier Malcolm Wood, who was introduced as the deputy head of the co-ordination centre. I noticed that beside him were staff drafted in from Downing Street and the Cabinet Office, including two of my former colleagues from the BBC: Bill Bush, who had been head of No. 10's research and information unit, and Lucian Hudson, formerly a BBC news producer and latterly director of communications for the E-Envoy group at the Cabinet Office, which was responsible for government websites. Reporters were handed a press release giving the latest statistics: 1,039,000 animals had been slaughtered; 541,000 animals were awaiting slaughter; and 408,000 carcasses remained to be disposed of. No statistics had been published on MAFF's website that week and once reporters were invited to ask questions they demanded to know why this information had been 'buried' for so long, as it showed the position was far worse than the government had been saying.

John Vidal of the *Guardian* said that what had happened was close to censorship. The Prime Minister was giving the impression the worst was over, but the figures which were being slipped out on Good Friday morning showed that the ministry was failing to keep up with the slaughter of infected animals. David Rossington, who handled statistical information for the co-ordination centre, said the new figures would be published on the internet as from 12 noon that day and would appear regularly from then on. The way information was being presented on the website had needed changing because the involvement of 1,600 vets and 1,900 soldiers had caused 'logistical problems' in the collection and transmission of data. 'We have taken a good look at the statistics to ensure they do reflect all the data that is out there. There is nothing more to it than that.' After the briefing Lucian Hudson was a little more forthcoming about the problems which the government had faced. He had been at MAFF for a week, having been taken on as the temporary deputy director of communications. 'I've just been transferred here from the office of the E-Envoy and it was obvious we had to do something about the ministry's website. All the statistics on it were crap. We just had to get on top of this and get them right.'

The main purpose of the briefing, however, was to provide an opportunity for Brigadier Wood to expand on the enormity of the task facing the army in providing logistical support. Preparations were being made to slaughter 20,000 animals a day; this required the biggest combined military and civil operation for thirty years, far outstripping the logistical effort needed in Bosnia or the Gulf War. 'We put thousands of tons of ammunition and equipment into the Gulf, but just think of it: a pallet load of ammunition weighing a ton is the equivalent of only two cows. The scale of this operation is enormous.'

On being told as we left the press conference that Nick Brown would be visiting the co-ordination centre at four o'clock that afternoon to thank staff for working over the holiday weekend, I asked if this could be filmed. To my surprise, Lucian Hudson agreed. The centre was on the eighth floor of the department's Page Street offices, and on entering the room with a BBC television crew I was struck by the number of uniformed army personnel working at computer terminals. A map of the United Kingdom was laid out in the centre of the room. Brown stood at one end of what in military terms is known as the 'bird table'. Standing around the map, alongside the minister, were a dozen army officers and an array of senior civil servants who had already started giving the minister a run-down of the day's events. George Trevelyan, director of the intervention board, responsible for the disposal of distressed or unwanted livestock was in charge of the proceedings. (Later I discovered he was the father of a fellow BBC political correspondent, Laura Trevelyan: on seeing the television footage of him briefing Brown, Laura said her father was wearing the tie she had given him for his birthday.) He reported that there had been some 'excellent' meetings with the agencies involved in finding landfill sites for animals carcasses. 'The environment agency can tell Cobra that we've upped the number of sites on offer to over a hundred . . . a French company is being asked about clay pits in Exeter . . . there are some objections in Sussex and East Surrey . . . we're still debating about whether to use powers of direction.' Although I was not entirely sure exactly what this meant, it caught my attention and I took a hurried note of what Trevelyan had said. Brown told the assembled company that he wanted to thank them for giving up their Good Friday to help in the 'largest peacetime logistical exercise which the army and government had ever had to undertake'. The aim was to eliminate foot and mouth and get disease-free status restored to the country. At this point one of the officers volunteered some fresh information: 'We now have military support for vaccination, if the vaccination button is pressed by the minister.'

While this exchange was taking place I saw that immediately behind Brown was a notice-board filled with newspaper cuttings and what looked like transcripts of radio and television broadcasts. The display was divided into two, under the overall heading 'Media monitoring unit latest report': one half bore the subheading 'What has been said' and the other 'What we should be saying'. I could not get close enough to read any of the text, but the press clippings included a story from the front page of the *Mirror* headlined 'The sheep shooter'. This referred to an episode in which the RSPCA had called for an inquiry into reports that a marksman had been employed to kill sheep in a field in south Wales. Video footage showed a man in white overalls taking pot shots at a group of sheep and lambs. I was anxious to get the minister's response to the video, and he agreed to answer questions in the few minutes which were left before we would have to leave. Brown said he had ordered an investigation. 'Those who carry out slaughter for the government are supervised and a code of practice must be adhered to . . . Animals are supposed to be penned up, brought forward in an orderly way, held still in a mechanical pen or between bales of straw, while clinically and swiftly despatched with a single shot at very close range.'

On being ushered out of the co-ordination centre, I felt the ministerial briefing I had witnessed, and the earlier news conference, had both been businesslike and impressive. There was clearly far more going on behind the scenes than was ever released to journalists. None the less, I could see that the routines being imposed by the Downing Street press office were proving effective and that the back-up was there to assimilate data and maintain a constant flow of information. The pressure that was being applied to news organisations in an attempt to persuade them to follow a positive agenda was relentless and had shown results. By making regular visits to the worst-affected areas, and by being seen talking to farmers, the Prime Minister had succeeded in influencing the news agenda for television and radio and had managed to keep the focus of much of the coverage on the steps being taken to control and eradicate foot and mouth.

Earlier that week a former head of information at the Ministry of Agriculture, Graham Blakeway, had criticised Blair for seeking to give the impression that he was in charge when in fact he was 'completely at the mercy' of government scientists and technicians. Blakeway, who said he was pushed aside in 1999 in New Labour's 'purge of government press officers', wrote about his experiences in the *Daily Telegraph*. He said the Prime Minister's attempt to become an instant expert on the epidemiology of foot and mouth had simply slowed down the process of decision-making. 'The Prime Minister may look as if he is taking charge when he is photographed talking to disgruntled farmers in Cumbria . . . But of course, he isn't . . . his vacillation about vaccination is a perfect example . . . he doesn't understand the biology of viral infections, and he knows it.' Blakeway mocked Blair's ineptitude in donning overalls and then declaring Britain was 'open for business' during a visit to a mass burial pit near Lockerbie on Friday 30 March. 'There he was, dressed in bright yellow protective clothing, looking for all the world like someone sent to investigate a melt-down at a nuclear plant . . . It made Britain look about as open for business as Chernobyl in 1986.' Blakeway had a point. The sight of Blair decked out all in yellow was so eye-catching that the picture had been reproduced repeatedly in the newspapers. Although not as memorable as the endless footage of animal carcasses being incinerated on huge fires, it was another negative reminder of the devastation which had been inflicted on rural life. However, the strength of photographs showing Blair in such poses was that they demonstrated his involvement in the problems facing the farming communities.

No sooner had I returned to BBC Westminster than the Downing Street press office was on the phone supplying statistics for Good Friday attendances at major tourist attractions around the country. No. 10 had a statement, embargoed for use on Easter Saturday morning, quoting Blair as having been encouraged by the 'better-than-expected' visitor and booking figures for the start of the holiday weekend. However, I had been working on my own story for the morning bulletins. My interest had been aroused at the co-ordination centre by the reference to the possible use of 'powers of direction' to secure landfill sites for burying animal carcasses. The duty press officer at MAFF, who was not present during the report back to Nick Brown, promised to find out and let me know what this referred to. Late that evening I was told the government was considering whether to invoke emergency powers to force local authorities and site operators to take animal waste on landfill sites. The issue was on next morning's agenda for the daily meeting of ministers and officials at the Cabinet Office. George Trevelyan had inadvertently provided me with an exclusive story for Easter Saturday.

Tuesday 17 April

Among the contentious issues which dominated the pre-election debate, the problems posed by asylum seekers had rarely been out of the news. For months Labour and the Conservatives had been competing with each other to sound the tougher in their approach to illegal immigration. On Wednesday 14 March, at a signing ceremony in the House of Commons, the Commission for Racial Equality obtained the support of the five main political parties for a compact that laid down a set of principles for the conduct of the general election campaign. It was designed to ensure that there was no attempt to 'incite or encourage, blatantly or covertly, racial hatred, prejudice and discrimination between others'. Elected politicians had to represent everyone, 'not pitch one group against another for short-term political or personal gain'. The commission accepted that political expression and debate in Britain had always been 'robust and uninhibited' and agreed that it was vital that issues like asylum and immigration were discussed in order to ensure that the country was 'a better place to live and work'. However, while the right to freedom of speech was essential, it should not be viewed as an absolute right, without any limits, and the right to free political expression could not be abused in the competition for popular votes. A requirement of the CRE compact was that in any dealings with the public, including door-to-door and telephone canvassing, candidates should not use words or actions which might 'encourage, instruct or put pressure on others to discriminate; or stir up racial or religious hatred or lead to prejudice on grounds of race, nationality or religion'.

Each of the five party leaders, Tony Blair (Labour), William Hague (Conservative), Charles Kennedy (Liberal Democrat), Ieuan Wyn Jones (Plaid Cymru) and John Swinney (Scottish Nationalist) agreed to ensure that his candidates abided by these principles; they promised that every alleged breach would be investigated; and they undertook to take action against any candidate who knowingly failed to comply. The strength of the Conservatives' commitment to the requirements agreed with the commission became headline news when the *Independent* revealed on Tuesday 17 April that the party chairman, Michael Ancram, had written to Conservative candidates and campaigners on Monday 26 March saying he believed they should have 'no problem with the compact'. He reminded them that the party was 'utterly opposed to racial discrimination' and believed in a Britain where what mattered was 'your talent and your effort, not the colour of your skin or your religion or who your parents were'.

The revelation that Ancram had thought it necessary to issue a reminder reignited the controversy sparked off the previous month when John Townend, the retiring Conservative MP for Yorkshire East, had made a speech in which he said he believed the late Enoch Powell had been right in his pessimistic forecast about the impact on Britain of 'massive immigration'. He had chosen the 'destruction of Britain' as his theme. 'Our homogenous Anglo-Saxon society has been seriously undermined by the massive immigration, particularly Commonwealth immigration, that has taken place since the war . . . If people had been aware that by the new millennium London, our capital, would have over 25 per cent of its population from ethnic minorities and that forecasts expect that by the year 2014 over half of the city will be non Anglo-Saxon, that Leicester and Birmingham would be vying as to which city would have a black majority first, Enoch would have been Prime Minister.'

Townend had given the speech at a constituency dinner on Saturday 17 March, but it was not until ten days later that most journalists were alerted to the provocative nature of his remarks, when on the evening of Tuesday 27 March the Labour Party faxed newsrooms a copy of the text. An accompanying press release claimed that Townend's remarks were 'outside the bounds of acceptable politics' and said the MP should have the Tory whip withdrawn. At this point Townend was out of the country, but his wife Jennifer told me on the phone that at the constituency dinner ten days earlier the prospective Conservative candidate for Yorkshire East, Greg Knight, suggested to her husband that he send a copy of the speech to the local paper. 'Liberal Democrats in the area have been making a stink about it ever since . . . John didn't use the word "coloured" in his speech. I saw him cross it out and put in "Commonwealth" instead. John wasn't being racist.'

Staff at Conservative Central Office must have known about the fuss caused locally by the speech, because within an hour of asking for reaction I was told by the party's chief spokesman, Nick Wood, that Hague totally repudiated what had been said. Townend, who was sixty-six, was not seeking re-election in 2001 and therefore was not a candidate; but Hague wished to make it clear that the repetition of such remarks by any Conservative candidate would not be tolerated as they would be in conflict with the compact which he had signed to avoid racist issues being exploited during the election. Hague's statement made no mention of his taking any disciplinary action against the Yorkshire East MP, and Wood told me that as the compact referred to the forthcoming campaign, in which Townend was not standing for re-election, there was no point taking action against him.

The leadership's reluctance to do any more than deliver a swift repudiation of the speech reflected the strength of feeling within the party over illegal immigration. Ann Widdecombe, the shadow Home Secretary, had been relentless in her criticism of the government for not doing enough to deter bogus asylum seekers and for allowing Britain to become 'a soft touch'. The stridency of her campaign had drawn support from across the party and had been endorsed by the former Conservative Deputy Prime Minister, Michael Heseltine. In a signed article published in the *Daily Mail* on Monday 1 January he had said that when chairing cabinet committees he had come to the conclusion that a very large number of those seeking asylum were 'cheats' and were 'quite deliberately making bogus claims'. Heseltine said he believed the government should enforce the laws against illegal immigration much more rigorously, and he stood by Hague's right to put similar views on to the political agenda. 'My record on race speaks for itself. I was the first Conservative MP to attack Enoch Powell's obnoxious "rivers of blood" speech . . . and Hague too, has an impeccable record on race.'

As it turned out, Heseltine's endorsement of the demand for tougher measures against bogus asylum seekers had been somewhat precipitate, because within a matter of weeks he was expressing dismay about the tone which his party leader was adopting. Hague caused consternation among one-nation, pro-European Tories when he delivered what became known as the 'foreign land' speech at the Conservatives' spring forum in Harrogate on Sunday 4 March. During a briefing at 5 p.m. the previous day to trail the speech, Nick Wood told political correspondents that Hague intended to describe what the country would be like if Britain joined the European single currency and the government failed to deal with the international trade in asylum seekers. Next morning the Sunday papers picked up the 'foreign land' theme. The *Sunday Times* said that Hague would warn that the 'threat posed by the Euro and a continuing influx of asylum seekers' would leave the country at risk of changing in a way few people would welcome. On the strength of the briefing, pro-European Conservatives said they were disappointed that Hague intended using such emotive language. Heseltine told the *Independent on Sunday* that he had faced 'a dilemma' over whether to vote Tory at the next election but had been a Conservative 'too long to do anything else'.

At a second briefing shortly before the speech was delivered, after correspondents had been given a copy of the text, Nick Wood was asked whether Hague intended to link the euro and asylum seekers in the way the Sunday newspapers had reported, in such a way as to suggest that Britain might become 'a foreign land'. Wood raised no objection to this interpretation, merely shrugging his shoulders and remarking that it was not for him to say. Whether inadvertently or by design, he gave journalists the clear impression he was happy for the connection to be made. The line from the briefing seemed quite clear: Hague intended to appeal to the party's core vote, and the leadership appeared relaxed at the possibility that pro-Europeans might be upset by the speech and consider it xenophobic.

As it transpired, when the speech was delivered, there was a space of a good ten minutes or so between the two most controversial sections. After his opening remarks, Hague said he wanted to set out what Britain would look like under four more years of Labour. 'Let me take you on a journey to a foreign land – to Britain after a second term of Tony Blair. The Royal Mint melting down pound coins as the euro notes start to circulate. Our currency gone for ever.' Hague turned later to illegal immigration, when attacking Labour's record on law and order. 'It's common sense that when we're dealing with an international trade in asylum seekers, we should make Britain a safe haven, not a soft touch . . . Where applications are unfounded, immediate deportation will follow.'

Next day the *Guardian* reported that Hague's supporters left Harrogate 'delighted that their leader had once again made waves with a headline grabbing speech'. But although the delegates had cheered Hague for spurning the middle ground, the 'foreign land' speech was regarded as a defining moment by the Conservatives' opponents and the first real indication of the ground on which the Tories were likely to fight in the election campaign. Paddy Ashdown, former leader of the Liberal

Democrats, told *Question Time* on BBC television that it was the 'most unwise and dangerous speech' uttered by a British politician since the days of Enoch Powell. 'It was intended to feed upon the base instincts of the people of this country in a way which will prove damaging to the fabric of the nation . . . We will fight an election that'll be the ugliest for fifty years because the Conservative Party has taken a right-wing path . . . That speech makes Hague unfit to be Prime Minister and Conservative leader.' Another of the panellists, the shadow Chancellor Michael Portillo, blamed journalists for linking asylum seekers to Hague's remarks about a foreign land. 'This was a trick of the press . . . I was sitting in the hall . . . His speech was mis-reported . . . He talked about the melting down of coins . . . and about ten to twenty minutes later, he talked about asylum seekers; it was completely unconnected. No one in the audience made that connection . . . Journalists then put it to Heseltine that Hague had made this speech. This was mischief by the press.'

Other members of the shadow cabinet did their best on the political programmes on Sunday 11 March to suggest that Hague had been misquoted and had not suggested that asylum seekers were turning Britain into 'a foreign land'. Francis Maude, the shadow Foreign Secretary, told *Breakfast with Frost* that there had been 'an error of inter-pretation' and there was 'not a racist thing' in Hague's body. Ann Widdecombe assured GMTV that her leader had not talked about the two issues in the same breath. None the less, the link had been made and it had stuck. John Townend's declaration that Enoch Powell had been right gave the controversy even greater momentum and provided Labour with an ideal opportunity to step up their efforts to undermine Hague's authority and to criticise his inability to exercise leadership or enforce discipline.

Having alerted newsrooms to the content of Townend's speech, Mo Mowlam, minister for the Cabinet Office, wrote to Hague on Wednesday 28 March, saying that unless he withdrew the whip from the East

Yorkshire MP he would be giving the green light to others in his party to go on making outrageous and intolerant comments. Blair kept up the pressure at Prime Minister's questions, telling MPs he would not allow Labour candidates to use racist language. Charles Kennedy said the 'foreign land' speech and the Tories' obsession with 'bogus asylum seekers' had given credence to offensive opinions within the ranks of the Conservative Party. Rather more ominously for Hague, the Conservatives' most prominent black politician, Lord Taylor of Warwick, added his voice to those calling for the whip to be withdrawn from Townend. As John Taylor he had faced racist abuse when he was selected as Conservative candidate for Cheltenham, a seat he failed to hold for the Conservatives in the 1992 general election. In a signed article published in the *Sun* on Friday 30 March, Lord Taylor, a barrister, said it was not good enough to excuse Townend by saying he was not seeking re-election. 'He is still a serving MP and in a responsible position . . . his comments could actually pander to more racism and more racist comments . . . Britain has moved on, we are now a multi-racial, multi-cultural society, and the Conservative Party has to as well.' But there were those on Townend's side, too, prepared to add their voices to the public debate. Christopher Gill, the retiring MP for Ludlow, became the first senior Conservative to express support for Townend, declaring that he too had been an admirer of Enoch Powell and believed that Anglo-Saxon Britain had been diluted by immigrants. Gill, who was sixty-five, said he was resigning from the Conservative Party after forty years' membership in order to become chairman of the Freedom Association.

The next day, Saturday 31 March, in an editorial headed 'Racism is an enemy within', the *Sun* said it did matter that two 'unknown' Tory MPs had made racist statements. 'We find their words depressing and abhorrent.' The paper's rebuke for Townend and Gill was welcomed the following day by Gurbux Singh, chairman of the CRE, who was interviewed on GMTV. 'I was delighted the *Sun* came out with such a clear position . . . I would like all newspapers to take the same strong line.' Michael Portillo told *Breakfast with Frost* that he had been appalled by the remarks of the two MPs. 'As John Taylor has said, the country has moved on and the Conservative Party needs to move on too. We are a party that extends absolute equality and esteem to every single person who's living in Britain.'

Friday 20 April

Having been bolder than the rest of his shadow cabinet colleagues in denouncing John Townend and Chris Gill for using offensive language, Michael Portillo then caused consternation in the news media by appearing to turn the story on its head. During a visit to the Welsh Assembly in Cardiff, he surprised journalists by announcing that he had refused to sign the compact on anti-racism drawn up by the Commission for Racial Equality. The shadow Chancellor said that having been as outspoken as he had about the need for inclusiveness, he did not see why he should sign every bit of paper that was thrust in front of him. 'I haven't signed it because I speak for myself and I say that I offer equality of esteem to everyone in this country. MPs are bedevilled with early day motions, questionnaires, pledge forms and everything else from pressure groups and they mainly arrive in the form of "When did you stop beating your wife?" type questions. I went into public life to speak for myself and I will use my own language, my own words.' Portillo's defiant stand was a deliberate but desperate attempt to demonstrate that even a Conservative MP who believed he had earned a reputation for tolerance was not going to be dragooned into signing the CRE's compact. He was in effect signalling a free vote on the issue and, by becoming a high-profile refusenik, he hoped to deflect the news media's attention from the growing list of MPs, mainly from the right of the Conservative Party, who were not simply withholding their signatures but calling for the CRE to be scrapped.

By the previous day, Thursday 19 April, nearly 400 MPs and candidates had signed the CRE document; the Commission published their names, and also identified those Conservative MPs who had registered their opposition. The objections came as no surprise to the CRE's press office. Journalists were told before the official signing of the compact in mid-March that the staff knew some Conservative MPs were unlikely to give it their backing. Gurbux Singh, the CRE chairman, told reporters that he was disappointed that three Tory MPs, John Townend, James Cran and Eric Forth, had notified the CRE of their refusal to sign. Cran and Forth were seeking re-election and Labour immediately issued a press notice calling for them both to the disciplined, and said that Cran should also be sacked from his post as an opposition whip. Journalists were being encouraged by Labour to check out the names of other Tory MPs likely to be critical of the CRE and, in an attempt to keep up the pressure, newsrooms were supplied with advance copies of a speech to be given that evening by the Foreign Secretary, Robin Cook, in which he intended to attack Townend and Gill, the two MPs who had complained that immigration had 'diluted' the British culture. Cook said that because of the 'foreign land' speech Hague had to accept 'a share of the blame' for the unprecedented step which the Conservatives had been forced to take in instructing their candidates not to make racist statements. The idea that Britain was a pure Anglo-Saxon society before the arrival of communities from the Caribbean, Asia and Africa was a fantasy. Legitimate immigration was the necessary and unavoidable result of economic success and was 'an immense asset' which the Foreign Secretary believed had contributed to the cultural and economic vitality of the nation.

'Creating an open and inclusive society that welcomes incomers is therefore a condition of growth and prosperity in the modern world . . . Our lifestyles and cultural horizons have also been broadened in the process . . . Chicken tikka masala is now Britain's true national dish, not only because it is the most popular, but because it is a perfect illustration of the way Britain absorbs and adapts external influences. Chicken tikka is an Indian dish. The masala sauce was added to satisfy the desire of British people to have their meat served in gravy.'

Cook's defence of Britain's ethnic diversity, and his attempt to ridicule the Conservatives by reminding them that curry was a true national dish, was headline news on Friday 20 April. 'Land of hope and curry' was the headline on the front of the *Mirror*, which also published a two-page spread entitled 'Rule Tikkannia'. The *Daily Mail* said the Foreign Secretary had sparked 'a furious row' by suggesting that Britishness could no longer be defined in terms of ethnic background. 'There is no such race as the British', said the front-page headline. An editorial inside argued that it was no surprise the race card had been played, even before the election was under way. 'And it is no surprise that the man so crassly playing it is Robin Cook, that smug architect of the "ethical foreign policy" . . . this master of hypocrisy.'

As Labour had intended all along, its taunting of the Tories was having an effect, and more Conservative MPs were lining up to express their anger about being asked to sign the CRE's compact. John Gummer, the former Conservative Minister of Agriculture, told *Today* that he intended to continue his long record of fighting racism in his own way, and that the Commission should not be seeking to undermine his relationship with his constituents. 'I am being asked to sign up under an implied threat. It is the CRE which has told the press that James Cran has refused to sign, that the implication must therefore be that he is a racist . . . He is not a racist . . . The CRE is using a measure of blackmail which is unacceptable.' Desmond Swayne, MP for New Forest West, said he feared that if politicians did not address the 'legitimate concerns of ordinary people' about asylum, it would encourage extreme parties on the right. Dr Julian Lewis, MP for the neighbouring seat of New Forest East,

accused the Commission of McCarthyite tactics. 'I am the third generation of a Jewish immigrant family and to ask me to sign a document
saying I am not a racist is outrageous.' Tim Butcher, the Conservative
candidate in Gillingham, did not see why he should be 'beholden' to the
CRE. 'I don't have to sign up to a piece of paper . . . We are a soft touch
for asylum seekers . . . We are genuine politicians, there should be a
genuine debate.'

The first public hint that a relaxed line would be taken by party
headquarters came in mid-morning when the assistant head of media,
Andrew Scadding, said Hague did not expect, and had not asked, all Tory
MPs and candidates to sign the pledge individually. However, when
Michael Portillo stepped into the spotlight an hour later with his pointed
and public refusal to put his signature to the document, he gave Labour
fresh ammunition with which to step up their charge that the Tories
lacked discipline and leadership. Portillo had effectively contradicted
Steve Norris, a Conservative vice-chairman, who had told *Newsnight* the
previous evening that Hague had informed the party chairman, Michael
Ancram, that he 'expects every Conservative candidate to be signed up' to
the CRE statement. Norris, who had been the Conservatives' candidate in
the May 2000 election for Mayor of London, tried to play down the
party's disarray when interviewed on The *World At One*. While insisting
that Hague had signed the compact on behalf of the whole party, he
stressed that the CRE was saying nothing which 'any decent person'
should not be happy signing. He did not share the argument that the
compact was 'patronising and politically correct'. The stand Norris had
taken in defending the CRE's attempt to outlaw racist electioneering was
welcomed by Simon Woolley, national co-ordinator of Operation Black
Vote. He told me that Hague's 'foreign land' speech had both emboldened
the British National Party, which had already organised two provocative
marches, and further encouraged the inward-looking stance of the
United Kingdom Independence Party. 'Portillo and Norris are the only

two senior Conservatives who are doing anything to try to pull the Tories back to the centre. The party leaders must do more to stop extremists playing the race card. They should remember the votes of the black community could decide up to eighty seats.'

That afternoon the *PM* programme provided a vivid illustration of the gulf which had opened up within the Conservative Party. Nicholas Soames, a former defence minister, accused the CRE of exceeding its role and helping Labour to destabilise the Tories by generating 'a fake, synthetic row' over its anti-racism compact. 'It is a loathsome and offensive document and a corpse of an idea which is trying to drag racism into a general election where no such desire would otherwise exist. It won't succeed, we won't play ball and the CRE can go to hell.' In her report that evening for *Channel Four News*, Elinor Goodman said two-thirds of Conservative MPs had not signed. The size of this potential revolt was seen by the former Conservative MP, Michael Brown, a columnist with the *Independent*, as the real reason for Portillo's high-profile rejection of the compact. He told Ms Goodman that by standing out, the shadow Chancellor had got the Conservatives 'off the hook' and enabled dozens of Tory MPs to throw off the CRE's interference without being labelled racists.

Although I had been taking note for some days of Labour's attempts to expose the views of MPs like John Townend, I was surprised by the extent of their success in exploiting the refusal of senior and long-standing Conservatives to sign the CRE's compact. During the long lead-up to the 1997 general election I had observed the ease with which Labour succeeded in fuelling Tory splits over Europe and in manipulating the news media's interest in reports about sleaze in the Conservative Party. I thought lessons had been learned from that defeat, and I could not believe that the media strategists of Conservative Central Office had been so inept in allowing so many MPs to walk straight into another Labour Party ambush. As I looked through the first editions of the next morning's newspapers I had to smile on reading the *Guardian*'s account of how, eight weeks from a general election, Tory MPs had eagerly queued up to divide themselves into signatories and non-signatories. Patrick Wintour, the paper's chief political correspondent, predicted that the damage to the party would reverberate for weeks, and he thought Hague had little time left to reclaim ground that had been lost as a result of the Tories' chaos. 'A textbook Millbank-inspired operation painting parts of the Tory party as racist only strengthened the image of a leader unwilling or unable to control extremism in his party.' I thought Wintour's column might prove an interesting read for Nicholas Soames, who had fulminated on *PM* about the lies which he claimed Labour were using to destabilise the Conservatives.

Sunday 22 April

Gurbux Singh sounded conciliatory, almost contrite, when asked to explain how the guidance which the Commission for Racial Equality had issued to the political parties had managed to cause so much antagonism and put race at the top of the pre-election agenda. Singh, who was being interviewed by Alastair Stewart on GMTV's Sunday Programme, knew he had some explaining to do. The Sunday papers contained blow-by-blow accounts of the panic and disarray which had engulfed the Conservatives' high command after the revelation that three Tory MPs had refused to sign a compact on political campaigning to which the leaders of the five main parties had all agreed. 'Race commissioners colluded with Labour to ambush Tories' was the *Sunday Telegraph*'s headline over a report quoting a former CRE executive member, Dr Raj Chandran, who believed the commission had become 'a political arm' of the Labour Party. 'It cannot be a coincidence that Robin Cook made his silly "chicken tikka masala" speech and, two days later, the CRE releases the names of

Tories refusing to sign the race pledge.' The *Mail on Sunday* revealed that it was on Thursday 22 March, eight days after the party leaders signed the compact, that Hague received an additional request from the CRE saying that 'it would be useful to know which MPs have pledged their personal support,' a request which started 'alarm bells ringing' at Conservative Central Office because there would be 'a revolt by some MPs who would then be branded racists'.

The *Sunday Times* said there was no doubt the names had been leaked because on the evening of Wednesday 18 April, Conservative Central Office took a call from the CRE's press office saying it had been approached by a daily newspaper which had obtained the names of John Townend, Eric Forth and James Cran, the three MPs who had refused on principle to sign the compact. The party was quoted as saying that, given that only the commission had the names, the information 'must have come' from within that organisation. It was on the following day that the CRE agreed to publish a list of the names of all the MPs, from all parties, who had responded.

Alastair Stewart put it to Singh that that CRE had leaked the three Tory names and was running 'dangerously close' to losing its political impartiality. 'I don't accept that. I have read the suggestions that we colluded with Labour . . . It is inappropriate for the CRE to leak these names . . . We thought it was important that the names of all those who signed should be made public, including those who said they would not sign.' Singh said the compact had first been agreed in 1996, in time for the 1997 general election, and that in discussions with the five party leaders earlier in 2001 it was agreed that the principle should extended to cover the forthcoming election and that all MPs should be asked to stand 'shoulder to shoulder' in signing the pledge. 'It was done openly and all the leaders welcomed this . . . but, yes, the compact has led to a debate which I am not terribly happy with. Rather than talking about the evils of discrimination, there has been a major deflection, to matters like political parties squabbling with each other to establish who is more or less racist than the other. I am saddened the debate has shifted to something which is not terribly helpful.'

Singh's emollient approach was of little comfort to the Conservative leadership which had been outmanoeuvred so comprehensively. 'Call me what you like, I will not be silenced', was the heading to a signed article by William Hague in the *Sunday Telegraph*. He said the charge that he and his party were racist could not go unanswered. The country was only a few weeks away from an election, yet Labour did not want anyone to talk about the increase in applications for asylum, which had jumped from 32,500 in 1997 to 76,000 in 2000. Britain had more asylum applicants than any other European country and it cost nearly £1 billion to support them, more than double the amount four years ago. The government, said Hague, was not interested in reforming the system or in acknowledging the anger that the 'current asylum chaos' aroused, so Labour politicians were trying to censor any discussion by labelling those who raised the issue as racist. He would not be browbeaten by the insults being thrown at him: 'It is a shabby and contemptible ploy . . . I and my colleagues will not be discouraged or bullied from making the case that we can make Britain a nation to be proud of again. Labour can call us all the names under the sun. We will fight this election our way.'

His defiant stand was supported by the shadow Home Secretary, Ann Widdecombe, who told *Breakfast with Frost* that she had signed this 'silly pledge' so that journalists did not use her refusal to deflect her from the case she wanted to make. 'I, more than anyone, will be talking about asylum and immigration during the election campaign and I do not want to be distracted by the media and sidetracked as to whether I have signed this silly pledge but I do regard it as an unnecessary pledge.' If she became Home Secretary, she said, she would set to work immediately building secure centres for asylum seekers and starting to have people detained.

I had been struck by the anxious demeanour of Gurbux Singh. However much he might been appalled by the outraged reaction of the Conservatives, he could not disclaim all responsibility for the provocation of which Tory MPs had complained. There were other ominous portents. The *Observer* reproduced a Tory insider's assessment of the impact which immigration could make on political campaigning. Andrew Lansley, the shadow Cabinet Office minister who was advising Hague on campaign tactics, had given a revealing insight into party thinking in September 1995 when he resigned as the Conservatives' research director after being selected to contest South Cambridgeshire in the 1997 general election. Lansley identified the topics which might again work to the Conservatives' advantage: 'Immigration, an issue which we raised successfully in 1992 and again in the 1994 Euro-elections campaign, played particularly well in the tabloids and has more potential to hurt.' Sir Brian Mawhinney, who had been party chairman during the 1997 campaign, was among the Tory grandees being interviewed that Sunday morning and he shared the determination of Hague and Widdecombe to continue raising the subject of asylum and immigration, an issue which he said people were talking about in the constituencies. 'We do have a robust political debate, I accept that, but John Townend did not cross the racist line . . . these issues cannot become taboo . . . This has become political correctness gone mad.' Sir Brian was impressed by the grip which Hague was exercising on the party. 'What we are seeing is just a periodic bout of "Tory turmoil" headlines . . . When the election comes people will have to choose between the common sense of the Tories and the gap between the rhetoric and reality of Blair.' His upbeat assessment was not shared by another of Alastair Stewart's guests, Sir Norman Fowler, who was also a former party chairman but was not seeking re-election. 'I am afraid we are kicking into our own goal and we must stop doing it.'

Robin Cook's claim that chicken tikka masala had become 'Britain's true national dish' attracted almost as much coverage in the Sunday newspapers as the strife in the Conservative Party. The *Observer* said the Foreign Secretary's special adviser, David Clark, who faxed Cook's speech to journalists, had noticed that this Indian curry topped a survey of the nation's favourite dishes and he thought it was 'a useful metaphor' for the strength and experience which could be drawn from multiculturalism. But Sir Herman Ouseley, a former chairman of the CRE, said Cook's suggestion that the popularity of chicken tikka masala illustrated the success of multicultural relations in Britain was 'insulting, crude and unnecessary'. Perhaps the cruellest insult was from the Foreign Secretary's former wife, Margaret Cook, who wrote in the *Mail on Sunday* that she could say with certainty that her ex-husband did not regard that 'bright red Anglo-Indian dish, chicken tikka masala' as a gastronomic treat when she knew him. 'He turned his nose up at my Indian curry (from a recipe by a grandmother who lived in India) because he liked to see chunks of meat undisguised by sauces.'

Wednesday 25 April

Stir in the British love of animals with the populism of tabloid journalism, add some crude electioneering, finish off with a dash of astute media manipulation, and the resulting mix is a pretty potent brew. As the grisly cull of farm livestock continued day after day during the first few weeks of the foot and mouth outbreak, there were frequent news stories about pet sheep and goats having to be slaughtered along with rare breeds and prize herds of cattle. The first hint of the emotional backlash waiting to be unleashed came in late March and early April when the newspapers were full of poignant photographs of spring lambs being rounded up for slaughter on infected farms. Easter weekend was obviously an opportune moment to appeal to the animal-loving instincts of the British people. All the journalists and photographers had to do was find a lovable creature that had been caught up in the horror and devastation which had engulfed the countryside. On Friday 13 April the newspapers had the pictures they had been waiting for: a colour photograph of a newborn lamb, covered in slime, barely managing to lift its head as it lay trapped in a pool of mud. It filled the front page of the *Daily Mail*, staring out, eyes just open. The headline read like a chilling epitaph: 'Portrait of an Easter lamb, Good Friday, 2001'. The lamb was one of an estimated half a million animals which had been trapped by the foot and mouth restrictions and could not be moved to fresh pasture. Farmers blamed their problems on the Ministry of Agriculture for not speeding up what was known as the 'welfare disposal scheme' which had been brought in to reduce the suffering of livestock which could not be moved or sold.

The lamb covered in mud had been photographed on a farm at Limpenhoe in Norfolk and was described as 'a heartbreaking symbol' of the blight on the British countryside. Ross Benson's account in the *Daily Mail* of the animal's 'pitifully short life of misery' pressed every possible emotional button in the psyche of the animal-lovers of Britain: 'Born on Wednesday. Unable to be moved because of the bureaucratic foot and mouth restrictions. Dead by the end of the week. By government order.' Next day's newspapers had the predictable follow-up: newsdesks had been inundated with calls from shocked readers, the lamb had been cleaned up, promised a new life, given the name Lucky and adopted by William Key, the four-year-old son of farmer Pat Key.

Lucky's lucky escape was merely a dress rehearsal for the outpouring of emotion over the fate of the aptly named Phoenix, a twelve-day-old Charolais calf found alive beside a pile of bloated carcasses five days after a foot and mouth cull on a farm at Membury in Devon. 'Save Phoenix from the ashes' was the *Mirror*'s headline on Wednesday 25 April over its account of how the 'tiny survivor', which had been missed by the slaughtermen, was found dehydrated, huddled beside the carcass of her mother.

The all-white Phoenix was photographed being fed with a bottle by her owner, Michaela Board, and the Ministry of Agriculture was quoted as saying the calf's fate would have to be decided after a blood sample had been taken. Mrs Board said that she and her husband Philip were begging the vets to spare the animal's life. Newspapers readers were asked to give their opinion by fax or email, and by lunchtime the calf had a starring role in television news bulletins.

Anna Ford's introduction to the *One O'Clock News* captured the moment: 'A twelve-day-old calf is at the centre of attention this lunchtime in a public struggle over whether she should be allowed to live . . . BBC news special correspondent, Ben Brown, has been at the farm all morning.' Brown's report had footage of the drama that was unfolding at Clarence Farm. A ministry slaughter team had returned to the farm that morning with a police escort to make a second attempt to kill Phoenix. Brown spoke to the three men, clad in white protective overalls, as they walked through the farm: 'Is the calf alive or dead?' Back came the reply from one man: 'I can't say anything . . . We are MAFF officials, so we've come to look at the situation here. Can't say any more.' Brown's report ended with the news that Philip and Michaela Board had sent the slaughtermen away, telling them they needed a court order. The stand-off continued all day. In his report for the *Six O'Clock News*, Brown had footage of the army arriving to take away the pile of animal carcasses beside which Phoenix had been found alive. When Peter Sissons opened the *Ten O'Clock News* his third headline told of a breaking story: 'Phoenix reprieved as Blair steps in to change the culling policy.' Sissons said that in the last half-hour the BBC had been told by Downing Street of 'a change in the culling policy which means Phoenix will be saved'.

Paul Rowley, a political correspondent at BBC Westminster, had taken a call from the chief press officer at No. 10, Anne Shevas, at 9.30 p.m. 'She said to me, "Phoenix has been reprieved, we have a new policy announcement coming out tomorrow." She said she had been told to get the message out in time for the ten o'clock news bulletins. She was in a rush. It was obvious she'd just been given the news by Alastair Campbell and was ringing round the BBC, ITN and the Press Association news agency to get the news out as fast as possible. She told me she didn't know how many healthy animals might be saved by the change in policy.'

But in its haste to hit the ten o'clock news bulletins, No. 10 had omitted to agree a consistent line with MAFF. A Ministry spokesman said Phoenix had been reprieved as a result of 'a refinement, not a change, in government policy'. The need to slaughter animals on neighbouring farms, in line with the requirement for what was known as a contiguous cull, was about to be 'refined' because of a fall in the number of foot and mouth outbreaks. Still, Paul Rowley was able to tell *The World Tonight* that by releasing the announcement that the government intended to reduce the slaughter of healthy animals on the suspicion that they might be infected, Downing Street had saved the calf and 'Phoenix had risen from the ashes'.

Thursday 26 April

No student of the British news media would have had much difficulty predicting the headlines in next morning's newspapers. 'Saved by the nation . . . Phoenix, a symbol of hope for everyone who has suffered in this crisis', said the front-page headline in the *Mirror*. Below a close-up of Phoenix's face, the paper said the whole of the foot and mouth crisis had come down to one small symbol, a tiny white calf which had 'touched the heart of this animal-loving nation'. On an inside page the *Mirror* reproduced a selection of the hundreds of faxes sent in by readers begging MAFF to spare the life of an innocent animal. 'Dear *Mirror*. My God! My God! Please, please, I beg you, don't kill this beautiful calf. He hasn't got a voice, we have.' Later that morning Phoenix had her own photo-call at

Clarence Farm, and the lunchtime news on ITN showed her surrounded by something like fifty journalists and photographers. Michaela Board said the survival of the calf would give a sense of hope to farmers throughout the country. 'When Phoenix is strong enough she will go out in the field with my horse for company.'

Having done so much to whip up the campaign to save Phoenix, reporters turned their attention to the villains of the piece: those who had dared to contemplate slaughtering the calf in the first place. Godric Smith, deputy press secretary at No. 10, faced some harsh questioning from what his boss Alastair Campbell had always said was the most cynical bunch of journalists in Britain, the lobby correspondents of Westminster. We were told at our afternoon briefing that Nick Brown had reported to Cabinet that morning that the outbreak was on a downward trajectory and that, on the advice of the chief scientific adviser, Professor David King, and the chief veterinary officer, Jim Scudamore, MAFF was widening the discretion on culling livestock on contiguous farms. Smith insisted that it was the falling number of cases, and not the 'life-chances of one calf', which had given the government the opportunity to 'look at the policy and refine it'. State vets had begun discussing the possibility of widening the discretion on slaughter the previous Friday, 20 April; a paper had been prepared for ministers to read over the weekend; and Brown had met senior officials the following Monday, 23 April. All this had taken place before the case of Phoenix came to light on the afternoon of Tuesday 24 April, and the final decision to relax the cull was made on Wednesday 25 April after a meeting between Brown, King and Scudamore and a further meeting that afternoon between Brown and Blair. 'The decision on Phoenix was made by MAFF on the advice of vets and officials. The idea this was taken by politicians or press officers is a little far-fetched, but inevitably if a case becomes a *cause célèbre*, it is not impossible there is going to be a discussion about it.'

Two political editors, George Jones of the *Daily Telegraph* and Philip Webster of *The Times*, challenged Smith's account. They insisted that their newspapers were told by MAFF on the evening of Tuesday 24 April that the calf would have to be slaughtered and that it was clear Downing Street had intervened. Eventually, despite his repeated refusal to reveal whether the Prime Minister had spoken directly to Brown about the fate of Phoenix, Smith finally acknowledged that media pressure had been a factor. He admitted that the announcement to save the calf had been released in time to catch the ten o'clock television news bulletins. 'That's really a media process question which I'm not going to get into but it was pretty clear Phoenix was going to be saved and newsrooms were told because we were getting lots of calls about it.'

The plight of Phoenix had brought to a head the growing anger of farmers who had been forced to watch the slaughter of healthy livestock. Jeff Bell, a farmer in Cumbria, told The *World At One* that his herd of ninety-one cattle had been killed the previous afternoon when the case of Phoenix was already in the news. 'MAFF were on the phone that morning telling me the slaughter team was on its way. The vets must have known then there was an element of doubt about the policy. Why didn't I get a call? My top-quality animals could have been saved. If it had been a cow that had survived that cull in Devon, it wouldn't have created any interest. It was just because it was a calf that the media got hold of it and the government definitely changed the policy because there's an election looming.' That afternoon other farmers complained to *Radio Five Live* about the needless killing of their livestock. The owner of a flock of rare sheep described her horror on seeing the slaughter of her great pygmy lambs. Frank Disney, who had lost a herd of 400 beef and dairy cattle on his farm at Bradworthy in Devon, said he had no idea the policy was about to change. 'Thirteen days ago they said I had become part of a contiguous cull. We staved MAFF off for ten days but last Saturday we were told we'd lost our appeal. They came in at 10 a.m. on Sunday to slaughter our herd. It's very quiet now on the farm. We're gobsmacked. It's totally destroyed my life.'

Nick Brown sounded tense when questioned by Eddie Mair on *PM*. He was clearly irritated on being asked when he had known that the calf in Devon would be reprieved. 'The final policy decision on culling was made yesterday afternoon but it had been evolving for some time . . . I don't know what was said on last night's news bulletins. I didn't see the news on television yesterday.' Mair put it to Brown that the suspicion was that Downing Street was driving the policy in order to announce that Phoenix had been saved: 'When did you know that the change of policy was being made public?' Brown: 'You tell me. I didn't hear it. I have no knowledge of it . . . I would love to tell you that the policy had been changed so that we could save Phoenix but that isn't what happened. Public policy cannot be extrapolated from the plight of individual animals. I know there is a tendency to look at young, appealing animals and say, "Oh, it's terrible," but the truth of the matter is that the only way we are going to defeat this disease is by culling it out . . . You say Downing Street announced it. I don't know whether it is true or not.'

Brown's tortured replies underlined the reality of life as a minister in Tony Blair's government. However galling it must have been to those wrong-footed by it, headline-chasing was deeply ingrained in Downing Street. Brown's statement to the House of Commons that afternoon announcing the change of policy had been pre-empted, and his job was now to catch up with the news as quickly as he could. He had been upstaged by Phoenix the calf. Alastair Campbell was anxious to avoid another day of harrowing headlines and pictures. He knew that even he could not face down the combined wrath of the tabloid press and the animal-lovers of Britain.

Friday 27 April

If there had been any thought that John Townend might moderate his opinions after the mauling which the Conservatives had received on the vexed issue of race relations, the leadership's hopes were well and truly shattered by the speed and determination with which the Yorkshire East MP returned to the fray. After being tracked down early in the morning in France, and being interviewed by *Today* on the telephone, he dashed back to the television and radio studios at Westminster to continue his tirade against the harm which he believed had resulted from the work of the Commission for Racial Equality.

Townend's renewed onslaught on its activities followed the release the previous evening of his letter of 13 March explaining why he had refused to sign the cross-party pledge designed to prevent racist electioneering. It was short and to the point: 'I am afraid that I am opposed to the whole concept of the CRE. I think it causes more racial problems than it solves. I passionately believe in individual freedom and in equality before the law. I believe that as a result of some of your activities some people are more equal than others. I therefore think it would be hypocritical for me to be associated with an organisation which I would like to see abolished.' Townend had used his release of his own letter as an opportunity to hit back at the Foreign Secretary, Robin Cook, who in a speech the previous week had ridiculed the MP's suggestion that Britain's 'homogenous Anglo-Saxon society' had been undermined by massive immigration.

Claiming to have the support of the vast majority of his constituents, the retiring MP fired off in all directions: 'Robin Cook and many of his colleagues challenge the very concept of our nation. Presumably he considers us a mongrel race. I can tell him my Yorkshire constituents are insulted by such comments.' Townend wanted all immigrants to be integrated so that English was their first language and they adopted English culture and history, rather than looking back to a motherland abroad. 'Everyone should be British, English, Welsh or Scottish, whether they are white, brown, black or yellow . . . I believe the concept of a multicultural, multiethnic, multilingual society is a mistake and will inevitably cause great problems.'

Townend's timing could hardly have been more devastating for his party. News of his latest outburst reached reporters as they were waiting for William Hague to arrive at the Hilton Hotel in Bradford to address West Yorkshire Conservatives. Hague's visit had taken in the Bradford West constituency, where over a third of the population were Asian. He was keen to show his support for the Conservatives' two Asian candidates in the city, Mohammed Riaz in Bradford West and Zahid Iqbal in Bradford North. On hearing what had been said about Britain becoming a 'mongrel race', Hague immediately repudiated Townend's remarks – but again insisted withdrawal of the Tory whip was not an issue because the MP was not seeking re-election. In his speech that evening, Hague pledged his support for a multicultural Britain: 'All people, all communities, all races and backgrounds are welcome in the Conservative Party . . . We were the first party to have a Jewish leader, we were the first party to have a woman leader and we will be the first party to have an Asian leader – though not quite yet.'

Townend, apparently oblivious to the efforts which his party was making, in his first interview of the morning told *Today* that although illegal immigrants were being caught at the rate of 100,000 a year, another 100,000 were probably getting through. 'Robin Cook says he wants to see an increase in immigration. Where are we going to put these people? . . . This is an important issue at this election and I think the CRE pact was aimed to stop discussion, and anybody like me who puts his head above the parapet is accused of being a racist.' Shortly after the interview Carole Walker, a BBC political correspondent, made contact with the MP, who by then was driving with his wife towards Calais; when asked, he agreed that on arriving at Dover he would make straight for the BBC's studios at Westminster to record a television interview for the lunchtime news bulletin. However, he hit bad traffic in south-east London and phoned in from Lewisham to say he might be delayed. Reeta Chakrabarti needed an immediate television interview for her report for the *One O'Clock News* and John Pienaar was anxious to talk to the MP at greater length before compiling his report for the *Ten O'Clock News*; but in the event Townend was too late for the lunchtime bulletin, and Ms Chakrabarti was recording her piece to camera as the MP arrived at BBC Westminster. Here he was welcomed by the Millbank duty meeter-greeter, Kenny Baker, who took him immediately to the remote camera position for *News 24*.

Baker's job involved adjusting the camera as instructed by the director in the studios at the News Centre in west London. Rachel Wright, one of the producers, offered to find someone else to operate the camera if Baker felt uncomfortable about doing so. 'I didn't mind at all. I was quite happy about having Townend look me in the eye as I looked at him down the lens of the camera. As I took him round the building, to the different studios, he kept saying to me that I was OK. He said he liked West Indians. We integrated well, we spoke English and played football. We weren't like the Asians who spoke their own languages which meant councils had to send out notices in nine different languages. He kept asking me for my opinion but I didn't say anything.' For his part, the Yorkshire East MP could not have been more obliging, responding to every interview request; but instead of the quiet Friday which had been expected, BBC Westminster suddenly found itself leading the news, as another instalment in the Townend saga gathered pace. For although the man of the moment had missed his slot, another Tory parliamentarian, the black peer Lord Taylor of Warwick, did meet the deadline for his interview with the lunchtime news bulletin and he renewed his demand, first made on Friday 30 March, for the controversial MP to be disci-plined, despite his imminent retirement. 'Towned is still a serving Member of Parliament. The reason the BBC is reporting his racist comments is because he is an MP in a responsible position. I believe it's time for the whip to be taken away from him.'

After his speech the previous evening in Bradford, Hague spent the morning at Pudsey, near Leeds, and addressed a rally in support of the Conservatives' 'Keep the Pound' campaign. He was jostled by three protestors wearing Hague masks who barracked him about Townend and called for the MP to be sacked. Hague told reporters he had no intention of withdrawing the whip. 'It would be just a gesture when he only has a few days to go. I believe in making the substance clear, that people of all races are welcome in the Conservative Party. That's how it will stay.' Hague's refusal to take action was put to Lord Taylor on The *World At One*. 'That's a cop-out . . . It's no good saying Townend has only a few days to serve and it doesn't really matter; it does matter. He has caused a great deal of offence.' Lord Taylor said he could only assume that Hague was failing to act because he was 'frightened of a certain right-wing element' in the party. 'Hague is not a bad man, but he's surrounded by people giving him bad, bad advice . . . He will say one thing one day and another thing the next day, and people feel uncertain as to where he really stands. When people feel uncertain they tend to, well, shy away, and certainly the ethnic minorities feel very uncertain about what he really is saying.' The only reason the black peer remained a member of the Conservative Party was in order to try to change it. 'It would be much easier for me to just walk across and join cool Labour. I have been asked to do so many, many times. But my fight is within the Conservative Party.'

At the end of the afternoon the two protagonists in the debate were interviewed one after another on *PM*. Lord Taylor described the battle going on within the party. 'There are those who realise Britain is changing, is multiracial and multicultural, and realise we need to be more inclusive . . . Townend is clearly determined to continue spouting his racist rubbish. It's as if Townend is laying down the gauntlet to Hague, goading him into action . . . I hope Hague will act because leadership is about action, not position. Hague is very proud of his judo and fourteen-pints-a-day macho image. He now has a chance to show real macho leadership by withdrawing the whip and booting him out.'

Townend responded by denying he was throwing down the gauntlet. 'If you say the Tory party should give up free speech and the right of MPs to give their views, that would be the end of the party. I don't think there's any reason to remove the whip from me. I haven't broken any rules.'

I was as perplexed and confused as were most other political correspondents about the leadership's tactics and response. If Townend had been told after his first outburst that he would be disciplined if he made similar remarks, then the whip could have been withdrawn in mid-morning, well before the lunchtime news bulletins, and Hague would have had the kind of headlines all day which Tony Blair obtained whenever he disciplined Labour dissidents. But instead of gaining positive coverage from his presence in Bradford, and his support for the city's two Asian candidates, Hague had allowed his visit to be obliterated by a story which had only drawn attention to his indecisive leadership of the party and his failure to slap down an MP who had spoken of the British becoming 'a mongrel race'. The only conclusion I could reach was that Conservative Central Office feared that if Townend were disciplined he would be treated as a martyr and this might encourage other like-minded Tory MPs to make similar statements. The party's chaotic response to the bedlam which developed over signing the CRE compact suggested that Hague remained reluctant, or unable, to assert his authority. Perhaps he was hoping the story would just go away.

Monday 30 April

After allowing the Conservatives' race row to continue unchecked for a month, leaving Tory MPs lurching from one crisis to the next and allowing doubts to be raised about his own abilities as leader, William Hague finally displayed clinical precision in silencing the two main protagonists. The day began inauspiciously enough. On the basis of news reports and interviews on *Today*, there seemed little that morning to suggest Hague was any nearer resolving what had proved to be a nasty and highly damaging pre-election spat. Firm action of a kind had been threatened the night before, but the Yorkshire East MP, John Townend, still appeared to be cocking a snook at the leadership and there were ominous signs that the party's most prominent black politician, Lord Taylor of Warwick, was on the point of defecting to Labour. Hague had acted with almost precipitate haste in December 1998 in sacking Viscount Cranborne, the leader of the Conservative peers, for going behind his back to Tony Blair to reach a compromise deal on reform of the House of Lords. A year later Hague had similarly shown no hesitation in dismissing Shaun Woodward from the Conservative front bench after the MP refused to vote in support of the retention of a provision known as Section 28 (of the Local Government Act 1986), which prohibits the promotion of gay sex in local authority schools. Woodward's subsequent defection to Labour, in mid-December 1999, was timed to cause maximum damage to the Conservatives, and Hague must have feared that another coup was in the offing. His outright refusal to contemplate removing the Tory whip from John Townend had dismayed Lord Taylor and deeply divided his MPs. Political journalists were confused as to Hague's intentions and failed to understand why he had not acted decisively much earlier to stamp his authority on the party.

The failure to discipline Townend – who appeared to have no comprehension of the offence he had caused and went blundering on, continuing to speak his mind – raised doubts about the strength of Hague's commitment to a multiracial, multicultural Britain. All weekend the storm clouds had been gathering. Saturday 28 April began with a stark reminder of the way Conservative MPs had alienated many in the ethnic communities. In a speech to a TUC conference in Perth, the black trade union leader Bill Morris said that thousands of doctors, nurses and other health workers, who were striving to save lives day in, day out, did not recognise the foreign country which Hague had spoken of. 'For too many of us, it is indeed a foreign land. A foreign land where ordinary black British families wake up almost every morning to listen on the radio to descriptions of themselves they do not recognise . . . They hear the CRE, which was established by an Act of Parliament, described as a pressure group and told to go to hell . . . In Hague's foreign country I do not fear the racists on the street, I fear the words of politicians which are sometimes taken by the racists as a licence to attack anyone who does not speak or look like them.' After his speech, Morris, general secretary of the Transport and General Workers' Union, told *Channel Four News* that as long as Townend continued to take the Tory whip, it had to be assumed his views represented 'a largeish proportion' of the Conservative Party.

Another unexpected twist was captured in the newspaper headlines on the morning of Sunday 29 April: Lord Taylor had been ordered to report to Lord Henley, the Conservatives' chief whip in the House of Lords. Lord Henley sent his summons to Lord Taylor by email. The *Mail on Sunday* said the message was timed 1.57 p.m. on Friday 27 April, which Lord Taylor thought was significant because it followed his interview on The *World At One* in which he accused Hague of being 'frightened' to discipline Townend and went on to reveal that he had been asked 'many, many times' to join the Labour Party. Lord Henley's invitation did not sound particularly welcoming. It said: 'I want to see you in my office next week.' On reading the email on Friday evening, the black peer said, the only conclusion he could draw was that he was about to be disciplined and might be expelled from the party for daring to criticise Hague's leadership. 'I presume they are not inviting me in to have a lollipop,' he said in an interview with the *Observer*.

Late on Sunday afternoon journalists learned of another surprise development: James Arbuthnot, the Conservatives' chief whip in the House of Commons, had told Townend that if he made any further 'intemperate remarks about race' he would be expelled from the party. The sudden change of tack caught the media by surprise, because earlier in the day Dr Liam Fox, the shadow health secretary, told *Sky News* that no action was required because Townend was leaving Parliament. 'Why would we want to make a greater issue out of this? Why would you want to create a martyr?'

The conflicting signals did little to reassure Lord Taylor, who told Sunday's *Ten O'Clock News* that he had not been pacified by the leadership's response. 'It's pathetic. What Hague is saying in effect is, "We know this man is racist, but we still endorse him as a Conservative MP. The only difference is he's got to keep his gob shut." That's not going to fool anybody. This is a fudge.'

A little later, when interviewed on *The Westminster Hour*, the party chairman Michael Ancram had the uncomfortable task of trying to respond to Lord Taylor's latest broadside. He insisted that Hague meant business, although Ancram calculated there were only ten days to go before Parliament was dissolved. 'This is not an empty gesture . . . I hope Townend will now understand that this is serious . . . His remarks about race relations are totally unacceptable and if he were to repeat them, his membership of the party would be untenable.' Ancram sounded edgy and flustered when asked why the party had not taken disciplinary action sooner and appeared to be on the point of threatening its only black peer with expulsion. The reason why Hague had not acted earlier was that if the whip had been withdrawn with only days of the parliament to go, the news media would have been 'the first to say this is meaningless'. Ancram insisted there was no truth in the suggestion that Lord Taylor was going to be 'told off', as Lord Henley had made it abundantly clear he was not intending to take disciplinary action.

If Ancram imagined he had injected some clarity into the situation, he was badly mistaken, because the fate of Lord Taylor dominated the Monday morning news bulletins. In an article for *The Times* he had intensified his attack on Hague's 'weak and pathetic' leadership for allowing Townend to escape with what 'is at best a belated yellow card issued by a timid referee against a player who has already committed numerous offences'. Lord Taylor piled on the pressure and, with an announcement about the general election expected within days, he knew just how to put Hague on the spot. Although the Conservative Party was 'a broad church, it cannot contain both Townend and people like me,' and if the MP was still in the party when campaign started his own position 'may well be untenable'. Hague's 'crass miscalculation' had battered the image of the Tory party among younger voters, committed Christians of all races and decent people from all walks of life. 'Hague is desperately trying to bury the race issue. In all probability, the race issue will end up burying his leadership.' The renewed challenge to Hague drew support from the Asian Conservative peeress Baroness Flather, who told *Today* that Townend's remarks had been 'offensive and hurtful' and that it did not matter whether he was leaving Parliament in 'six weeks, six months or six years': he should have been expelled immediately.

The morning's news coverage left political correspondents with the clear impression that Lord Taylor was intent on provoking a confrontation with the Tory high command, almost as though he was looking for a justification to defect to Labour. His line of attack, accusing Hague of weak leadership, appeared to mirror the tactics adopted by Shaun Woodward after he was dismissed from the front bench and then crossed the floor of the House in a blaze of publicity. The suspicion grew that the black peer had been lined up for the leading role in the latest sting to be engineered by Millbank Tower and was acting out the lines which had been scripted for him by Alastair Campbell.

At the morning lobby briefing Downing Street was asked about an interview on GMTV the previous morning by the Secretary of State for Trade and Industry, Stephen Byers, who said Lord Taylor was 'a politician of great principle' who would be welcomed in the Labour Party if he wished to defect. Campbell told political correspondents he had not been in discussion with Lord Taylor and knew of no contact with him by any member of the government. 'I know your attention span doesn't last longer than a day but this is a story about the Conservatives, not Labour . . . Lord Taylor has friends in all sorts of parties and places and I cannot be expected to know what everyone in the Labour Party has been up to every hour of the day.' Lance Price, Labour's director of communications, agreed it was not impossible that someone had spoken to the peer, but insisted that his defection was not something which appeared on the party's 'pre-election grid' and a reception committee was not waiting for him at Millbank Tower. Campbell and Price could hardly believe their good fortune. Most of the morning newspapers had front-page reports about Hague's failure to sack 'a Tory race bigot', yet the inside pages were filled with picture spreads of Tony Blair meeting the former President of South Africa, Nelson Mandela, at a concert in London marking seven years of democracy in his homeland.

As Campbell had indicated at the morning briefing, the curtain had yet to go up on the final scene in the Townend drama. Interviews for the lunchtime news bulletins gave a hint of what was to come. First Giles Marshall, chair of the Tory Reform Group, urged Lord Taylor to remain in the party; then the shadow Foreign Secretary, Francis Maude, hinted that further action had not been ruled out. He said racist sentiments had no place in the Conservative Party. When Townend talked of 'Commonwealth immigration' and 'Anglo-Saxon society' he meant 'coloured immigration' and 'white society', and even though his racism had been dressed up in euphemisms, it was unacceptable in a modern democratic party. Maude had been taking part in a frantic round of discussions at Conservative Central Office and, along with several other members of the shadow cabinet, he was said to favour firm action against Townend. Earlier in the morning I had spoken to one of the party's media officers, Mike Penning, as he headed to Smith Square for a meeting, saying he was about to get briefed on what had been decided. Shortly after the lunchtime programmes went off the air, the news came through: Hague would make an announcement on the steps of Central Office at 3 p.m. Soon after the reporters, photographers and television crews had assembled, party officials trooped out to give support. Heading the line-up were Hague's parliamentary private secretary, John Whittingdale; the head of the policy unit, Danny Finkelstein; the head of media, Amanda Platell; the chief spokesman, Nick Wood; and the assistant head of media, Andrew Scadding. But after a few minutes they all turned on their heels and trooped back inside Central Office.

Hague had been held up for fifteen minutes because he was being filmed with a party of schoolchildren for *Sky News*. Elinor Goodman, political editor of *Channel Four News*, used the delay to tease her four main competitors for their habitual jostling with one another as they tried to get into the best position to put the first question to Hague. There tends to be a strict pecking order for doorstep interviews. Newspaper reporters usually hold back, allowing their colleagues from television and radio to make the running, at least to begin with. Ms Goodman had seen it all before and was usually happy to let her rivals on the airwaves, John Sergeant (ITN), Andrew Marr (BBC), Nick Robinson (*News 24*) and Adam Boulton (*Sky News*) fight it out for the first question. On seeing that her tease had been greeted with some embarrassed shuffles, she said it was a pity Michael Brunson, who had retired from his post as ITN political editor the previous year, was no longer with them. 'Mike always knew how to get in first and he loved it when politicians used his first name and said "Mike" in their reply. He'd always use that answer in his report. I hate it when politicians say "Look, Elinor . . . "; I think that excludes the viewer. The public don't like it when we're seen talking to each other on first-name terms.' In the event there was little need for supplementary questions. When the party officials trooped out for a second time to line up outside Central Office, they were joined by one of the party's black candidates, Judith Edwards, who was to contest Liverpool Riverside. Mike Penning told the media throng that he would be handing out two separate press releases once Hague had spoken, a hint that one related to a decision about Townend and the other to Lord Taylor.

The formal statement barely did justice to the brinkmanship which had evidently taken place. Hague said he had told Townend that unless he was prepared to apologise for his 'ill-chosen words and withdraw them, undertake not to repeat them, and accept that racism has no place in the party', then he could no longer remain a Conservative. Townend had signed a statement to that effect. Hague announced that he was asking Lord Taylor to join the party's nine black and Asian candidates in supporting an open letter in which they declared their belief in a Conservative Party which was 'an open and tolerant party' and which valued the rich variety of Britain's multicultural society. It amounted, in effect, to a loyalty oath which Lord Taylor had to sign if he wished to remain in the party. Hague told the assembled reporters that he recognised issues could blow up unexpectedly in politics and they did provide a chance to say 'what you are and what you mean'. His ultimatum to Townend had been an unprecedented step, but people had got the impression that the MP's views were representative of a larger section of the party, and he would not allow that inference to stand.

Once Hague had returned to his office, the party's media officers were anxious to put the best possible spin on their leader's handiwork. Nick Wood said that Townend had asked for half an hour to 'think about it' after Hague told him about the ultimatum but then rang back and agreed to sign 'a grovelling apology' saying he was 'very sorry' for his 'ill-chosen words'. Andrew Scadding pointed to what he thought was the technical precision of the move against Lord Taylor, who could face disciplinary action unless he signed the loyalty oath. 'Obviously there was a lot of head banging inside Central Office but we do seem to have sorted it out at last.'

Lord Taylor himself sounded distinctly dubious when giving his first reaction on *PM*; indeed, he dismissed Townend's apology as worthless: 'It is too little and too late.' However, he agreed to sign the open letter in which the party's black and Asian parliamentary candidates reaffirmed their faith in the 'inclusive and welcoming nature' of the Conservative Party. When asked if there was still a danger he might defect, Lord Taylor said the suggestion that he had been cosying up to Labour was ridiculous. 'It's anonymous and faceless Tories who are saying this. It's not true, it's a lie.' Later that evening, when interviewed on the *Ten O'Clock News*, he sounded far more positive about his future with the Conservatives. 'I don't want to damage the party and I want to stay and fight my cause.' Townend beat a hasty retreat that evening when reporters met up with him at King's Cross station in London. Television news pictures showed him dashing through the crowds hotly pursued by a BBC producer, Rachel Wright, who was easily identified by the blue coat she was wearing. 'No comment,' was his only answer to her persistent questioning.

Hague's closest advisers spent much of the evening briefing journalists, insisting that the Conservative leader had acted decisively and put an end to the row. But *Newsnight* provided a further illustration of support within the parliamentary party for the views of the Yorkshire East MP. Laurence Robertson, MP for Tewkesbury, said Townend's remarks were 'basically true' because 'cramming together too many people from different multiracial groups' made society very difficult to manage. Judith Edwards, the black Tory candidate who had stood with Hague outside Central Office, looked shocked and disappointed on seeing the interview. She told *Newsnight* that she hoped Robertson's comments would be studied 'very closely' by the party and that he too would be required to give an explanation and make an apology.

Hague's failure to act sooner in disciplining Townend had dismayed the former Conservative Prime Minister, Sir Edward Heath, who told *News 24* that the MP should have been expelled 'straight away' – though he acknowledged that Hague had been in no position to act with the same speed with which he had acted himself when he sacked Enoch Powell from the shadow cabinet after the 'rivers of blood' speech in March 1968. The real 'culprit' of the affair was that the party had ended up even further 'on the extreme right', and Hague could not have moved any faster because so many Conservative MPs shared Townend's views. Sir Edward's greatest fear was that Hague's slow response had ensured that race relations would become an issue in the election campaign. 'Look at the publicity Townend has got. Look what he's done to the party.'

Inevitably there had been a price to pay for the month's postponement in calling the general election. Hague had urged Blair to delay the campaign for as long as possible because of the difficulties posed by the outbreak of foot and mouth disease. If there had been any tactical advantage to the Tories in putting off polling day, it had been well and truly dissipated by the self-inflicted wounds of the following few weeks. If Hague had been able to fall back on the sense of urgency and self-discipline usually generated by a general election, he might have been able to save himself and his party from a disastrous lead-up to the campaign that lay ahead.

Tuesday 1 May

Dire predictions about the low turnout which was expected for the 2001 general election had been commonplace for weeks. Tony Blair's decision to delay announcing polling day for a month had disappointed many political strategists and psephologists who feared the postponement would encourage cynicism in the news media, which in turn would only add to voter disenchantment. In his valedictory contribution to his final Queen's Speech debate in December 2000, the former Conservative Prime Minister John Major had told MPs he could make one prediction with certainty. He was convinced the turnout in 2001 would be 'far lower than for any election in modern times', and he believed Blair should shoulder much of the blame for having allowed one of the 'most unscrupulous spin machines Britain had ever seen' to fuel the public's distaste of politics and distrust of politicians. Major could speak with bitter experience about voting intentions because turnout had fallen from 77.7 per cent in the 1992 general election to 71.4 per cent in 1997 when he was defeated by Blair. I remembered Major's foreboding as I set off for the Attlee Suite in Portcullis House, the new block of MPs' offices opposite Big Ben, to attend a seminar on 'Stirring Up Apathy' organised by the Hansard Society in an attempt to pull together efforts by inter-ested groups in the hope of attracting publicity for increased voter registration and participation.

Dr David Butler, a fellow of Nuffield College, Oxford, and co-author of *British Political Facts*, remained optimistic. He said the campaign to encourage postal votes and the introduction of rolling electoral registers, allowing voters to register as late as mid-April for a June election, should have an effect. He thought the postal vote could go up from an average of around 2 per cent since the 1950s to perhaps 4 or 5 per cent, and that held out the possibility of a higher total turnout. Shelagh Diplock, director of the Hansard Society, shared Dr Butler's optimism about the impact of the publicity drive which the government had promised to promote the simplified procedure for obtaining postal votes. There had been forecasts of a 4 per cent drop in the overall turnout on polling day, but she did not think the level of apathy would be as bad as some opinion pollsters had been predicting.

Wednesday 2 May

Alastair Campbell's ability to enunciate government policy with greater clarity than Tony Blair seemed to intensify the closer it came to the general election and his promised departure from the combative world of Westminster lobby briefings. At what MPs accepted was the penultimate session of Prime Minister's questions, William Hague asked for an indication of government policy on the American proposal for a nuclear missile shield, known as son of *Star Wars*. Following his inauguration in January 2001, President Bush had backed moves to develop protection against nuclear terrorism and if Britain's closest ally was taking the lead, Hague thought the government should give its support. Blair refused to give a definite answer and stuck rigidly to the line which ministers had been advancing for several months, namely that Britain intended to wait until the United States made a specific proposal. He stressed that there was still no indication as to whether the Americans intended to use sea-based or land-based technology for its new anti-missile system.

Political correspondents took over from where Hague left off when they got the chance at the afternoon lobby briefing to see if the Prime Minister's official spokesman could throw any more light on the government's thinking. To begin with the questions got nowhere, but then, when asked if the government thought a global missile defence system was a good idea, Campbell was quite specific in his answer: 'Broadly, yes, in that the Americans are the last remaining superpower. They are the only ones who can develop this new technology and they are going ahead with it.' I was not present at this briefing, but Susan Cornwell, political correspondent with Reuters news agency, had no doubt that Campbell knew what he was saying. 'He'd answered a lot of questions and hadn't given anything away, but when he was asked, "Was it a good idea?" and he replied, "Broadly, yes," everyone began taking a note. You could hear the pens suddenly start scratching as everyone wrote down what he'd said. I thought he'd take it back or play it down but he didn't. What he was really saying was that America was the only remaining superpower and they'd do it anyway, so he was really saying to us, "Look, you lot, get real." There was no doubt he knew what he'd said.'

The fallout from Campbell's briefing was fast and furious. Iain Duncan Smith, the shadow defence secretary, told *PM* that it was breathtaking that Campbell and not Blair had announced such an important shift in policy. 'At question time Blair says this is not the time to make a decision. Half an hour later, under pressure from the press, his spokesman changes the position. Who is governing the country, for goodness sake?' Duncan Smith thought Blair probably wanted the Americans to hear an expression of British support but knew he could not give it in the House of Commons because Labour MPs hated the prospect of a new missile shield, so he had 'quietly slipped this out' through the lobby. Campbell's skill in defusing issues which could cause Labour trouble in the election campaign was identified by the Liberal Democrats' foreign affairs and defence spokesman, Menzies Campbell, as the likeliest explanation for what had happened. 'What Alastair Campbell did was pull back the curtain and let us see what the government is thinking . . . I think he knew that Blair didn't want to go through the election campaign with missile defence being a live issue.'

Geoff Hoon, the Secretary of State for Defence, did his best to stonewall Jeremy Paxman's questions on *Newsnight* but finally had to concede that Campbell's answer was in line with government thinking. 'We have made clear we wish to be sympathetic to US concerns and we would want to be helpful . . . What Alastair Campbell is talking about is a situation which will arise when the United States make a specific proposal.' His answer did not satisfy the Liberal Democrats' deputy leader in the House of Lords, Baroness Williams of Crosby, who thought a press secretary should not have said missile defence was 'a good idea without qualification' when the Prime Minister was promising to discuss the details. 'I think it is unacceptable constitutionally of Alastair Campbell to give an answer on the most important foreign policy issue of our decade.'

3   The Home Straight –
and the Stalls Open

Thursday 3 May

If a cynical political correspondent had dared to suggest at one of Alastair Campbell's lobby briefings that Tony Blair would use the day on which the general election should have been held to declare that the foot and mouth crisis was over, I am sure the reply would have been crisp and to the point. The hapless journalist would have been accused of having become obsessed by 'processology' and reminded that in the policy-driven world inhabited by the Prime Minister's official spokesman, spin does not exist and the art of presentation is merely a mundane process that is part and parcel of the everyday mechanics of politics. A front seat at the carefully choreographed news conference held at 10 Downing Street would have dispelled any such notions. Blair and Campbell had agreed a soundbite which they knew would be included in every news bulletin and would secure headlines in next day's newspapers. The No. 10 press office had been busy the night before trailing the announcement that Blair was due to make and the top line on the early-morning lead story on the Press Association wire service said it all: 'The fight against foot and mouth is finally being won, Tony Blair was saying today, just days before he is expected to call the next general election.'

At the midday news conference Blair was followed into the room by Brigadier Malcolm Wood, the deputy head of the foot and mouth co-ordination centre; the government's chief scientific adviser, Professor David King; and the Minister of Agriculture, Nick Brown, whom I had seen a few minutes earlier being briefed by his department's deputy director of communications, Lucian Hudson. Blair's first task was to welcome journalists and broadcasters from France, Germany and the USA, whose presence, he said, he appreciated because one of the biggest casualties of the outbreak had been the British tourist industry. He had called the news conference because he wanted to pay tribute to all those who had worked so hard to fight the disease and bring it under control; to the vets from Britain and all over the world; to the armed forces who had shown once again they were a force for good; and to the scientists, civil servants and police. There was a special word of tribute to the farmers themselves, who had suffered greatly from this 'terrible disease' and yet had still co-operated with the 'dreadful business of culling out their livestock'. The government had 'all but completely' cleared the backlog of animals waiting to be slaughtered as well as the backlog of carcasses waiting to be disposed of. Then, the preliminaries over, the Prime Minister had to get to the real point of this news conference. He had to prepare the ground for an election campaign which was expected to start within days. 'It has been a vast logistical exercise. We must carry it on until the disease is fully eradicated. The battle is not over yet, but I believe we are on the home straight.' In his well-crafted soundbite Blair went as far as he dared towards giving the impression that the epidemic was over: he was winning the 'battle' and, as he was on the point of completing the task which had forced the postponement of the election, he was ready to go to the country.

The chief scientific adviser immediately endorsed the Prime Minister's assessment. Providing the restrictions remained in force and were fully observed, Professor King was sure the weekly figure for new cases, which was down from an average of thirty-two a day to eight a day, would continue to fall on a fortnightly basis. 'I remain convinced that the epidemic is fully under control . . . I am convinced but not complacent. We must be vigilant and maintain the current controls.' Brigadier Wood was then asked by Blair to give the latest run down on the 'biggest peacetime logistical challenge' the army had faced. Up to 60,000 animals had been slaughtered every day and the military had organised the removal of 350,000 tons of animal carcasses for disposal. Brigadier Wood said the sites for ammunition and petrol needed for the Gulf War had been dwarfed by the scale of the mass burial sites which had been constructed in such a short period of time. Nick Brown thanked the 2,000 military personnel for their contribution to the slaughter programme which had kept the number of cases on a downward trend since the disease peaked at the end of March. Over 2.4 million animals had been killed – 2.5 per cent of the national herd and flock – but the culling of infected farms and animals at risk would have to continue because there were still likely to be 'sporadic' outbreaks.

In the questions which followed Blair picked out journalists from the foreign media to answer what he said were the myths which had been reported. The truth was that the disease had not been passed to humans: all fifteen possible human cases had tested negative. A reporter from Radio WGN in Chicago asked whether he could report that food in Britain was safe. Blair insisted there was no human risk at all. 'Foot and mouth – hoof and mouth as you say in the States – is not BSE. It is nothing to do with that . . . and in respect of the countryside, I cannot think of anything which the average US tourist does or wants to do, which they cannot do . . . .the last pyre has been lit in Devon and will be through in a week.'

Blair had invited political correspondents to a news conference on the very day they thought they would be reporting a general election in order to convince them that the decks had been cleared and that Britain was ready to the go to the polls; but when the moment came, he indicated he had no intention of being so inept as to be seen or heard electioneering in public. On being asked when polling day would be announced, and whether he felt vindicated in having delayed it for a month, the Prime Minister displayed an air of injured innocence: 'No, the reason for speaking to you today is to bring you up to date . . . I am not going to breach the golden rule and talk about general elections until they are called.' Blair and his campaign manager, Gordon Brown, had no such inhibitions that evening when a series of meetings were held in Downing Street with media proprietors and newspaper editors. Among those seen either entering or leaving the front doors of No. 10 or No. 11 were Rupert Murdoch, owner of News International, which publishes the *Sun*; Rebekah Wade, editor of the *News of the World*; and Charles Moore, editor of the *Daily Telegraph*. Murdoch was observed leaving by the front door of No. 11, the official residence of the Chancellor of the Exchequer, but when Nick Robinson, chief political correspondent for *News 24*, asked for further information on the meeting he was told there would be no statement. He protested, saying it was a matter of public interest that the country's biggest newspaper proprietor had met Labour's campaign manager on the eve of a general election; but Brown's special adviser, Ian Austin, gave him short shrift. 'No, it's not. You are a mad, paranoid wanker.'

Sunday 6 May

Television and radio journalists can find it difficult, once a general election has been called, to continue reporting the activities of those MPs who pursue their own enquiries and who like to make a name for themselves by investigating highly contentious issues. Editorial guidance on maintaining a fair balance among the parties starts applying almost immediately to news bulletins and current affairs programmes, and it can become even harder getting airtime for one-off political stories when Parliament is formally dissolved and MPs have reverted to the status of candidates. As an announcement about the election was still a day or two away, I was sure there was sufficient time to follow up a claim by the Conservative MP for Chichester, Andrew Tyrie, that he had new information relating to what had become known as the Hinduja passport affair. Tyrie had apparently obtained leaked copies of correspondence between Downing Street and two millionaire Indian businessmen, Gopichand and Srichand Hinduja, whose passport applications had been the subject of an inquiry by Sir Anthony Hammond following the second resignation from the Cabinet of Peter Mandelson, in January 2001. Tyrie told me he had been handed a bundle of letters which he believed were highly significant because they revealed that the two Hinduja brothers, who in February 1998 offered to become sponsors of the Faith Zone in the Millennium Dome, had visited 10 Downing Street and met Tony Blair in June 1998, shortly before a disputed telephone call by Mandelson to Mike O'Brien, the immigration minister at the Home Office. Previously the only known contact between Blair and the Hindujas had been at social events like the Diwali celebrations, and there was no public record of the brothers having met Blair officially or visited No. 10.

After getting the go-ahead from the newsroom I set off with a cameraman for Chichester, where Tyrie had said he would meet us at 12 noon at the cross in the centre of the town. I was glad to get out of London, where the May Day bank holiday weekend had turned into a waiting game for political correspondents. Most MPs seemed to be enjoying the break, realising that there would be little chance to relax once the election campaign was under way, and Blair, celebrating his forty-eighth birthday, was spending the day at Chequers with Cherie and their four children; but ministers were being required to give up some of their bank holiday weekend because they had been told to return to Downing Street for a special meeting of the Cabinet on Monday afternoon, in order to approve the contents of Labour's manifesto. On our arrival in Chichester, we walked as directed towards the cross and after a short wait saw Tyrie emerge from a throng of visitors. He was holding a sheaf of documents. As promised he handed me a copy of one of the letters. It was signed by Srichand Hinduja, addressed to Jonathan Powell,

Blair's chief of staff, and said the two brothers, together with their 'Indian friend' (Brajesh Mishra, representing the Indian government) looked forward to meeting Blair and Powell later that day (4 June 1998) to discuss the international initiatives which were being made in the wake of tension over nuclear testing by India and Pakistan.

Tyrie said the letter showed that the Hindujas met Blair during June and July 1998, which was the period Sir Anthony considered held the key to his inquiry into whether improper approaches had been made over the passport application for Srichand Hinduja. By not revealing his meeting with the Hindujas to his own investigator, Tyrie said, Blair had 'made a monkey' of Sir Anthony, whose inquiry had cleared ministers of any wrongdoing over the issuing of British passports to the Hindujas. Tyrie would not reveal the identity of the person who had handed over the letters, but I had heard that some senior civil servants were uneasy about the government's links with the Hindujas and I formed the impression that the leaked correspondence must have come from someone somewhere in Whitehall. Tyrie was a member of the House of Commons Select Committee on Public Administration and had established a reputation for his persistence in pursuing the Cabinet Secretary, Sir Richard Wilson, about instances where he believed the Blair government had politicised the work of the civil service. He told me he intended to ask Blair to make a statement in the Commons on Tuesday about the circumstances surrounding his meeting with the Hindujas. He insisted that he was not in any way involved in an attack on Blair being orchestrated by Conservative Central Office; he had spent many months investigating the Hindujas' links with the government, and had released the letter as soon as he got the agreement of his informant.

On the drive back to London, I telephoned Downing Street and the duty press officer, Tanya Joseph, promised to enquire whether No. 10 intended to comment on the letter. Two hours later she rang back with a statement. Blair did have a photo-call on the day in question with a representative of the Indian government, Brajesh Mishra, who saw Jonathan Powell; but he did not meet the Hindujas. An hour later Ms Joseph clarified her statement: the Hindujas had been in the delegation which accompanied Mishra when he handed Blair a letter from the Indian Prime Minister. Blair had no time for a meeting with the delegation but greeted Mishra, who then had discussions with Powell and other Downing Street officials. 'Nothing improper took place . . . Yes, the Hindujas were in the delegation but they were not there at our behest or invitation. This visit was about issues surrounding the nuclear tests; it's clear it wasn't about passport applications.'

Within minutes of my radio report about Tyrie's leaked letter having been broadcast, both No. 10 and the Labour Party were on the phone complaining about what I had said. Tanya Joseph took issue with my reference to Mishra, the Indian official, having 'met' Blair. She said that 'sounded as if they had had a meeting' when in fact it was 'just a handshake and the handing over of a letter'. I said I doubted whether listeners could possibly have come to that conclusion. Saying that Bishra had 'met' Blair meant exactly that: the two men had met one another at the handing over a letter at a photo-call inside No. 10. 'Look, it's very difficult for me,' said Ms Joseph. 'I am caught between No. 10 and Millbank Tower on this one.'

My second call, from Mary Maguire, the duty press officer at Millbank Tower, revealed the close contact there must have been between the party headquarters and Downing Street. My broadcast at 6 p.m. was the first news report about the leaked letter and Ms Maguire said she was annoyed with me for not having made contact with her because Millbank wanted to respond. Hardly pausing for breath, she insisted on reading out a statement from Ian McCartney, minister of state at the Cabinet Office, who spoke for the government on Labour Party affairs: 'This is a despicable and transparent attempt by Andrew Tyrie, a member of the Tory campaign team, which is clearly panicking at even the mention of a general election, to use a non-story to distract the media's attention away from the issues which are important to the British people, like economic stability, which Labour has brought about, and the cuts in public services which the Tories are promising. People will not be taken in by such opportunism as this.'

The speed of Ms Maguire's call, the discomfort of Ms Joseph and the vehemence and irrelevance of McCartney's denunciation were all elements of my first pre-election brush with the infamous rapid rebuttal unit at Millbank Tower. I had to admire Labour's efficiency. Even before the newsreader had finished the 6 p.m. news bulletin on May bank holiday Sunday, I had registered two complaints – and we were still waiting for Blair to announce the date of the general election.

Monday 7 May

William Hague and Charles Kennedy were anxious to ensure that Tony Blair did not steal all the limelight by parading his ministers at a bank holiday Cabinet meeting, so the Conservatives and the Liberal Democrats both staged events to secure their share of any pre-election publicity. Hague unveiled his party's manifesto for the council elections which had been delayed until Thursday 7 June, the date which every political strategist was confident would also be confirmed as polling day for the general election. In the hope of livening up any television or radio coverage of the launch of their local authority policies, the Conservatives gave journalists the first public hearing of the party's election theme tune, devised by Mike Batt, who had composed the music for the Wombles. Kennedy sounded equally upbeat when he went campaigning for the first time in his election battle bus. On a visit to Portsmouth South, where the Liberal Democrats were defending a seat which they had won by just over 4,000 votes in 1997, Kennedy predicted his party would win even more seats in 2001. Alan Milburn, the Secretary of State for Health, and the Secretary of State for Education, David Blunkett, spoke on behalf of the Cabinet as their colleagues left Downing Street. They gave voice to the campaign strategy which had just been agreed. Milburn said the whole emphasis of the campaign would be on delivering what the public had a right to expect. 'The heart of our manifesto, our top priority, will be reform of the public services; a manifesto based on the foundations that we've laid of economic stability that put schools and hospitals first.' Blunkett's soundbite, aimed at countering apathy and the speculation that Blair would win by a landslide, was already beginning to sound rather familiar. Labour had always failed before to get a sufficient majority to complete a second term in Parliament; now, for the 'first time ever', Labour had the chance to reverse the betrayal of the British people by Labour's previous failure to deliver.

Earlier there had been much discussion on *Today* and The *World At One* about some cautionary words from two senior Labour politicians who had found themselves on the sidelines of the campaign. Roy Hattersley, who wrote increasingly about the complaints being made by Old Labour, berated Labour MPs for their toadying and for having turned Prime Minister's questions into 'a weekly meeting of the Blair fan club'. In an article for the *Mail on Sunday*, he said Labour had 'played fast and loose' with its manifesto with 'barely a squawk from the most subservient Parliament in history'. Lord Hattersley had fought the 1987 and 1992 campaigns as Neil Kinnock's deputy, and he feared that a 'second successive massive majority' would not convince Blair that what the country needed was the politics of change. He wanted to see Labour re-elected with a majority that made parliamentary democracy a reality and allowed the party to remind its leader of the ideas on which it was founded.

Peter Mandelson had also found the opportunity to give advice from the wings one he could not resist. After his second resignation from the

Cabinet, the former Secretary of State for Northern Ireland had announced that he intended to dedicate himself to the task of getting re-elected as Labour MP for Hartlepool, the seat he had held since 1992. Mandelson, who had directed a highly acclaimed election campaign for Kinnock in 1987 and who had been a powerful force behind Blair's victory in 1997, used an article in the *Observer* to highlight the themes which he thought should inspire Labour's campaign in 2001. Economic competence had been the foundation for New Labour's success in the first four years of government, but the party had to be far more ambitious in its aspirations for a second term and needed a range of coherent policies and programmes rather than a patchwork of initiatives to tackle the worst social and economic problems and give every individual and family the chance to get on. 'Britain, therefore, needs more than competence . . . A second-term Labour government cannot simply be about the completion of "work in progress" . . . Ambition must be New Labour's compass for the second term and beyond.'

Labour's response to these twin calls for Blair to be more daring came from Douglas Alexander, the party's campaign co-ordinator. Alexander, MP for Paisley South and an ally of Gordon Brown, was being put forward increasingly often as a spokesman for the leadership after his responsibilities at Millbank Tower had been enhanced following Mandelson's return to the back benches. He said he agreed that every Labour voter wanted to see higher standards in schools and sustained investment in hospitals. 'Peter Mandelson has recognised the scale of what Labour has achieved, but I agree with him we could afford to be more ambitious.'

By the *Ten O'Clock News* the focus had switched to the imminent dissolution of Parliament. Andrew Marr, the BBC's political editor, said Blair would definitely see the Queen next morning and ask for the dissolution of Parliament. However, the Prime Minister would not stand in Downing Street to make his announcement about polling day but would go 'somewhere else' to make his declaration. 'This is all going to be about surprising people . . . it will be a different kind of campaign and tomorrow will be a different kind of opening to that campaign.'

Tuesday 8 May

Broadcasters can pay a price for getting too close to, or becoming too involved in, the action at big events, and they do occasionally live to regret what they have said in a live commentary or in their first, instant report. I think my initial hurried description of the Prime Minister's launch of the general election campaign at St Saviour's and St Olave's Girls School, at Southwark in south London, would probably have made a worthy entry for either Pseuds' Corner or the Colemanballs column in *Private Eye*.

The moment Tony Blair completed his address at afternoon assembly I had to file a forty-second voice piece. The speech was being taken live by several of the television networks and an up-to-date report was required for the next radio news summary. I was trapped right at the back of the room, having to look over the heads of the 650 girls who were packed into the hall. There was an enormous media scrum in attendance: easily a hundred or more broadcasters, journalists, photographers and various other producers and technicians working for television and radio. It felt like the hottest day of early summer and I noticed that the Prime Minister took off his jacket after he walked on to the stage. I could just see his face as the choir sang a South African song, 'Wa Wa Wa Emimimo', and then a millennium song for schools, 'We Are the Children of the Future'. Blair was late arriving and in starting his speech, and, from the advance copy of the text which had been distributed to journalists, I could see that it was going to last much longer than I had expected. I was already hot and sweaty and realised I would be up against a tight deadline. I thought I had better start writing my short script straight away, while Blair continued giving his speech.

I tried in my report to capture a flavour of what I could see: 'After the grandeur of his audience with the Queen at Buckingham Palace, not for Tony Blair the traditional backdrop of Downing Street but a location well away from the hothouse of Westminster politics – the hall of a girls' school just off the Old Kent Road. Behind him on the platform for afternoon assembly, the sun was streaming in through the blue stained glass windows . . . ' Immediately Blair finished I rushed out to record my piece, not having time to stand back and think for a few moments, or the chance to talk to the camera crews or other journalists to discover how they were reacting to what we had seen and heard. On returning to the hall a few minutes later, having filed my report from the radio car, and starting to talk to the other correspondents, I realised I had probably gone over the top and that I had been rather too lyrical in my description. Looking again at my script, I thought I should perhaps have submitted it to *Private Eye*'s editor, Ian Hislop, for inclusion in St Albion Parish News, the weekly newsletter about the activities of the Revd A. R. P. Blair MA (Oxon). The newspaper reporters still inside the school hall told me about the bored looks on the faces of the girls as Blair's speech droned on for over twenty minutes; a number of the pupils were being asked to give their opinion. I soon picked up talk of unease among some of the teachers and staff about the speech having been far too political for afternoon assembly at a girls' secondary school, especially as they were all too young to vote.

What seemed to have aroused the greatest interest was the scene that I had missed while I had been filing my report. When the television lights went off, shortly after Blair completed his speech, he walked off the stage while the choir was only halfway through singing the final hymn, 'I, The Lord of Sea and Sky'. I sensed immediately that the live television pictures had probably captured the awkwardness of the occasion and might have led viewers to question whether a school was an appropriate venue for a highly political speech and a sustained attack on the Conservative Party. Had New Labour been too clever by half in trying to use an inner-city girls' school with a multicultural intake as the backdrop for such a high-profile political event? Would there be complaints about it? I was annoyed with myself for not having paid greater attention to what was going on while Blair was speaking, and for failing even to have considered whether he would have been wiser to have stuck by tradition and announced the election in Downing Street.

Journalists had been told at the 11 a.m. lobby briefing that Blair's audience at Buckingham Palace would be at lunchtime. He would ask the Queen to dissolve Parliament and then go to St Saviour's and St Olave's. On arriving at the school I had noticed that Blair's advance guard seemed to have taken full command of both the school and the proceedings, issuing instructions to the staff and ordering journalists where to sit. Anji Hunter, Blair's special assistant (described in the tabloid press as his 'gatekeeper'), was much in evidence, as was one of the Downing Street press officers, Hilary Coffman, and Labour's director of communications, Lance Price. Outside the school entrance security was strict. Half a dozen Tory protestors shouted: 'Education, education, education . . . failed, failed, failed.' On walking into the school hall I passed the stage and noticed the blue stained-glass windows which bore the inscriptions 'Heirs of the Past' and 'Makers of the Future'. In the middle of the stage was a new, glass lectern. Most of the journalists were sent to the back of the hall. The girls filed in and took their seats; then, after Blair walked on to the stage, one of the party's press officers, Matthew Doyle, handed out a Labour press release which contained the text of the speech. Blair told the girls he had already been to see the Queen to ask for a dissolution of Parliament so that there could be a general election on Thursday 7 June. He explained to them that every vote was precious. 'No one's support should ever be assumed. That is the strength of our democracy. We earned the trust of the people in 1997 – after eighteen long years of opposition. Today we have to earn that trust again.' It was after these few initial sentences and a glance down at the text that my heart began to sink and I realised time would be against me. I knew from past experience that politicians were usually advised to keep their remarks at school assemblies down to about five minutes; but Blair had seven closely typed pages. After a short introduction, he intended to go on, point by point, describing the 'foundations' which New Labour had laid and then listing in more detail what was at stake in the election for education, the National Health Service, welfare reform, pensioners, transport, inner-city regeneration and so on. It was not until page six that Blair started to develop his theme about why the election offered a more fundamental choice than for many years.

This was pretty detailed stuff, bearing in mind that the youngest girls present were eleven and had probably been expecting to hear something about the Prime Minister himself, his own children or perhaps a description of life in Downing Street. But Blair was deep into politics. The differences between the two main parties were starker than at any time since 1983. 'Today's Conservative Party would take us back to negative equity, high mortgage rates and boom and bust; back to cuts in public services; back to social division; back to the margins of influence in Europe and the wider world.' His peroration was written as though he were rousing his supporters at a Labour rally with an appeal to the nation. 'My goal at this election is this: it is not just to win your vote, but to win your support, win your heart and mind in the fight for change that I am leading.' Finally he addressed the girls themselves: 'Britain is a great nation. It has so many strengths. But its biggest strength is its people. They, you young people here today, are the nation's potential. This is the time, and ours is the task, to set your talents free and build a land of hope and opportunity for all. Now you, the people will decide.'

After Blair departed, the headteacher, Irene Bishop, told reporters it had been an historic day for the girls. She dismissed suggestions that her Church of England foundation school had been used a television backdrop for some blatant electioneering. 'It's fantastic for the children to meet the Prime Minister. It's nothing to do with an impending election. He's the most wonderful Prime Minister in the world. We didn't ask him to come, we were just told "an important minister" wanted to visit the school. I didn't know it was the Prime Minister who was coming.'

In hurrying back to the hall after filing my report I had seen Alastair Campbell talking to a group of reporters. He was frowning and did not seem too pleased with the questions he was being asked. Campbell had resigned that morning from his post as chief press secretary, in line with the guidance issued to the seventy-nine politically appointed special advisers recruited to assist Blair and his ministers. Special advisers had the status of temporary civil servants, and as their annual salary bill of £4.4 million was paid for by the taxpayer, the Cabinet Secretary, Sir Richard Wilson, had reminded them that they had to resign if they wished to help in the election and that they would be required to 'physically have left' their departments before embarking on the campaign trail. Conservative MPs had complained that by doubling the number of special advisers, Blair had built up a ready-made campaign team which could be transferred from Downing Street and Whitehall direct to Millbank Tower once the election was called. In view of this concern, Sir Richard had stipulated that Campbell and his colleagues must surrender all government property, including mobile phones and pagers, and that they would no longer have preferential access to government papers or officials. Any request from them for information would be treated in the same way as an enquiry from a member of the public.

It was not only the special advisers who had a sudden change of role to contend with. Civil servants had been preparing for the expected cut-off point for several days: as soon as the election was announced they had to cease advising ministers and do no further work on new policy initiatives. I heard about the last-minute rush when talking to fellow contributors before the start of a media seminar that morning organised by the charitable trust Common Purpose. Sian Jarvis, head of media at the Department of Health, told me that her staff had immediately stopped briefing their Secretary of State, Alan Milburn, whose special adviser, Darren Murphy, intended to resign that evening. Milburn had been due to join the television presenter Loyd Grossman at the launch that day of the *NHS Recipe Book*, which contained fifty new menus prepared by celebrity chefs for use in hospital kitchens. 'We had to pull Milburn out of the recipe launch. If he'd been there it would have been seen as a political stunt and we didn't want to damage a positive story.' The main speaker at the seminar was the publicist Max Clifford, who told me of his pride in helping to bring down John Major in 1997 by exposing the financial irregularities and sexual misdemeanours of Tory ministers and MPs. 'The last government destroyed the NHS and I felt an effective way of damaging them was to get the word "sleaze" put up in lights alongside "Conservative".' He was not aware of any scandals about Labour MPs which were about to hit the newspapers and damage Tony Blair's government. 'Anyway, if someone was trying to sell a story like that they wouldn't come to me because everyone knows I am a socialist.' If asked to advise William Hague, he would urge the Tories to find ways of concentrating on the NHS because there was still real concern about its future. Clifford thought Alastair Campbell was 'extremely happy' about having Rupert Murdoch on Blair's side, backing Labour again at the election. 'Among the newspapers, the *Sun* really has become the government's most important ally, but the public are far less influenced by what they read in the press than the political parties think. It's when people see a politician on television that they really make up their minds.'

Hague and the Liberal Democrat leader Charles Kennedy needed no reminders from Max Clifford about the importance of television, and they had both laid on photo-opportunities for the evening news bulletins. Charles Kennedy was out again campaigning in his election battle bus, having declared he was glad the 'long drawn-out phoney war' was at an end. He planned to spend the next three days on the road visiting every region of the country so that he could be interviewed by as many local television and radio interviews as possible. For Hague the first stop was Watford where, flanked by his wife Ffion, he spoke on a soapbox in the town centre. Despite having to compete with a few hecklers, he told a crowd of mainly Conservative supporters that Labour had failed to deliver. 'When Tony Blair called the election this afternoon, he wasn't so much running on his record but running away from his record, not so much asking for a second term as asking for a second chance.' As he left to make his way to a helicopter to take him to Taunton, a BBC political correspondent, Laura Trevelyan, asked Mrs Hague if she was looking forward to the campaign. She smiled. Her husband replied: 'She certainly is! She's enjoying it already. And I'll answer the questions!'

The opinion polls did not look encouraging for either the Conservatives or the Liberal Democrats. Blair was as powerfully placed as any Prime Minister ever had been at the start of an election campaign, and no leader of the opposition had ever been as far behind as Hague. Opinion surveys over the previous five weeks showed that Labour's support averaged 50 per cent; the Conservatives were on 31 per cent; and the Liberal Democrats had averaged 13 per cent.

Wednesday 9 May

My irritation at not having been quicker in spotting Labour's own goal over the election launch was only aggravated by the headlines in the morning newspapers. 'Clammy with sincerity, he sounded like an American TV evangelist,' was Quentin Letts' take in the *Daily Mail* on

Tony Blair's shirtsleeved appearance at St Saviour's and St Olave's. Every parliamentary sketch writer had a ball describing what Matthew Parris told readers of *The Times* was a nauseating event which should have been swept away on a great wave of national revulsion. 'It was breathtakingly, toe-curlingly, hog-whimperingly tasteless. It was unbelievably ill-judged . . . If the PM sanctioned the arrangements for this dire event and if there is a Hell, he will go there. To prepare for his entry, the choir sang an ethnic song whose predominating lyric was wa-wa-wa . . . Wild rumours swept the audience that Phoenix the calf was coming on . . . Blair grinned soupily . . . Alastair Campbell clapped caringly.' Most newspapers published the same colour photograph, taken by Kirsty Wigglesworth of the Press Association: a close-up of Blair standing on the school stage, looking upwards, singing with an open hymn-book in his hands, framed by the blue stained-glass windows behind him.

The source of my discomfort at having been so roundly put to shame by almost every other correspondent and commentator was William Hague's good fortune, because the atrocious press for Blair's speech was an ideal source of material for the final Prime Minister's questions before polling day. Hague went hard on Europe and warned that a re-elected Labour government would bounce Britain into the single currency. He quoted from a speech made just before the 1997 general election in which Blair described his emotional attachment to the pound and claimed to know exactly what the British people felt when they saw the Queen's head on a ten-pound note, because he felt it too. 'Wasn't the Prime Minister's emotional exploitation of the Queen's head before the last election just like his emotional exploitation of schoolchildren at this election? And why doesn't he come clean, be straight with people and admit that he wants to ditch the pound as soon as he can get away with it?' When Blair countered by reminding MPs that it was a Labour government which had cut class sizes for five-, six- and seven-year-olds, Hague was ready for him: 'Even the schoolgirls saw straight through him. As we read in this morning's press: "One girl covered her head with her pullover as Blair rambled on about devolution. One wrinkled her nose and said, 'He's a big crook.'" No wonder they made it a beacon school.' Blair had by far the worst of the exchanges, and his uncomfortable demeanour during his final pre-election appearance at the dispatch box showed how annoyed he must have been at Labour's miscalculation in choosing a girls' school for the election launch and his own ineptitude in ploughing on with a twenty-minute speech which – if nothing else – was far too political for children who could not even vote.

Hague had promised that he would start campaigning the instant Blair confirmed the election date, and to demonstrate his determination to get a head start on Labour he gave the go-ahead for the launch next day of the Conservatives' manifesto. The process of approving Labour's manifesto had not been completed and Millbank Tower, anxious not to be upstaged, brought forward publication of the party's latest pledge card as a way of promoting some of the party's key policy commitments. Pledge cards were used by Labour for the first time in the 1997 election and proved highly popular with party workers, who liked to distribute them when out canvassing or at campaign meetings. No bigger than a credit card, they carried on one side a picture of Blair and on the other a series of five pledges, the first of which in 1997 card was to cut class sizes to thirty or under for five-, six- and seven-year-olds. Political correspondents learned about the hurried decision to advance the release of the 2001 pledge card at a lobby briefing called by Alastair Campbell immediately after Prime Minister's questions. I wondered who had given authority for the briefing, because the deputy press secretary, Godric Smith, had told journalists at the 4 p.m. briefing the day before that the government would be holding no further briefings now that the election had been called. Smith said that Campbell and other Downing Street press officers and aides who were special advisers and who intended to take part in the election campaign were resigning in accordance with the guidance issued by the Cabinet Secretary and would have to 'rely on the Labour Party for administrative support'. Smith said he would continue to speak for the Prime Minister, but he thought the circumstances would be 'very limited'. Downing Street's website, which publishes a summary of the lobby briefings, announced that afternoon that 'in keeping with established precedents, only essential new information will be posted for the duration of the election period'.

Afternoon briefings are always held in the lobby room in the House of Commons, which is a short walk from the press gallery, along the committee corridor and up several flights of stairs. Campbell was late, and he arrived together with the Secretary of State for Social Security, Alistair Darling, and Labour's director of communications, Lance Price. To my surprise he was also accompanied by Godric Smith and the chief press officer Anne Shevas, who were still in their posts at No. 10 as they were both civil servants. Campbell took charge of the proceedings and announced that Blair would be holding a question and answer session that evening at St Albans in Hertfordshire, where he would launch the new pledge cards. Darling ran through the five pledges for the next five years which, he said, set out the dividing lines between Labour and the Conservatives: to keep mortgages as 'low as possible'; to recruit 10,000 extra teachers, 20,000 extra nurses and 6,000 extra policemen and women; and to retain the pensioners' winter fuel payment. Jon Smith, the Press Association's political editor, asked whether any voter would believe these undertakings as Labour had not honoured the five previous pledges. Darling replied that three had been delivered: low inflation, cutting hospital waiting lists and getting 250,000 under-25-year olds into work. The promise to cut class sizes would be honoured at the start of the next school year and the pledge on youth justice would be delivered by March 2002. Other journalists asked why Labour's 1997 pledge not to increase income tax had not been repeated. Darling denied there was 'a hole' in the pledge card: Labour's promises were based on the strength of the economy. Campbell said Blair's central message for the campaign was that the economy was generating the money needed to invest in public services. 'That is why this is such an important election. We can finally bury the idea that you have to choose between economic prosperity and social justice.' He explained that although the task of preparing the manifesto had not been completed, there were strong tactical reasons for bringing forward publication of the pledge cards. 'They are very good campaigning material for the doorstep and we thought the earlier we got them out the better.'

While the questioning continued I looked across to where Godric Smith and Anne Shevas were sitting. They both seemed to have no hesitation about remaining in the room and continuing to give their support to Campbell and Darling, although it was abundantly clear the proceedings related entirely to promises Labour was making to the electorate; the briefing had nothing to with existing government policy and could hardly have been said to be dealing with 'essential new information'. I had noticed for some months that civil service press officers were being asked increasingly to cross the line and either support ministers at Labour Party events or back up party policy initiatives; but this was the first time in many years at Westminster that I had ever seen senior civil servants attend a party briefing about an election campaign after the declaration of polling day. In my view Campbell should not have asked his Downing Street press officers to back him up by their presence at the briefing, and it should have been obvious to Darling, the one elected politician in the room, that civil servants should not have been in attendance. But Darling seemed deferential in Campbell's presence, and I wondered whether he lacked the courage to overrule the Prime Minister's official spokesman and remind him of the official guidance.

Campbell and Darling were in a hurry and were the first to leave. The journalists who remained asked Smith if he could comment on the publication of further leaked correspondence between Blair and the Hinduja brothers. At a news conference in the House of Commons that morning Andrew Tyrie had released five letters, including three signed 'Yours ever, Tony', dated during the period in 1998 and 1999 when the Home Office was considering Srichand Hinduja's application for a British passport. In one letter to Gopichand Hinduja, the Prime Minister referred to his decision in May 1999 to appoint the Leicester East MP, Keith Vaz, as parliamentary secretary to the Lord Chancellor, saying it was 'always a pleasure to appoint people of talent and ability to the government'. Vaz had been dogged by investigations into his financial links with the Hindujas, and although the House of Commons Standards and Privileges Committee recommended in March 2001 that no action should be taken against the MP, the Parliamentary Commissioner for Standards, Elizabeth Filkin, had reopened her investigation following further complaints. When Alastair Campbell was asked about the contents of Blair's correspondence with the Hindujas and the connection with Vaz, he told journalists the letters were 'wholly unremarkable' and their publi-cation simply a diversionary tactic by the Conservatives, who wanted the news media to talk about anything other than jobs, the economy and health. 'There will always be people in the media who will assist the Conservatives and I don't intend to help them. We have set the agenda for the election and that is what we will stay focused on.'

Although Campbell made no further mention of the letters at his afternoon briefing, I asked Smith if Downing Street was making any comment. I had expected him to decline to get involved in the discussion, as the letters were being treated by Labour as an election issue and, as a civil servant, he was again in danger of getting dragged into party politics. But Smith had no hesitation in responding: he repeated Campbell's answer that the correspondence was 'wholly unremarkable' and that the letters were standard responses on foreign affairs and made no mention of passports.

At Labour's question and answer session in St Albans that evening, the chair was taken by the actress Maureen Lipman. When Blair walked on to the platform he immediately took off his jacket and was greeted by Ms Lipman, who described herself as 'a long-term Labour supporter and a long-time spectacle wearer', a dig at what the newspapers said were the trendy new glasses which the Prime Minister had worn for the first time the previous week and which he said he needed in order to refer to notes when making detailed speeches. In response to one question, Blair said he intended to resist the pressure from some Labour MPs and party activists for the top rate of income tax to be increased to 50p in the pound. 'I think it's important that we keep incentives for people in the taxation system. I know many people who support us might like us to change tax rates at the top, but I believe the best thing we can do is offer real opportunity at the bottom.'

While I was watching the live television feed of Blair answering questions I took a telephone call from David Hill, the former Labour director of communications who was on leave from Bell Pottinger Good Relations and had temporarily rejoined his former colleagues at Millbank Tower. Hill was anxious to get down to business: 'Look, Nick, I've got a spoiler for you for the morning news bulletins ahead of the Conservatives' manifesto launch. It's something on tape that Michael Portillo said and it gets right to the heart of the Tories' tax and spending plans.' Within half an hour Labour handed out a cassette box which carried a picture of the shadow Chancellor and was labelled 'The Portillo Tapes'. Hill said the cassette was a recording of a lecture that had been given earlier in the year but had not previously been reported, and in which Portillo admitted that the Conservatives' plan to allow young people to build up their own pensions could leave 'a hole' in the national insurance fund which might have to be filled by increased taxation. By publicising this on the eve of the Conservatives' manifesto launch, Labour were doing their best to target Portillo and provide journalists with some awkward questions which could be used to embarrass William Hague.

Thursday 10 May

Michael Portillo had no need to fear the 'spoiler' which Labour had been touting around the previous evening, because the Conservatives succeeded in capturing the news agenda with the one headline-grabbing pledge contained in their manifesto: a cut of 6p a litre in the price of petrol and diesel. While David Hill was contacting newsrooms and trying to arouse interest in 'The Portillo Tapes', the BBC's *Ten O'Clock News* was breaking the news that in his first Budget, the shadow Chancellor intended to reduce fuel duties. The promise of a 6p a litre reduction was aimed at wrong-footing Labour and capitalising on the continuing campaign by road hauliers and farmers for lower fuel prices. Ministers had been caught off guard in September 2000 by widespread protests which included blockades of major oil refineries, fuel shortages and several days of disruption. The loss of confidence in the government had been so great that for almost a fortnight the Conservatives moved ahead of Labour in the opinion polls for the first time since John Major's 1992 election victory. Now the promise of a reduction in fuel prices made the headlines in the morning news bulletins, and although it meant the Conservatives pre-empting their own announcement, the publicity was seen as helping generate interest for the 10.30 a.m. launch of the manifesto, entitled *Time for Common Sense*.

Michael Ancram, the party chairman, opened the proceedings by explaining that the Conservatives had succeeded in starting their campaign faster than ever before. On the day Blair called the election, Tory party workers had spent the evening handing out leaflets at railway and bus stations in key seats, and the following day, at his final confrontation across the dispatch box, Hague delivered 'a blistering demolition' job on Blair. 'We want to leave no one in any doubt about what we are proposing. We are a party ready for government and ready to serve.' Ancram declared that the Conservatives' vision for the twenty-first century was the 'vision of one man', William Hague, who had shown 'a courage and a determination and a clearness of vision which has been inspiring'. Hague presented what he said was the 'most ambitious Conservative manifesto for a generation', which would go further than any government before in handing back to individuals and families the 'power to shape their own lives and their own communities'. People would be set free by allowing them to keep more of their own money. He would lead a tax-cutting government which would 'reverse the most unfair, indiscriminate and hated stealth tax of all' by cutting 6p a litre off petrol and diesel prices; introduce a new married couple's allowance worth up to £1,000 a year; and also cut taxes for businesses, savers and pensioners. His aim was to halt the steady erosion of Britain's independence. 'We will lead the argument for a different kind of Europe. A flexible, open Europe that respects the independence of national government. Above all, we will keep the pound.' Voters had to choose between a Labour Party that trusted government instead of people and a Conservative Party that trusted people instead of government. 'I trust the British people. I trust their common sense. It's time for common sense.'

Hague's speech had been well crafted and I felt he had done well to seize his opportunity and build on the momentum which his party had generated. Though there was nowhere the near same excitement which Labour succeeded in creating before their manifesto launch in 1997 and there were also fewer reporters attending than I had expected, I was struck by the youthful appearance of many of the headquarters staff and campaign workers who helped to fill out the hall – a sign, I thought, of the regeneration within the party which Hague had been trying to encourage. Television and radio journalists dominated the questioning and, after taking five broadcasters in succession, Hague made a point of calling some newspaper journalists. Most of the enquiries related to the 6p a litre fuel tax reduction, which would take 27p off a gallon of petrol. He said it would be financed out of the £8 billion worth of savings in government expenditure which Michael Portillo and his shadow Treasury team had already identified. Hague accepted that it was the last Conservative government which had brought in the fuel escalator and introduced annual increases in duty. 'Yes, that's true, and when you get to the top of an escalator, you are meant to get off, a common sense principle which Labour have forgotten.' The tenth journalist to be called was the *Guardian*'s political editor, Michael White, who said the reporters had all been given copies of 'The Portillo Tapes' and told the question which Millbank Tower thought should be asked. The shadow Chancellor said the idea there could be a secret tape of a public meeting was ridiculous and any changes which the Conservatives made to the national insurance fund would be 'prudent and self-financing'.

There were fifty separate pledges in the Conservative manifesto and all but a handful had been well trailed in advance, especially most of the promised tax cuts. Once the launch was over, the party's media team were bombarded with questions. I asked the chief spokesman, Nick Wood, whether Alastair Campbell had been right the day before when he taunted the Tories about devoting thirteen days of their campaign to saving the pound. Wood refused to discuss the party's election timetable but he was in no doubt about the strategy. 'We will campaign hard, vigorously and very frequently on Europe, but I am not putting a number of days on it.' I was anxious to ask Andrew Scadding, the assistant head of media, how he thought the Conservatives would perform against Labour's slick publicity team at Millbank Tower. Earlier that morning, in an interview on *Today*, Portillo had said he was looking forward to the four-week campaign. 'We will, at last, have the air time and the media space to explain our policies.' Scadding shared Portillo's confidence about the Conservatives' ability to use the broadcast media to offset the hostile coverage which they were getting in much of the press. 'So far I think we are getting our fair shout on television and it's Labour who seem to be having a rough time of it.'

Wood and Scadding had been cheered up no end by the drubbing which Blair had received for his insensitivity in launching the election during afternoon assembly at a girls' secondary school. They pointed to reports in the *Daily Mail* and *Daily Telegraph* which both quoted Irene Bishop, the headteacher at St Saviour's and St Olave's, as saying she regretted the way Blair had used his speech to attack the Conservatives when schools should be apolitical. I was still keeping my head down, hoping no one had heard my lyrical reporting from the launch, when my brother George Jones, political editor of the *Daily Telegraph*, walked over to join us. I sensed a put-down was in the offing. 'You were poetical, weren't you? What got into you?' he harrumphed, to the amusement of other correspondents. I got little sympathy from Joy Johnson, a former BBC political news editor who had served briefly as Labour's director of communications. She thought I sounded as enthusiastic as the broad-casters who were at the much-criticised rally which Labour held in the 1992 general election at Sheffield, where Neil Kinnock punched the air, shouting out, 'We're all right! We're all right!' in a style reminiscent of a 1960s pop concert. 'We could all see in the newsroom that the television pictures coming back from Sheffield were ghastly and triumphalist but I remember the BBC's political editor, John Cole, reporting that it was like being at a Kennedy rally. It was the same with Blair's launch at the school. The television pictures were just as ghastly but the broadcasters who were commentating live from the scene got overwhelmed and they just couldn't see it.'

I was able to continue ruminating about my inept response to Blair's speech because I had to spend much of the afternoon and early evening in the company of Labour's publicity team. Matthew Doyle, the press officer who had handed out copies of the speech, thought Blair should have gone to a sixth-form college instead of a girls' secondary school. David Hill agreed that the newspaper reports had not been favourable, but he did not think the television coverage had backfired. 'I know it was a bit churchy but don't underestimate the number of people who do feel comfortable seeing Blair holding a hymn book.'

My first assignment at Millbank Tower was Labour's afternoon news conference to attack the Conservatives' manifesto. On a screen in front of reporters was a message all in blue: 'The Tories' boom and bust cuts manifesto. Why their sums just don't add up . . . ' The Chancellor, Gordon Brown, who headed the line-up on the platform, argued that the savings of £8 billion which Portillo claimed to have identified in public expenditure did not stand up and that the promised tax cuts would threaten schools, hospitals and other public services. 'The Tory bandwagon is on the road to boom and bust and public spending cuts.' An hour later I had to return to Millbank Tower to doorstep what is known as Labour's 'Clause Five' meeting: the moment when a Labour cabinet and the party's national executive committee meet to approve the manifesto. In the 1970s and 1980s these meetings were often tense and difficult occasions and the scene of much hard bargaining, as the trade union leaders who helped finance the party demanded their say on policy. The reorganisation and restructuring pushed through by the New Labour modernisers since then had given Tony Blair almost total control over the party, and I doubted whether the handful of left-wing representatives who had seats on the executive were likely to raise any serious objections to the manifesto proposals.

One of the first to arrive for the meeting was the Prime Minister's chief of staff, Jonathan Powell, followed by Blair's special assistant, Anji Hunter. The prime ministerial Jaguar swept into the concourse a few minutes later. Campbell held back for a few moments, anxious to avoid getting into the shot. 'Nice to see you, Alastair,' I shouted across as he approached the swing doors at the entrance to Millbank Tower. 'No, it's not,' came back the reply. I feared I was in for a long wait. There had not been much news interest in the meeting, and I had only a BBC and an ITN camera crew for company. However, it was a pleasant evening and there seemed to be plenty happening. Sian Jarvis, head of media at the Department of Health, walked by on her way home. She told me that the launch of Loyd Grossman's recipe book for hospital chefs had been highly successful. 'We got fantastic coverage and I think it helped not having Alan Milburn there. There wasn't a politician in sight and it really did make a difference.'

The next diversion was the arrival of the two coaches hired to transport the journalists and photographers assigned to follow Blair's battle bus. Written in large letters on the sides of each coach was Labour's campaign message, 'The work goes on. Strong leadership', and in smaller letters underneath, 'www.Labour.org.uk'. I had noticed already that for the first time each of the three main parties was displaying an internet address on publicity material and beneath the party logo on the platform at news conferences. The few reporters who got out of the coach had been on the road all day and complained about ending up way behind Blair, who had returned to London much earlier. He had been on a campaign visit to the midlands which included a meeting with business leaders at Warwick University and tea with a group of Labour supporters at a café in the Pump Room at Leamington Spa. Susan Cornwell of Reuters, one of the journalists on the trip, said it had been a tiring day. Nigel Morris, a political correspondent for the *Independent*, looked relieved to back in London. 'One day down, twenty-seven to go.' Also on the coach was Labour staff member Rory Scanlan, a volunteer in 1997, who had taken a month's unpaid leave from his job as a public affairs consultant to help with the campaign.

Two Labour MPs were among the first to leave the manifesto meeting. Bruce Grocott, who had been Blair's parliamentary private secretary since

1994 and who was not seeking re-election, told me he was returning to the House of Commons to say farewell to the forty Labour MPs who were standing down. Dennis Skinner hurried away, but he did shout across to the television crews: 'It's all done and dusted, a second Labour victory.' My suspicion that there had not been even a whiff of dissent was confirmed by Christine Shawcroft, one of the representatives of the centre-left Grassroots Alliance. She was a regular contributor to *Labour Left Briefing* and when standing for the national executive had campaigned against the government's use of the private finance initiative in schools and hospitals and in favour of public ownership of the railways. However, having been selected as Labour's candidate for the target seat of Meriden, she had no intention of saying anything which might damage her chances or bring her into conflict with the party. Ms Shawcroft could hardly have been any more enthusiastic about the manifesto. 'I think it's excellent. It's a very full and comprehensive document and will help us win an increased majority.' When I expressed surprise at her keenness, given her support for controversial causes like the campaign to link pensions to average earnings, she insisted the left of the party would be satisfied with the manifesto. 'There's a great deal in there about eliminating poverty and improving housing. I think the left will be very happy with it.'

While interviewing Ms Shawcroft, I noticed that several chauffeur-driven Jaguars with their engines running were lining up around the concourse. Philip Gould, Blair's leading pollster, got into one of the cars. Another was waiting for the Labour peer and media strategist Lord Ali, founder of the television production company Planet 24 and best known as the creator of *The Big Breakfast* on Channel Four. By the time Blair departed I had been joined by another reporter, Chris Buckland of the *Sunday Mirror*. On seeing Blair leave, he shouted: 'Good meeting, Prime Minister?' Blair smiled, but did not say anything as he got into his car. Dr John Reid, the Secretary of State for Northern Ireland, who was put forward as the party's spokesman, used his interview to attack the Conservatives' manifesto which, he said, 'fell apart before the ink was dry' and contained sums which did not add up. 'We have produced an original, forward-looking manifesto based on sound management of the economy.'

It was all very different from the many Labour meetings which I had covered in the past, which had often ended up with the arguments that had taken place inside continuing in the street outside during noisy and sometimes bad-tempered radio and television interviews. Setting off from Millbank Tower to return to BBC Westminster with barely anything worth reporting, I felt as if I had spent my evening standing on the doorstep outside a well run extraordinary general meeting of New Labour plc.

Friday 11 May

Political correspondents who had avoided my fruitless assignment on the doorstep outside Millbank Tower had far greater success than I did in piecing together what transpired at the Clause Five meeting to approve Labour's manifesto. 'Tax war: Labour pledges no rise' was the headline over an exclusive report in the *Guardian* which said the party leadership had decided to go into the election with a commitment not to raise the basic or higher rates of income tax. Tony Blair did not deny the story when he gave his first interview of the morning on GMTV. 'What's in the paper comes out of our manifesto meeting, but you'll have to wait for the details of that in the manifesto when we publish it. In the last Parliament we said we wouldn't raise the basic or top rates of income tax.' Blair was keen to regain the initiative after an uncomfortable two days. The tax cuts promised in the Conservatives' manifesto had secured widespread publicity, and the omission from Labour's pledge card of any undertaking about future levels of income tax had put pressure on the Chancellor, Gordon Brown. 'Labour refuses to rule out tax increases', had been the *Daily Mail*'s front-page headline the previous day over a report which quoted a warning from the Institute for Fiscal Studies that there could be a £5 billion a year shortfall in the Chancellor's spending plans from 2004. Blair and Brown were at a tactical disadvantage, unwilling to pre-empt the launch of their own manifesto but anxious to put an end to the claim by the Conservatives that voters faced a choice between a massive cut in petrol duty or looming tax rises under Labour. All day there were off-the-record briefings by media strategists at Millbank Tower, confirming that Labour's manifesto would have reassuring news on income tax for middle Britain: the basic and higher rates would remain the same.

Charles Kennedy took immediate advantage of Labour's discomfort to accuse Blair of failing to recognise that without higher taxes the government could not deliver the improvements in public services which he was promising. 'What this demonstrates is the sheer timidity of the Labour government, the sheer poverty of ambition. A Labour government should be prepared to say to people, yes, there are howling social priorities out there and we're so angry about them and so determined to tackle them, that we will use the tax system.' Blair's refusal to give a straight answer allowed the Conservatives to open up another line of attack and claim that it was Brown's sums which did not add up. In a BBC interview Andrew Dilnot, director of the Institute for Fiscal Studies, repeated his warning that if the Chancellor wanted to go on increasing public spending after 2004, the government would have to increase taxes or borrowing. William Hague threw down the gauntlet to Blair: 'I challenge him to say that he will not increase taxes at all, and if he is not prepared to say that, then everyone will know that Labour plans yet more stealth taxes on the people of Britain.'

Hague was delighted at the chance to go on the offensive and distract attention from Labour's attempt to cost the commitments in the Conservatives' manifesto. Gordon Brown calculated that it contained promises of tax reductions which could amount to £16.6 billion over three years, which was 'way in excess' of the £8 billion quoted by Michael Portillo. When he tried to defend his own calculations on The *World At One*, the shadow Chancellor found himself at a disadvantage because Nick Clarke persisted in challenging him about an acknowledgement on *Newsnight* the evening before by the shadow social security secretary, David Willetts, that the £8 billion figure did not add up. When pressed to set out the reductions in public expenditure which would be needed to finance the tax cuts, Willetts had been £1 billion short in the savings he could identify and had said he was prepared to settle for '£7 billion out of the £8 billion'. Portillo refused to admit that a figure of £7 billion had been mentioned and in his replies to Clarke he made no reference to Willetts by name. 'My £8 billion figure for tax cuts has not been dented by anyone and it won't be dented by anyone in the campaign.'

Saturday 12 May

Photo-opportunities are ten a penny during general election campaigns, and the political parties dream up all sorts of stunts in the attempt to interest the news media. If an eye-catching idea is to stand any real chance of forcing its way to the top of a peak-time television news bulletin when there is so much footage for the picture editors to choose from, it has to relate as closely as possible to the main political news of the day. A repainted petrol tanker with huge letters on the side saying '£6 a gallon under Labour' provided an ideal image against which William Hague could repeat his warning about the higher 'stealth taxes' which the Conservatives claimed a re-elected Labour government would need to impose. Having been caught off guard by the rapid publication of the

Conservatives' manifesto and Hague's pledge to take 6p a litre off petrol and diesel prices, Labour was in the uncomfortable position of having to stall the news media. While Tony Blair and Gordon Brown implored journalists to await the publication of Labour's manifesto, their aides were doing all they could to reassure the press and broadcasters that the government had no plans for further tax increases. Hague knew he had to move fast to exploit Labour's vulnerability, and by campaigning at Newbury in Berkshire with a fuel tanker that proclaimed the arrival of petrol at £6 a gallon he believed he had found a sure-fire way to attract attention. He predicted that petrol prices could soar after the election, provoking the possibility of further protests about rising fuel costs, because Labour would have to increase taxes by £10 billion to fill a black hole in their spending plans. 'If you add that to the price of petrol then it would reach £1.30 a litre, nearly £6 a gallon. That is what would happen if all of Labour's tax increases in the coming Parliament were added to the price of petrol.'

Hague's success in putting Labour on to the defensive in the opening days of the campaign was seen as a vindication of the tactics being pursued by two of the Conservatives' leading policy strategists, the shadow Cabinet Office minister Andrew Lansley and Tim Collins, a senior vice-chairman of the party. They had worked together at Conservative Central Office before becoming MPs in 1997 and had played key roles in John Major's 1992 general election victory; Lansley was director of the party's research department and Collins was the press officer who accompanied Major on his campaign tour. Lansley often deputised for the party chairman, Michael Ancram, and in the long build-up to the 2001 election he was a frequent visitor to the studios of BBC Westminster, regularly doing the late-night interviews on behalf of the party which had to be prerecorded for use in the morning news bulletins. He told me that launching the manifesto within forty-eight hours of Blair's calling the election had always been their plan, and he was pleased by the momentum they had established. 'So far it's all gone along as we planned, just as we've hit petrol again today. It'll be the shot of the petrol tanker and the £6 gallon that's used on television and gets into the newspapers and that's what people will remember. We're having great fun kicking Labour around again on tax. It's just like a re-run of 1992 and the "tax bombshell" campaign that destroyed John Smith's shadow Budget, when I was director of research and Tim was out on John Major's tour bus.' Lansley said the great strength of the Conservatives' latest campaign was that Blair had promised in 1997 that there would be no tax increases under Labour, and yet his government had imposed forty-five stealth taxes and raised £28 billion, which was the equivalent of 10p on income tax.

The *Financial Times* quoted 'senior Labour insiders' as conceding that the Conservatives had won the first week of election campaigning, and Lansley's bullish interpretation of the opening skirmishes was certainly shared by some of the newspaper correspondents who gathered at Labour's morning news conference. As we waited for the Chancellor to open the proceedings, Alastair Campbell walked across to hear what we thought of the campaign. He saw me taking notes and pointed this out: 'Look, there's Nick Jones, writing it all down, remember everything in life is on the record.' Almost before he had finished he was challenged by a correspondent from the *Mail on Sunday*, Peter Hitchens, who demanded an apology for what had happened to him the previous Tuesday during an altercation which he said occurred after 'Blair's St Nauseous School speech'. Hitchens had tried without success to speak to the Prime Minister. 'When Blair walked off the stage in the middle of the final hymn I attempted to follow him out but Anji Hunter stopped me. Who does she think she is? I asked her when it was she'd signed up as a special constable.' Hitchens had made a name himself during previous general elections because of his fearless and persistent questioning of Labour Party leaders, and Campbell let him have his say before rounding on both of us: 'You two will always put as much focus on process as on policy but our research shows people were clocking what Blair was saying at the school. People were hearing the message that he'd called the election and it was important he did so in a way which emphasised the significance of education.'

Campbell predicted that I would soon get 'very bored' with the campaign because Labour would be focusing relentlessly on their election promises. Blair had an interview planned for next morning on *Breakfast with Frost* and he would then make the first of six big speeches, which would all go back to 'where it started for Blair, to his core beliefs'. Campbell seemed relaxed about some of the favourable headlines being obtained by the Conservatives. 'Yes, the *Mail on Sunday* will say tomorrow that the Tories have made a better start than expected, but Hague hasn't got what it takes and the public have formed that view already.' Campbell said Hague's problem was that he could not control his own party, and he pointed to the headline on the front page of *The Times*: 'Hague ally issues Hitler warning over Europe.' The story referred to a speech by Sir Peter Tapsell, the Tory MP who had nominated Hague for the party leadership in 1997 and who was seeking re-election in Louth and Horncastle. In predicting that the British people could rise in 'an explosion of anger' against the European Union, Sir Peter said he would never agree to Britain joining the euro and then issued a dire warning about the likely blueprint for a European government: 'The German Chancellor Gerhard Schroeder wants Britain to be governed by a European federal superstate modelled on the present German constitution. We may not have studied Hitler's *Mein Kampf* in time but, by heaven, there is no excuse for us not studying the Schroeder plan now.' Sir Peter's outburst was a gift for the Chancellor at the news conference which Labour had called to promote the government's promise to protect the elderly by giving single pensioners an increase of £3 a week from April 2002 and married couples an extra £4.80 a week. Gordon Brown called on Hague to do more to curb extremism, having made the mistake of not taking action early enough against the racist remarks by the outgoing Yorkshire East MP, John Townend. 'I believe it's a test of Hague's leadership as to whether he can make it clear to all his candidates that the kind of language used by Sir Peter Tapsell should have no place in British politics.' Charles Kennedy backed Labour in urging Hague to discipline Sir Peter: 'Drawing analogies with Adolf Hitler, for Heaven's sake, comparing that to an elected European leader in a long-standing now democratic European country, I think that is abysmal talk.' Ann Widdecombe, the shadow Home Secretary, indicated her displeasure on *Today*. She doubted whether many Conservatives would support the expression Sir Peter had used: 'You don't need to evoke Hitler to oppose the single European currency. Colourful language can sometimes give a wrong impression.' Miss Widdecombe refused to repeat her remarks for television, which suggested she might have been silenced; Andrew Lansley took over the task of responding for the leadership and tried to use the story as an opportunity to reinforce the Conservatives' opposition to the euro. 'Yes, in referring to Hitler, Sir Peter's language was inflammatory and exaggerated, but it's his own choice of language in a speech in his constituency. It's not the view of the Conservative Party and I don't think it's something which requires us to reprimand him. Candidates speaking in their own constituencies should have a right to free speech.' After the interview Lansley told me he thought the story was orchestrated by Labour to divert attention from the Conservatives' campaign on tax. 'You can tell the story is a Labour plant in *The Times*. It's a desperate attempt by Labour to slow the pace of our attack.'

Sunday 13 May

I did not get the chance to see Tony Blair being interviewed on *Breakfast with Frost*, as Alastair Campbell had recommended, because I had to make an early start in order to get to the constituency of St Helens South on Merseyside. My assignment was to report a last-minute selection meeting later that morning at which Shaun Woodward, who had defected to Labour from the Conservatives in December 1999, seemed poised to win the nomination and inherit a 23,000 majority in one of Labour's safest seats. On the long drive north from London, on the M1 and then the M6, I had only the radio for company, and the news that Woodward was being parachuted into St Helens commanded considerable airtime. There was much discussion about the likely outcome. How would party members in an area with high levels of social deprivation respond to the apparent imposition in their constituency of the former Tory MP for Witney in Oxfordshire, whose wife Camilla was a Sainsbury heiress? What would the people of this Merseyside seat have to say about being represented by a wealthy MP who lived in a mansion and kept a butler? There had already been much comment that weekend about the circumstances surrounding the hurried decision by two long-serving Labour MPs to step down, thereby releasing seats for Woodward and David Miliband, head of the No. 10 policy unit. Miliband's selection meeting was also taking place later that morning, in the constituency of South Shields, where Dr David Clark, a former minister for the Cabinet Office, had surprised his constituency party by announcing on Thursday 10 May, two days after Blair called the election, that he intended to retire from the House of Commons. Gerry Bermingham, who had held St Helens South since 1983, had caused consternation in his constituency by his announcement on Wednesday 9 May that he was not seeking re-election. He told the Press Association his the decision to step down had not been an easy one; but he was sixty-one, he had a son who was two and wanted to spend more time with his family.

The sudden departure of these two senior Labour MPs fitted a pattern of events which had occurred repeatedly in the run-up to previous general elections. By agreeing at the very last moment not to stand for re-election, sometimes in return for the unspoken promise of a peerage, an outgoing MP with a big majority is able to provide his or her party leader with a vacancy which can be filled by a favoured insider or perhaps a defector like Shaun Woodward who requires a seat but who would not stand much chance of winning the backing of party members in a safe constituency. In order to smooth the way for candidates being parachuted into safe seats at the last moment, the Labour party takes control of the selection process in the final weeks before the likely announcement of polling day. The right of a constituency party to draw up its own shortlist is removed. Instead, candidates have to be interviewed by a panel representing Labour's ruling national executive committee, which approves a shortlist, which is then presented to a constituency meeting where a decision is made on the basis of one member one vote. Labour's manipulation of the selection process in order to find seats for Woodward and Miliband had encouraged journalists to investigate what was happening to other senior MPs who it was thought might be under pressure from the leadership to step down.

Mark Fisher, a former junior minister at the Department of Culture, Media and Sport, was one of those approached to see if he would make way for a younger candidate. He told the *Mirror* that the day after Blair called the election he made it abundantly plain that he was not interested in doing a deal or accepting a peerage. 'The request was clear and my response was equally clear. I won't tell you the official's name but he obviously doesn't know me very well.' Fisher said that when he finally decided to retire he intended to make sure his constituency party in Stoke-on-Trent Central had ample time to choose a successor and would not have to 'brook any outside interference'. Fisher's refusal to step aside was in marked contrast to the willingness of another former Labour MP, Dr John Gilbert, to accede to the leadership's bidding before the 1997 general election. He was approached on his seventieth birthday on 5 April 1997, twenty-six days before polling day, when 'someone high up' in the party told him he would definitely get a peerage if he vacated his seat of Dudley North. When the news emerged that Bermingham and Dr Clark had both agreed to step down, Lord Gilbert had no hesitation in describing to The *World At One* the procedures which were followed in his case. He knew that Blair was anxious to have more high-powered lawyers in his government if Labour won the 1997 election and, in standing aside, he made way for Ross Cranston, who was appointed Solicitor-General when Blair took office. Lord Gilbert acknowledged that his hasty departure had let down his local constituency party and meant that the election literature which had already been prepared had to be pulped.

It was the first time I had heard a former Labour MP speak so openly about the ruthless efficiency of the party machine over which Blair presided, and as I headed north towards St Helens South I mulled over what Lord Gilbert had said. I knew there was likely to be considerable local opposition to the moves to get Shaun Woodward installed as the candidate, but the process had by now become a well-oiled routine and was hardly likely to fall apart. During the many years I had spent reporting the affairs of the trade unions and the Labour Party I had seen at first hand the way in which Neil Kinnock, then the late John Smith and then Blair had tightened their grip on internal party procedures. In the years preceding the 1992 general election I covered the hearings which led to the expulsion from the party of supporters of the Militant Tendency, including Dave Nellist, one a Labour MP, now candidate for the Socialist Alliance in Coventry North East. Nellist had become national chair of the Alliance, which was attracting growing support from the left and intended to field a total of ninety-seven candidates in 2001. One new recruit was the former Labour NEC member Liz Davies, who was deselected as the Labour candidate in Leeds North East in the run-up to the 1997 election. Blair's subsequent interference in the procedures for choosing a Labour leader in the Welsh Assembly and for selecting

Labour's candidate in the contest for Mayor of London had led to accusations that he had become a control freak; but once a general election was called party headquarters took charge, and if the Prime Minister had decided that Woodward should be installed in St Helens South, then I was sure that was what would be delivered.

Two seasoned observers of the Labour scene had formed the same impression in their columns in that morning's newspapers. Roy Hattersley, writing in the *Mail on Sunday*, said that when he was Neil Kinnock's deputy he helped devise the fast-track route which was now being used to install a 'Tory renegade and unlikely Socialist'. In his view, Woodward's expressions of affinity to New Labour were being made out of 'personal convenience' rather than political conviction. In his column in the *Sunday Times*, the author Robert Harris said Millbank's 'shabby deal' suggested there was 'something truly loathsome' about the modern Labour Party. Woodward's value to Blair was that he was a walking rebuke to the Conservative Party, 'a capture from the enemy, a trophy to be led in the triumphal procession behind the emperor's chariot'.

Woodward's imminent arrival on Merseyside and his chances of getting selected provided a topical talking point for Nick Robinson, who was presenting the breakfast programme on *Radio Five Live*. He was keen to discover what had prompted the last-minute departure of Gerry Bermingham and Dr David Clark. An on-the-spot report from South Shields revealed the astonishment of local party workers when they heard of Dr Clark's sudden about-turn after having been reselected and telling the constituency that he intended to serve a full term. Robinson suggested to Labour's campaign co-ordinator, Douglas Alexander, that in view of the experiences of Mark Fisher and Lord Gilbert, it appeared another fix was being arranged in order to hand David Miliband a safe seat where he would inherit a 22,000 Labour majority. Alexander insisted that the procedure being followed was 'above board' and that the final selection would be made on the basis of one member one vote.

Robinson's next guest, Tim Collins, leapt at the opportunity to taunt the Labour leadership about the dangers of accepting renegade MPs. 'If Shaun Woodward walked out of his first party in a fit of pique, how can a second party ever trust him? He voted against the minimum wage, the ban on hunting and attacked Blair vitriolically.' Fraser Kemp, Labour MP for Houghton and Washington East, who frequently spoke on behalf of the Labour leadership, defended the St Helens South procedure but dodged the question when Robinson challenged him to say what a Labour constituency on Merseyside was going to make of a former Tory MP who had 'a butler, cook, chauffeur and three houses'; he simply followed the line taken by Alexander and denied that Woodward was being imposed as the candidate. 'It is not a shoo-in. It's a one member, one vote selection.'

At this point I was in two minds whether to stop the car and ring up *Radio Five Live*, because Robinson was obviously unaware of the latest position. In fact, candidates who lived or worked in the two constituencies had been excluded from both shortlists, and the absence of local candidates meant there was indeed every likelihood of the 'shoo-in' which Kemp had just tried to deny would take place. Although I had grown accustomed to the chilling proficiency of Millbank Tower when handling Labour's selection procedures, I must admit I was taken aback by the sheer brutality displayed by the party's chief press and broadcasting officer, Steve Bates, when I spoke to him late on Saturday evening and asked for a rundown on what was likely to happen. He said the selection panel had met at Warrington and spent the day interviewing candidates. Four had been selected for the shortlist in St Helens: Julie Hilling, a youth worker from Leigh; Barbara Keeley, a Trafford councillor, who had been on the shortlist for seats in Leigh and Preston; Munaver Rasul, a chartered accountant from Manchester; and Shaun Woodward. No feelings were spared or confidentialities respected when I asked what had happened to the four candidates who worked or lived in the constituency, including the two who were being tipped as the local favourites: Marie Rimmer, Labour leader of St Helens Metropolitan Borough Council, and Martin Bond, a young solicitor who had the backing of one of the local trade unions, the GMB, and whose father, Jim Bond, was chairman of the constituency party. Bates casually spelt out the reasons why neither had made it to the shortlist: Ms Rimmer, who had been a Labour Party member for thirty-two years and had risen to become a council leader, 'did not do well at interview' and Bond, 'whose dad is something in the constituency, didn't have a fantastic interview, but probably found it a useful learning experience'. Bates gave me the names of the three candidates on the shortlist for South Shields: Liz Atkins, sister of the Labour MP Charlotte Atkins; Andrew Howard, who had stood in the Romsey by-election in May 2000 and fought Reigate in 1997; and David Miliband. Again, no candidates who lived or worked in the constituency had made it to the selection meeting. The tactic of excluding local favourites, who were usually well known to constituency party members, was a ploy which Labour had used before. If a selection meeting is presented with a list of outsiders it makes things much easier for the preferred candidate, who invariably comes armed with the strong endorsement of the national leadership and sometimes has a high profile or perhaps has attracted a degree of notoriety. I knew firm instructions would have been given to party officials to do all that was possible to guide Woodward through the selection process. His defection had been exploited shamelessly by Blair, as had Alan Howarth's decision to cross the floor in 1995. Howarth had had to complete a similar odyssey, turning his back on the ultra-safe Conservative seat of Stratford-on-Avon before eventually ending up, just ahead of the 1997 election, in rock-solid Newport East, another secure berth in a traditional Labour heartland. If Labour were to succeed in encouraging other Tory MPs to defect, Woodward too had to be installed in a safe seat.

St Helens, like Newport, relied on heavy industry and had seen many redundancies, especially in coal-mining and glass-making. West Sutton Labour Club, where the selection meeting was taking place, was opposite the reclaimed site of the former Sutton Manor colliery, which had been one of the last remaining pits in the Lancashire coalfield. A blue and yellow British Coal sign, skewed at an angle outside the old pit gates, was the only visible reminder of its former existence. When I arrived the car park was almost empty. Some of the club's doors and windows were protected by steel shutters. Tattered plastic bags had attached themselves to the barbed wire which ran along the outer walls. There were posters up for the next big event, a concert by the Cockney duo Chas'n'Dave. I noticed that a cleaner was busy inside preparing the main room where the contest would take place.

Kevin Maegher, Labour's regional press officer, was one of the first to turn up. Soon I was joined by other reporters, photographers and television crews. Once party members started arriving we found that most of them had no idea that the St Helens council leader, Marie Rimmer, had been excluded and to begin with they would not believe it. Quite a crowd gathered when Anne McCormack, an observer at the meeting for the public service union Unison, confirmed that all four local candidates had failed to reach the shortlist. 'Unison represents 9,000 people who live in the borough. Most of our members belong to the Labour Party but they're being denied the right to vote for a local candidate. It's a stitch-up if even our council leader, Marie Rimmer, a party member for thirty years, can't get on to the shortlist.' Ms Rimmer's sister, Marlene Quinn, who was also a borough councillor, blamed Gerry Bermingham for depriving the constituency of the normal selection process. 'His last-minute resignation has prevented local members and affiliated associations from having a proper say. It's a castration of democracy.' There was quite a buzz when Ms Rimmer herself arrived and expressed her disappointment at failing to reach the final four. When I told her that Labour were saying she had not done well at her interview, she looked shocked and demanded an explanation. 'I find that very insulting. Who told you that?' Despite her evident anger, I sensed she had probably agreed to fall into line with what the party leadership wanted. 'Yes, of course, I will support whoever is chosen and I will work for the Labour candidate. I've been in the party for most of my life and I'll definitely be in it for the rest of my life.'

Shaun Woodward was one of the last to arrive. Television crews and photographers had been looking out for a chauffeur-driven car, but he had planned his entrance with the care one might have expected of a former television producer and Conservative Party director of communications. Woodward and his wife Camilla were first seen some distance away along the main road, almost opposite the pit gates, walking together towards the club. As he approached the main door, and before being hustled inside, he told journalists that his message to party members was that if he became the MP he would speak up for the area and become 'a champion for St Helens and the north-west of England'. We estimated that around 200 party members went into the club; we were told the candidates would each be given thirty-five minutes to present their case. In the event the result was far closer than I had anticipated. Woodward won by only four votes. On the first count no candidate cleared the 50 per cent hurdle. When second preferences were included Woodward obtained eighty-one votes, just ahead of Barbara Keeley on seventy-seven votes.

As party members left the meeting and gave their opinions, it became obvious that the constituency had been split down the middle. Woodward had won over many of the waverers with what one member, Mike Davies, considered was an impressive speech. 'There's no doubt he will raise the profile of the town and that'll do nothing but good for St Helens.' Helen Shaw, who voted for Barbara Keeley, was not convinced. 'Woodward said he left the Conservatives because of Hague's extremism, but if they weren't so extreme would he still be a Tory MP? I'm not sure I know the answer.' Anne McCormack, the Unison observer, thought that a working-class town like St Helens would not accept 'a renegade Tory' and she predicted the Labour vote would go down.

After a short wait we were ushered into the main room next to the bar. Woodward, who was sitting with the three other candidates amid tables strewn with glasses, promised to represent 'all the people' of St Helens. He intended to buy a house in the constituency, which he had visited for the first time the previous Wednesday, although he said he had worked in the north-west when he was a producer with *That's Life*. 'This is a fabulous constituency and I'm in a party which recognises we are one nation whatever people's background or race . . . If you work together you can actually make a difference . . . As for the Conservatives, they're moving so far to the right it's impossible to tell how extreme they've become. It's inconceivable they could be fit to govern.' Marie Rimmer sat next to Woodward. He thanked her for her support and undertook to work closely with the local council.

Woodward's narrow victory in the face of such deep discontent reflected the underlying strength of the party machine, and I thought the speed with which leading members of the constituency united around the new candidate was impressive. Even safe seats like St Helens had not escaped the force of New Labour's reforms, and the will to win which Blair had injected into his party ensured that the differences which had been exposed would be rapidly set aside, especially in the presence of the news media.

Outside the club there were quite a few local youngsters who had been attracted by the television cameras and photographers. Some were sitting on the wall drinking lager and enjoying the sunshine. When I took up my position for the BBC camera crew, ready for the next live interview with *News 24*, our producer started attracting wolf-whistles from some of the drinkers and she ordered us inside to find a new location, fearing their presence would prove distracting to viewers. When I was interviewed at lunchtime my audience had been slightly younger and I did manage to persuade one group of small boys dressed in football shirts to move out of shot while they continued celebrating Liverpool's 2–1 win over Arsenal in the FA Cup. On re-entering the club, the only free space we could find was in a passageway next to the bar. It was hot and noisy and beginning to feel rather tacky underfoot. The moment I finished my report I headed for the front door to get some fresh air. Ahead of me was Camilla Woodward, who walked straight out into the crowd of youngsters drinking lager in the club forecourt. She looked lost for a moment, but regained her composure and headed off to join her husband, who had been escorted out through a rear door and ushered towards a waiting car. I thought his wife must have found a sunny Sunday afternoon outside a Labour club in St Helens hardly the place to loiter, and quite a contrast from the calm and ordered existence of their family home in the Oxfordshire countryside.

Monday 14 May

When Andrew Lansley told me the Tories were 'having great fun kicking Labour around again on tax' he made one fatal miscalculation. Labour had not forgotten the lessons of the 'tax bombshell' which Lansley and his colleagues at Conservative Central Office had helped orchestrate in 1992 and which blew apart the shadow Budget of the late John Smith. In preparing for the 1997 and 2001 general elections, Gordon Brown had drilled it into his Treasury team that they must never, ever, deviate from the figures on which Labour was campaigning. Estimates for likely levels of taxation and spending had to be watertight, and once they had been published they had to be adhered to, come what may, so as to prevent a repetition of the way Neil Kinnock's 1992 campaign was destabilised by the Conservatives' ability to unpick Smith's figures and run scare stories about the impact of Labour's tax plans. When Lansley spoke to me on Saturday 12 May he was riding high on the initial success of William Hague's campaign, and he ignored two ominous warning signals. On *Newsnight* the previous Thursday the party's social security spokesman, David Willetts, had said he would settle for '£7 billion of the £8 billion' savings which Michael Portillo had proposed; and the following evening, again on *Newsnight*, another frontbench spokesman, Howard Flight, had admitted that in addition to the Conservatives' £8 billion in tax cuts, there could be some other 'changes of tax plus or minus' and that, if there were an economic downturn, borrowing would have to go up.

The cracks which were already appearing in the Conservatives' platform, and which were being exploited day by day by Gordon Brown, grew even wider after the *Financial Times* printed an interview with an unnamed shadow cabinet member revealing that the tax cuts the party was planning could reach £20 billion a year by the end of the next Parliament. The Conservatives' 'aspiration' for the second half of the parliamentary term went far beyond the public pledge of £8 billion by the end of the third year because Portillo and his team were confident that 'vast savings' could be found. The zeal which the Tory front bench was displaying in its drive to talk up the prospects for public spending cuts and tax reductions gave Brown the ammunition he was looking for following the battering he had taken in the Sunday newspapers for his failure to provide an early and categoric undertaking that Labour had no intention of raising the basic or higher rates of income tax. The Chancellor claimed Portillo's credibility was 'in tatters' because of the speed with which the spending cuts had escalated from £8 billion to £20 billion. With the help of his party chairman Michael Ancram, the shadow foreign affairs spokesman, Francis Maude, had to close down the Conservatives' morning news conference after only nine minutes when he faced a barrage of questions. Maude insisted they were committed to 'cast-iron reductions' of £8 billion and aspired to 'further tax reductions beyond that'.

By the time William Hague's plane reached Cardiff for the launch of the Welsh Conservatives' manifesto, the line had changed again and the 'aspirations' being talked of by Flight, Maude and the unidentified front-bencher were no longer being mentioned. Like Portillo the previous Friday, Hague did his best to re-establish the original line: '£8 billion is the only figure we've given and that is the correct figure. Thank you very much.' Did the Tory leader intend to reprimand the shadow cabinet member who had upped the figure to £20 billion? 'No, £8 billion is the figure. Next question.' But the damage had been done, and Tony Blair had further evidence to justify Labour's claim that the Conservatives were planning reductions in public spending which would cut deep into the fabric of the state. 'If you tried taking £20 billion out of the economy, you would have massive cuts in key public services like schools and hospitals.'

In another inauspicious development for the Tories, Labour press officers began telling journalists that the unnamed cabinet minister quoted by the *Financial Times* was the shadow chief secretary of the Treasury, Oliver Letwin. The infamous rapid rebuttal unit inside Millbank Tower had been put to work and Excalibur, the party's computerised retrieval system, had come up trumps and found that in a letter published by the *Daily Telegraph* on Tuesday 6 March, Letwin had mapped out a strategy which mirrored the quotes reproduced in the *Financial Times*. After stressing that his party was committed to 'something significantly more radical' than £8 billion in tax cuts, Letwin's letter explained that by 2004 the Conservatives' spending path would be delivering reductions of £8 billion a year and beyond, allowing taxes to come down even further in the later years of the Parliament. When political correspondents reported on the teatime new bulletins that they were having difficulty tracking down Letwin to get his reaction to these developments, a 'Wanted!' poster bearing his photograph and offering a £20 billion reward was rushed out by

Labour's publicity department in time for it to be held up by the BBC's political editor, Andrew Marr, on the *Ten O'Clock News*.

Millbank's prompt unmasking of Letwin recalled the flair which Peter Mandelson had shown in the years he controlled Labour's campaign team; but after his second resignation Mandelson had been banished from the war room and was devoting his energies towards fighting off some high-profile challengers in his Hartlepool constituency. Arthur Scargill, president of the National Union of Mineworkers, was contesting the seat for the Socialist Labour Party, and John Booth, a former press officer sacked by Mandelson in the mid-1980s, planned to stand as Genuine Labour. Mandelson found his exile hard to take, as he had when he found himself left on the sidelines in the 1992 campaign, but he had no intention of remaining silent about the tactics which Labour was adopting. During the long, traumatic day that followed Neil Kinnock's second defeat, Mandelson joined other Labour MPs in denouncing the 1992 campaign. He said Kinnock had been wrong to raise the issue of proportional representation so close to polling day because it was not 'a strong suit' for Labour. I included his remarks in my diary of the campaign, *Election 92*, and subsequently Mandelson complained about this, saying that if I had not written up his comments in my book, Kinnock would never have known that he had been critical of the campaign. Now, nearly a decade after that campaign, the main headline on the front page of the *Independent* showed that the party's former director of communications had lost none of his flair in offering advice from afar: 'Mandelson urges less spin, more vision.' In a signed article, he set out what he thought was the dimension missing from Blair's campaign. He maintained that he had always recognised that the emphasis which Labour placed on effective presentation should not appear to dilute the party's core social-democratic beliefs. However, Mandelson thought more needed to be done to build positive support for the New Labour vision. 'We have to lift our sights, explain the vision coherently and not simply rely on the well-worn methods of campaigning, message delivery and rebuttal to achieve our ends.'

In an attempt to spruce up another 'well-worn' method of campaigning, Labour had offered a cameo appearance in the party's first election broadcast to the former Spice Girl Geri Halliwell. The one-time Ginger Spice, who famously declared that Margaret Thatcher was the founder of 'girl power', was shown making the tea and then serving it to pensioners. Instead of featuring a number from the singer's new album, *Scream If You Wanna Go Faster*, Labour's official campaign song, *Lifted*, by the Lighthouse Family, was used as the soundtrack for the broadcast, which was entitled *The Work Goes On*. Ms Halliwell had helped get publicity for Labour at the official launch of her new album earlier in the morning, when she expounded on her shift in political allegiance from Thatcherism to Blairism. 'I wouldn't claim to know the ins and outs of the manifesto but I genuinely admire and believe in Tony Blair . . . Tony and Cherie are great parents and we all need good parents. I see Britain as a whole as a child that needs bringing up with good care, and that's what Tony can do.'

If the Prime Minister had read the morning papers and taken on board Mandelson's advice about the need to add more vision to Labour's campaign, his first interview of the morning did not provide a reassuring platform from which to lift his sights. He was being interviewed down the line from his constituency home in Sedgefield by John Humphrys, who was in the *Today* studio at the BBC's news centre in west London, and after ten minutes he complained that he had not been asked a single question on the economy, crime, schools or Europe. Humphrys stood his ground, saying he had no intention of apologising for persisting with questions about whether the government had been 'purer than pure', as Blair had promised in 1998, after complaints about the way commercial lobbyists had told clients they could gain access to ministers and government departments. Much of the interview revolved around whether the

Prime Minister retained 'absolute confidence and trust' in Keith Vaz, the Minister for Europe, and Geoffrey Robinson, the former Paymaster-General, who were both seeking re-election although they remained under investigation by the Parliamentary Commissioner for Standards, Elizabeth Filkin. Blair said that until the allegations against them had been proved, it would be 'very unfair' to say they could not stand as candidates.

In his irritation at not being asked about what he thought were the 'issues of fundamental importance to the country', Blair tried to stop Humphrys on four consecutive occasions, saying each time, 'Hang on John, now hang on a minute' – a phrase and a form of interruption which the impressionist Rory Bremner had taken to using when satirising life in No. 10 for his sketches on Channel Four.

Tuesday 15 May

Charles Kennedy was able to proclaim a break with tradition when he launched his party's manifesto. Instead of setting out their stall to the electorate in the usual glossy pamphlet, the Liberal Democrats produced a document which looked more like a tabloid newspaper. Drawn by the use of brash headlines and plenty of photographs, and pledges highlighted in bold type, the eye of the casual reader would not necessarily have lit upon some of the small print and especially the two short sentences, tucked away on pages four and ten, which underlined the real difference between the Liberal Democrats and their opponents. Unlike Labour and the Conservatives, they were prepared to countenance higher taxes; but mention of the two increases which were being proposed was not front-page news and took some finding. On page four, which set out a programme to boost investment in education, the headlines heralded a cut in class sizes, more books and equipment and the abolition of university tuition fees. Slipped deep into the text was the sentence that mattered: to fund the additional cost of around £3 billion a year, 'we will put an extra penny' on the basic rate of income tax. Mention of the second tax hike was just as brief: on page ten, where the Liberal Democrats outbid Labour and the Conservatives in the increases they were proposing in the state pension, they stated that the rises would be financed by introducing a new top rate of income tax of 50p on earnings of over £100,000 a year.

Alongside Kennedy's photograph on the front page of the manifesto were three words in black capital letters: 'Freedom Justice Honesty.' It was the theme of his introduction at the launch: 'It's freedom because we want everybody to have the opportunity to make the most of their lives. It's justice because we believe that freedom depends on fairness. And it's honesty because where fairness has a cost we explain how it will be paid for.' There was not much to choose between the Liberal Democrats and the government over the number of extra nurses, doctors, teachers and police officers which they each wanted to hire. Kennedy said the one difference was that he did not believe Tony Blair could reach his recruitment targets without raising taxes. 'We know that these are big priorities, they are the priorities of the overwhelming majority of people in our country today. That's why we're not afraid to be honest and ask those who can afford to, to pay a small price for a big benefit.'

Labour responded by accusing Kennedy of deceiving the public. Gordon Brown calculated that when the various commitments were added together, the manifesto would necessitate an increase of 3p on the basic rate of income tax. The Conservatives joined in by suggesting there was no party in British political history which had 'spent a penny' as often as the Liberal Democrats. Michael Portillo's chief preoccupation was his attempt to try a new tack in the continuing debate over spending cuts, and he indicated publicly for the first time that he was ready to promote the 'aspirations' which had got Oliver Letwin into so much trouble, forcing the number two in the Tory Treasury team to retreat to his constituency of Dorset West and take a vow of silence.

I picked up a sense of the shift in thinking that was taking place in the Tory high command when talking to the shadow Foreign Secretary, Francis Maude. He told me the feedback they were getting on the fuss about the size of their spending reductions was that it was reminding the public of the Conservatives' reputation for tax-cutting and was doing them no harm. 'If the only argument is whether to cut taxes by £8 billion or £20 billion, we don't think that's unhelpful to us.' Bernard Jenkin, another frontbencher, agreed: 'The punters are getting the message now that we're really serious about tax cuts. Hunting down Oliver Letwin might seem a great game for the Westminster cognoscenti, but it's doing us a lot of good.'

None the less, Portillo struggled on The *World At One* to make sense of the positioning which was under way. The Conservatives' aspiration, he stressed, was to deliver tax cuts. 'I don't think we are hung up and we are not in a mess . . . No Conservative has ever mentioned £20 billion. Oliver and I and William Hague are all talking about exactly the same thing.' Later, in a speech to an afternoon rally at Putney in south London, Portillo said that he wanted to thank Gordon Brown for helping to publicise the Conservatives' tax-cutting agenda. If possible, in the second half of the Parliament, it would be his aim to find room for reductions in the higher rate of income tax, inheritance tax and capital gains tax. 'It is indeed our intention to not just have £8 billion of tax savings at the end of the first two years but also to go on throughout the Parliament cutting taxes. The choice is between a Conservative Party that is indeed committed to cut taxes throughout the next Parliament and a Labour Party which is bound to raise taxes.' By indicating so clearly that the £8 billion figure was no longer meant to be regarded as an upper limit, but was simply his starting point, Portillo played into Labour's hands and only drew attention to Letwin's disappearance from Westminster and his absence from the party's news conferences. In ordering Letwin not to give interviews to journalists, the Tory leadership merely egged on the media plotters inside Millbank Tower, who printed more 'Wanted!' posters and stepped up the hunt for the missing frontbencher by hiring three bloodhounds and a Sherlock Holmes lookalike who poked around Smith Square and made fun of campaign workers and staff on their way in and out of Conservative Central Office.

In sharp contrast to the caring image of Labour's opening election broadcast, which showed the former Spice Girl Geri Halliwell serving tea to pensioners, the Conservatives used shock tactics to publicise their promise to strengthen the criminal justice system. To a background of menacing music, reconstructions of violent crimes were enacted to strengthen the argument in favour of the party's pledge to abandon the government's scheme for the special early release of prisoners. An old lady was seen about to be mugged; a house was broken into; and drugs were shown being sold on a street corner. Two rapes were listed among the crimes committed by prisoners who had been let out of gaol up to two months early. William Hague told the *Ten O'Clock News* that the broadcast was completely factual in illustrating the government's 'disgraceful record', which he believed would become a major issue during the campaign; but it sparked a political row by omitting to explain that out of the 35,000 prisoners released early under the scheme, only 3 per cent had reoffended, when the average for all released prisoners was 57 per cent. The Home Office minister of state Paul Boateng accused the Conservatives of descending into gutter politics, excoriating the broadcast as 'desperate, dire. In itself a damning indictment of the way the Conservatives clearly intend to run this campaign. Negative advertising of the worst kind.' According to the *Guardian*'s website, *Guardian* Unlimited, the broadcast was a replica of the infamous 'Willie Horton' television advertisement in the 1998 campaign of the former United States President George Bush Snr, which highlighted the case of a murderer let out to kill again and which was blamed for damaging the Democrats' campaign for the Massachusetts governor, Michael Dukakis.

4 Losing Control

If I were asked to choose one illustration of the change which has taken place in political campaigning since I started reporting general elections, I would probably select the tiny personal microphone which I noticed being clipped with increasing regularity to Tony Blair's tie or to the lapel of his jacket. It was a symbol of the tight control which the Labour Party tried to exercise when Tony Blair met party members or the public under the ever-watchful gaze of the news media. His personal microphone is wired up to a small transmitter tucked into a back pocket or fixed to the waist of his trousers. The signal it sends out, relaying what the Prime Minister is saying, is picked up by a sound system and is then fed to camera crews and radio engineers for use in television and radio broadcasts.

Personal microphones with pocket transmitters are commonplace in theatres and concert halls, allowing actors and singers freedom of movement. I first noticed some years ago that Blair was occasionally being wired up in this way for big occasions such as conference speeches, question and answer sessions or fund-raising events. I was not surprised, because I had grown accustomed to the emphasis which he placed on the importance of presentation; and it was only as the 2001 campaign got under way, and I saw that he was wearing a personal microphone much more frequently, that I began to realise the full potential of a system which allows a political leader to operate in an environment where the output from his conversations can be controlled.

Labour used to have a well-earned reputation for being notoriously ill-equipped when trying to communicate through television and radio, and as late as the 1983 general election Michael Foot was at a severe disadvantage when up against a media-conscious Margaret Thatcher. Conservative Central Office understood the importance of regular and well-timed photo-opportunities, and it had a long record of investing in advanced sound systems and visual displays for news conferences. Once Neil Kinnock became leader and Peter Mandelson was appointed director of communications in 1985, Labour started using its own equipment and began to master the latest techniques. I cannot put a date on precisely when Labour's technical competence overtook the Conservatives: they certainly seemed to be more effective in the 1987 election; they were definitely well ahead in the 1992 campaign; and they had far outstripped the Tories by 1997. Labour had the edge where it really mattered, out at events around the country, and by using their own sophisticated equipment they began to impose greater control. Camera crews and radio engineers were told they could not install their own microphones and were required to use a sound feed provided by the party.

In some ways the increased stage management of political events has benefited the news media, facilitating more ordered coverage and better television footage, as shown by the care and attention paid in Downing Street to ensuring that the view is not cluttered up with unnecessary microphones and cables and that there is a clear picture of the Prime Minister outside the front door of No. 10. Moreover, fear of terrorist attacks and other unprovoked assaults has necessitated far closer co-operation among the police, political parties and the news media, and there is a general recognition of the need to have agreed procedures out on location in order to curb the free-for-all which might otherwise develop with cameramen, photographers and reporters all jostling with one another for the best positions. Security is so tight at some events, such as a tour of a school or hospital, that the media pack has to be penned in, unable to move out of their designated area, along the entire route of a visit. As a result, television crews frequently find themselves corralled some distance from the action, and if Blair were not wearing a personal microphone, transmitting a signal back to a sound system or direct to the individual camera positions, there would be no clear audio of what he is saying.

Increasingly, Labour are allowing only one television crew and photographer to attend small or intimate photo-opportunities, so that their material has to be pooled with other broadcasters and news outlets. Again, this can often work to the media's advantage as it prevents competing channels from getting exclusive footage. In return for the promise of access inside a location, even though this might be provided on a limited basis, Labour tries to impose restrictions on what can be reported outside an event, and party officials often go to inordinate lengths to control the opportunities to take pictures on Blair's arrival. Here the party tends to have the upper hand, because television channels are usually desperate to obtain the best footage and competition between rival services is so intense that few broadcasters dare take the risk of being excluded and thus losing the opportunity to obtain their own footage and interviews.

Major events are planned in advance with the same precision as a military exercise, because there is every likelihood they will go out live on one or more of the television news channels and the political parties are keen to get maximum exposure for the images they want to promote. By agreeing to relinquish our freedom of movement, broadcasters have accepted that we will have far fewer opportunities to film an unexpected confrontation or eavesdrop on an unscripted conversation which was intended to be out of range of the cameras and microphones. Therefore it came as no surprise to me that the two unforeseen events which all but obliterated news coverage of the launch of Labour's manifesto had one telling similarity. Both incidents took place during what can still be a dangerous moment for a party leader or any prominent politician: the short space of time it takes to get out of a car and walk across a pavement or along an approach path before entering the controlled environment of the location which is to be visited. Newspaper photographs of a shocked Prime Minister being harangued in Birmingham by Sharron Storer, the anguished partner of a cancer patient, illustrate the point I am making. Look at Tony Blair's tie or the lapels of his jacket: there is no tell-tale microphone to be seen. He was not within the protection of a well-ordered sound system, and he had been ambushed not only Mrs Storer but also by television crews who were filming his arrival and who managed to get in close enough to film and record her unstoppable tirade about the government's failure to spend more on the National Health Service.

John Prescott's confrontation later in the day with an egg-throwing protestor at Rhyl in north Wales was another example of the same phenomenon: an uncontrolled photo-opportunity which took place during the few moments it took the Deputy Prime Minister to walk from his coach towards the theatre where he was due to speak. Security for Prescott was not as heavy as for Blair and a cameraman from HTV, Sion Jones, had had the foresight to pick the right spot from which to film the arrivals; in the process he captured Prescott's left jab and secured the most memorable footage of the entire campaign.

Labour's determination to impose the tightest possible control on the news media's access to Blair was evident from the day he launched the election at St Saviour's and St Olave's Girls' School. Television cameras had to remain inside a pen, just behind the school choir, and it was the refusal of a crew from Panorama to be corralled in this way which produced the first complaint of the campaign. Lance Price, Labour's director of communications, said the behaviour of the programme's staff had been appalling. According to the *Daily Telegraph*'s account of what happened, the police were called when Panorama's reporter John Ware and his team objected to being ordered to go to the agreed position. Ware said that he and his colleagues were 'a model of politeness and civility' during Blair's visit to the school, and he accused Labour of 'a massive over-reaction' when his crew was subsequently refused permission to film any of Labour's daily news conferences.

On the day after the election launch, when the actress Maureen Lipman joined Blair for his first question and answer session at St Albans, I noticed as soon as he took off his jacket that the transmitter for his personal microphone was attached to the waist of his trousers; but it was not until the day after, Thursday 10 May, that I discovered that Labour's control over media access had reached a level of sophistication far greater than anything I had previously witnessed. Reporters who followed Blair's tour that day, and whom I met outside Millbank Tower on their return to London, told me that when the Prime Minister had tea in a café at Leamington Spa they were issued with headphones and were able to listen in to his conversation with a married couple who had been carefully chosen for the occasion. Not only did Labour control the camera positions at the Pump Room; they had also kept the journalists so far away that unless they plugged themselves into the sound system they would not have been able to hear what was going on.

I saw shots of Blair having tea with Kevin and Louise Finnan on the *Ten O'Clock News* and I thought the event looked rather staged. The café was filled with party supporters and the couple, seated at a small table in the middle of the room, were joined by Blair who engaged them in a conversation about mortgage rates. In the extract used in the television report, Louise Finnan spoke first: 'We pay less now than when we first entered the housing market.' Blair mentioned the 0.25 per cent interest rate cut announced earlier in the day and then asked: 'You will be pleased about the interest rate reduction? There was such a long time when interest rates were whizzing about.' Kevin Finnan replied: 'It will make a big difference for us.' I was eager to read what the newspapers made of this encounter. The *Guardian*'s correspondent, Kevin Maguire, described how 'the apparent reluctance of the self-styled people's premier to meet ordinary people' had led him to have a cup of tea with 'Mr and Mrs Middle England . . . a couple straight from the Millbank school of casting'. Much of Maguire's report concentrated on Blair's conversation, which was as 'artificial' as the election launch at St Saviour's and St Olave's and 'as toe-curlingly embarrassing'. One sentence in his report confirmed what I had been told: 'Microphones allowed the world to eavesdrop a conversation through headphones which could not have gone better for the Labour leader if it had been scripted in advance which, of course, it could have been.' The *Guardian*'s photograph had the other tell-tale evidence I was looking for: pinned to Blair's tie was the personal microphone which had supplied the sound feed to the television crews and for the headphones provided for the journalists.

A report that weekend in the *Mail on Sunday* had a fresh angle on the story, claiming that the Finnans felt they had been used by Labour because their criticism of the government had not come across. 'Reporters listening to the conversation through a microphone on Blair's tie said the device failed to pick up her concerns. Instead, they only heard the Finnans' praise for Labour over mortgage rate cuts.' The Finnans' experience revealed the tactical advantage which a sound system gives Labour when seeking to exercise control over media access. As Blair is the only one wearing a microphone, his voice tends to dominate and remarks by other people are not always audible or of sufficiently high sound quality to be broadcast. Indeed, until Blair's transmitter has been switched on and the feed has started, there might be no sound at all. Even though most cameras have a built-in microphone, if the crews are being held some distance away they would be unable to pick up normal conversation with any great clarity in a busy place like the café at the Leamington Spa Pump Room. To overcome the effects of the background noise, a soundman or reporter would have to get in close with a hand-held directional microphone.

That kind of access would certainly have been required on Monday 14 May if the crews had been allowed to follow closely in the path of the Prime Minister when he visited a building site in Inverness. Blair, who was again fitted with a personal microphone, donned a yellow fluorescent jacket and a safety helmet and was taken over to talk to a group of construction workers who were engaged in excavating a new shopping centre. Reporters, also kitted out in fluorescent jackets and hard hats, were corralled in a roped-off enclosure some distance away. In her report for the BBC's Six O'clock News, Carolyn Quinn said the journalists were 'under orders to stay in their pen' while the Prime Minister's chat was piped to them through their headphones. Benedict Brogan, the *Daily Telegraph*'s political correspondent, captured a flavour of Blair's conversation: 'His remarks to the workers included "What does a quantity surveyor do?" and "Those cranes are amazing things, aren't they?" He was invited to stare into the 300,000 sq ft hole, but not to climb in.'

During the Prime Minister's highly regimented visit, which lasted for fifteen minutes, journalists had no opportunity to get near to the action or ask questions. Afterwards, Blair denied he was being insulated from ordinary voters and assured reporters that he would do some walkabouts during the election and meet members of the public who had not been vetted first. 'I'm sure we will do that. The most important thing is that we have a dialogue with people. I'm answering the questions that are difficult.' On his visit to the construction site Blair would have realised that as he was being filmed and his conversations recorded, the wisest precaution was to restrict himself to small talk. Over the years I have grown to admire Blair's self-discipline in front of the news media. Press officers who have worked with him have told me that once he is aware that reporters and photographers are present they can be sure he will do nothing unplanned or unexpected, and will always check with his support staff before responding to media demands. Blair is caught out so rarely that when it happens it makes headline news – like the occasion in

June 2000 when he was unnerved by a slow handclap during his address to the massed ranks of the National Federation of Women's Institutes. Despite the look of panic on his face when he was accosted by Sharron Storer outside the Queen Elizabeth Hospital after Labour's manifesto launch, he kept his cool for what must have seemed like an interminably long four minutes.

He was walking with Gisela Stuart, the Labour MP for Birmingham Edgbaston, towards the entrance to the hospital when Mrs Storer pushed her way through the security cordon and stopped him. Party officials felt they were to blame for not seeing her approaching; but they could not consult Alastair Campbell because he had gone on ahead with the reporters who were being held inside the hospital and could now not get out of the building to listen to what she was saying. Blair's measured response to the verbal assault that followed would have won plaudits from any media manager; at no point did he lose his patience. Mrs Storer's sense of presence in front of the cameras, the forcefulness of her attack and the clarity of the case she made about the inadequacy of the treatment her partner was receiving for cancer, made gripping television and dominated the teatime news bulletins. She said the hospital staff were 'absolutely incredible' but the conditions in accident and emergency where her partner had spent 'a horrendous twenty-four hours' were 'absolutely diabolical' and she wanted to know what Blair was going to do to give them better facilities. Despite his reassurance that the government was taking action on the NHS, she urged him to go inside and see how 'really terrible' it was. It was at this point, after Blair said he was sorry about the situation, that Mrs Storer, keeping her nerve, laid into the Prime Minister: 'No, you're not very sorry, because if you was, you would do something about it. They're understaffed, they've got terrible facilities, the toilets are appalling. The nurses and staff are doing their best and you're just not giving them the money to make the facilities better for them.' Wisely, Gisela Stuart left the Prime Minister to do the talking and he tried again to insist that his government was doing something; but it had no effect. 'You are not, you are definitely not. You walk around and make yourself known but you don't actually do anything to help anybody.'

Realising that he was surrounded by television crews who were recording every word of Mrs Storer's vehement censure of the NHS, Blair tried patiently, but without success, to persuade her that she should go into the hospital with him so that they could sit down and talk about it; but Mrs Storer would not be budged. Despite his repeated attempts to explain that the extra investment going into cancer and heart services would take time to have an effect, Mrs Storer persisted with her account of the way her partner had been taken to accident and emergency because he could not get a bed in the bone marrow ward. She asked again: 'Are you going to do something?' Blair said she must let him explain – but at this point she pushed past him, walked off through the media pack and disappeared out of shot.

After his visit to the hospital, where he was shown a new cardiac unit which had cost £13 million, Blair said he had a message for Mrs Storer and her partner. 'The whole reason why we're putting such a big invest-ment into the health service in the next few years is precisely so that cases like that can't happen . . . If we don't invest, then cases like the lady I talked to are going to carry on.' Alastair Campbell told reporters that Mrs Storer's protest reinforced Labour's promise to increase health spending. Blair had made it clear to her that he would look into what happened to her partner and said that his offer at the time to sit down with her and talk about it was 'a pretty reasonable approach'.

Although Mrs Storer's criticism made uncomfortable viewing in the early evening bulletins, the event did relate to the politics of the campaign, and as it kept the focus on Labour's plans for the NHS, Campbell insisted the party was relaxed about the coverage. John Prescott's altercation with an egg-throwing protestor was of a wholly different order in its potential to damage Labour's chances in the election. The first I heard of it was on *Radio Five Live* shortly before 7 p.m. when I was driving home. Tim Hirsch, a BBC correspondent following William Hague's campaign, had just filed a report about how the police had bustled the Conservative leader back on to his coach after a mêlée in Wolverhampton when there was a newsflash about Prescott having been 'manhandled' on his way to give a speech at Rhyl. I got home in time to see the last half of *Channel Four News*, which had an interview with a Press Association reporter who described how Prescott had been pushed up against a low, narrow wall and looked 'very shaken and angry'. Police and party officials had intervened to separate him from some protestors and one person had been arrested.

The fight made the top headline on the *Ten O'Clock News*: 'John Prescott is attacked tonight before a Labour rally in north Wales. The Deputy Prime Minister exchanges blows; a man is arrested.' However, Peter Sissons, the newsreader, proceeded with considerable caution when describing the fight and said the pictures 'appeared to show that Prescott threw the first punch'. ITN used pictures from HTV, taken by Sion Jones, who was in a different position from the cameramen from BBC and *Sky News*, and from these there was no doubt about what had happened: when an egg was thrown at him at close range, Prescott retaliated and hit the protestor on the chin with a left jab. *Newsnight* had film of Prescott making a short statement to reporters. He described what happened when he had got out of his coach, the Prescott Express, and met a hostile crowd as he walked the short distance towards the theatre where he was to give his speech: 'I walked though the jostling and I was attacked by an individual. In the mêlée that followed I clearly defended myself. I believe someone is being questioned by the police and it would be quite improper for me to add any further comment.'

Although reaction to the Prescott punch dominated the late news, the main bulletins did give prominent coverage to the launch of Labour's manifesto at the International Convention Centre in Birmingham. Reporters covering this event had to be at Euston station by 7 a.m., and on the train north Gordon Brown went from table to table in the media coach, talking to each group of journalists. David Cracknell, the *Sunday Telegraph*'s political correspondent, told me that some of his colleagues had purposely spread out on their tables in front of them copies of the *Sun*, which had a front-page exclusive by its political editor, Trevor Kavanagh, claiming that Blair had decided to appoint David Blunkett as Home Secretary immediately after the election and this meant that Blunkett rather than Brown was 'increasingly seen' by Blair as a future Labour leader. 'Brown seemed a bit rattled by the *Sun*'s story and he was busy chatting everyone up.'

In his briefing the night before about what would be announced in Birmingham, Campbell said Labour's aim was to present the electorate with a programme for improving and modernising education, health and criminal justice which would take until 2010 to complete. Most of the policy objectives had already been announced and the party had deliberately chosen a headline-free launch because the government wanted to emphasise the extent of the change which would be required and the challenge this would pose to powerful vested interests in the public services.

In presenting the 44-page manifesto, *Ambitions for Britain*, Blair said Labour had chosen to 'reject the quiet life' and were asking the British people to let the government get on with the job of real and radical change. A start had been made in repairing the neglect they had inherited, but there would have to be far-reaching reform of public services which would otherwise be threatened with 'being broken up, torn down, sold off'. There was no more radical mission than to give Britain world-class public services; but money alone was not enough, and no barriers, dogma or vested interests should stand in the way of reform. 'With this manifesto as our route map, we now ask the British people for a mandate to get on with the job. A mandate for investment. A mandate for reform.'

Several of the questions followed up the *Guardian*'s front-page exclusive that morning, which revealed that the government's reform programme for a second term was likely to include proposals for private contractors to run vast swathes of the public services, including clinical health, school management and many aspects of local government. A report drawn up by the Institute for Public Policy Research, a think-tank close to the policy advisers of Downing Street, had warned that an injection of private-sector competition was the only way to bring about innovation and improve services. Blair insisted there was a role for the private sector in both education and health, and said that, in order to guarantee shorter waiting times, the government intended to open specially built surgical units which could do non-emergency operations and which could be managed by the NHS or the private sector. And, after the controversy the previous week about the failure to use the party's pledge card to renew Labour's 1997 promise on income tax, the manifesto repeated the undertaking not to raise the basic or top rates.

Blair's vision of what Britain could achieve by 2010 evoked a scornful response from both the Conservatives and the Liberal Democrats. William Hague said the manifesto seemed to be a watered-down version of what Labour had promised in 1997, and that for the first time a government was seeking re-election by promising to deliver in the next two terms what it had already promised to deliver in the first. Charles Kennedy thought the biggest disappointment was Blair's 'poverty of ambition'.

Labour's manifesto launch was chosen by Oliver Letwin as the moment to break cover and admit that he was the unnamed shadow cabinet minister who had told the *Financial Times* that the Conservatives' aspiration was to cut tax by as much as £20 billion a year by 2006. By ordering him not to speak to journalists for two days, Central Office had given Labour a free hand to go on distributing 'Wanted!' posters for the missing Treasury spokesman and to run scare stories about the spending cuts which William Hague and Michael Portillo would be required to make to achieve such savings. Now Letwin told journalists the *Financial Times* story was 'a perfectly accurate representation' of the comments he made but that, as he pointed out at the time, the £20 billion figure was 'an aspiration' and he had not made 'any commitments to a specific level of tax cuts' for the second half of the Parliament. But his belated explanation could not repair the damage which had been done to the credibility of the Conservatives' figures: the accuracy of the pledge to cut public spending by £8 billion had been badly dented, and by failing to act sooner the Tories had given Labour ministers ample time, through speeches and interviews, to establish £20 billion as a figure which was likely to be used by the news media rather than the more cautious estimate given in the Tory manifesto. Moreover, Letwin's measured explanation received far less coverage than he might have expected because of the battering Labour were taking from the unforeseen events of the day. Sharron Storer's confrontation with Blair coincided with a drubbing for the Home Secretary, Jack Straw, which might otherwise have dominated the early evening news bulletins. Delegates at the Police Federation's annual conference in Blackpool heckled and jeered him throughout his forty-minute speech. To begin with there was mocking laughter when he insisted that police numbers were rising for the first time in seven years while wastage was 'stable and low'; then the protest turned into a slow handclap, and Straw was forced to stop speaking for more than half a minute.

When the news started coming through about the fracas in Rhyl and the accuracy of John Prescott's left jab, Labour's media strategists were not sure how to react. Carolyn Quinn, one of the BBC's correspondents on the campaign trail, told me there was no chance to interview the Prime Minister that evening to get his response. Journalists travelling on the battle buses got the impression initially that the incident was being treated rather light-heartedly. 'All we could find out was that when Alastair Campbell got the news that John Prescott had thumped someone, Tony Blair's response was pretty hilarious.' Later, once the police confirmed that a protestor had been arrested on suspicion of assault, and after the television news bulletins started showing pictures of Prescott looking shaken and subdued as he explained that he had defended himself after being attacked, the mood in the Millbank war room changed. Concern about the potential gravity of the disturbance was heightened by reports that the egg-throwing might have been connected with a demonstration by fuel protestors and rural campaigners. Questions were also being asked about the way Prescott had chosen to retaliate rather than get out of the way. Attention started to focus on the daily news conference which Blair was to host at Millbank Tower next morning. Wednesday 16 May had seen Labour assailed from all sides, and there was a real fear that in the newspapers next morning Blair might undergo the kind of hammering not seen by a Labour leader during a general election since the disasters which befell Michael Foot in 1983 campaign.

Thursday 17 May

After having been hit for six so spectacularly by a sequence of events which no spin doctor could possibly have predicted, Labour had no alternative but to prepare for the worst and wait to see what the morning newspapers would make of a disastrous day's campaigning. No other western country has ten national dailies which can claim to have anything like same circulation or readership of the British press and, as a succession of Prime Ministers and party leaders can testify, the newspapers do have the power to make or break a politician. Indeed, the ability of the daily papers to set the political agenda for days on end and to influence news coverage on television and radio has been condemned down the years by all the major parties. What would the newspapers make of John Prescott's left jab, Sharron Storer's ambush of Tony Blair and the Police Federation's scathing reception for Jack Straw? Among the all-important headline writers there was no contest when it came to deciding whether to adopt a hard cop or soft cop routine. 'Two jabs Prezza bops a voter', was the *Daily Star*'s contribution and possibly the most succinct of the banner headlines, although the *Daily Mail* came a close second with 'The two Jags floor show' over a front-page photograph showing the 'astonishing scene' as the Deputy Prime Minister, flat on his back, brawled on the pavement with a countryside protestor. The *Independent*, having the advantage of more space, had perhaps the best take on the day: 'Eggs fly. Prescott cracks. And Labour's big day is scrambled.'

The light-hearted, jokey nature of the headlines had an immediate impact in the war room at Millbank Tower, where it had been feared that the overnight coverage might be far more censorious. Early morning news programmes carried the first political reaction. Prescott's explanation that he was acting in self-defence got short shrift from William Hague, who said the Deputy Prime Minister should not have got so rattled. 'If he was in my party I would demand an explanation from him. In public life we are all in a position where people try to provoke us. It happens every day out on the campaign trail and I think he should learn to keep his cool.' The Liberal Democrats considered that both John Prescott and the egg-thrower were wrong to have acted as they did and, at his morning news conference, Charles Kennedy suggested a degree of self-control all round would have been better. When political journalists reached Millbank Tower there was still an air of uncertainty as to how Labour would respond. In a statement issued that morning, in which he described the incident as 'frightening and regrettable', Prescott said he assumed he had been punched and thought that the egg running down his face was blood. The Prime Minister faced a difficult moment squaring up to the news media. He wanted to go as far as he could in backing Prescott while not saying anything which might prejudice the police enquiries which were continuing following the release on bail of the egg-thrower; and, while he was anxious to acknowledge the seriousness of what had happened, he thought it best to adopt a light, low-key approach.

David Blunkett, the Secretary of State for Education, was also on the platform, and Blair's opening line of introduction went down well: 'Right, well, good morning everyone. I know you are waiting with bated breath for David's announcement on classroom assistants!' The laughter of the assembled journalists gave him the cue he was waiting for: 'I have spoken to John Prescott last night and this morning. Of course he regrets the whole incident ever happened. He felt a blow on the side of the head and reacted instinctively . . . I tell you, you know, in the last seven years you get to know someone pretty well when they're as close to you as he has been to me as my deputy. John is John and he has got very, very great strengths . . . [laughter] . . . not least in his left arm [renewed laughter].' From then on Blair knew that his deft approach had done the trick. However, he was challenged after getting slightly carried away in his paean of praise for the politician whose left jab had wiped Labour's manifesto off the front pages: 'You could not wish for a deputy to be more loyal, more true or more decent. He cares about his country, cares passionately about his politics. I tell you I am lucky to have him as a deputy.' Nick Robinson, chief political correspondent for *News 24*, caught Blair off guard and managed to connect: 'Prime Minister, isn't there a danger when you say that "John is John" you sound like the mother of a hooligan. That's what they say.' Blair retreated swiftly to his corner: 'I mean, you know, I can't go back over what I've said. If you read his statement, he explains it.'

David Blunkett did his bit to keep up the run of puns when Blair escorted him by the arm towards the podium, remarking as they went: 'I'm watching the right hook there, David.' Blunkett did not need much prompting: 'Better with the left than the right.' And, to make his point, the Secretary of State smacked the knuckles of his left hand into his right palm. Later, William Hague, never one to miss the chance to use humour to make a political point, managed to sharpen up his rebuke to John Prescott while taking a side-swipe at the Prime Minister's official spokesman. Alastair Campbell had made it to the front page of the *Daily Star* on Wednesday 16 May because of a report that the nineteen-year-old pop star Britney Spears had sent him a good luck message for the election campaign. After taking his six-year-old daughter Grace to a Britney Spears concert at Wembley Arena and attending one of her parties at Planet Hollywood, Campbell was described regularly in showbusiness columns as a self-confessed fan of the 'teen singing sensa-tion'; to his discomfort, he found that Hague had also taken an interest in the repertoire of the 'princess of pop' – and used it to good effect when asked to deliver his verdict on the Prescott punch. 'Perhaps the Deputy Prime Minister should have taken advice from the real Deputy Prime Minister, Alastair Campbell. He's a great fan of Britney Spears and Campbell should have told him that her latest number, "Hit me baby, one more time", isn't meant to be the theme tune of Labour's campaign.'

The lunchtime news bulletins had pictures of Craig Evans, the 29-year-old farm worker and hunt supporter who threw the egg, posing outside his home near Denbigh after being released on police bail. When asked if he regretted what he had done, he said nothing but shook his head. North Wales police told reporters that the Deputy Prime Minister would also be interviewed in connection with the incident. Evans's solicitor, Gwyn Jones, read out a statement saying his client did not deny that he threw the egg, in 'pursuit of a peaceful protest' which became 'rather heated and got out of control'. Evans was a 'quiet and private person' who wished to live his life without 'further massive media intrusion'. Prescott, who was determined there should be no interruption to his campaign, spent the day in Scotland. He travelled by car instead of his coach, the Prescott Express, and avoided walkabouts. Traffic cones and a police cordon kept the entrance clear to a Labour club at Prestonpans, near Edinburgh, where he met party supporters and cuddled a baby in classic campaign style. The only excitement was when seven-month-old Coll MacAskill made an affectionate jab at Prescott's chin. 'I had better not put a fist in her face,' he quipped.

Prescott was enjoying his celebrity status and, after numerous requests, he agreed to give an interview to STV's Scotland *Today*. 'Of course, I regret the incident. I felt a bang on the back of my head . . . Two of my female assistants went down . . . I responded to defend myself . . . It was a hostile environment. Who'd want to be in that? I regret it happened as much for me as my staff, who all suffered. It's the same when the Chumbawumba group threw water over me at the Brit Awards. They did it for publicity. Why should we be subjected to that kind of protest? I think it's all wrong.' Prescott, who had already visited thirty constituencies, said he hoped it would be possible for him to continue walking into crowds and having a sensible debate, but if he was going to become a focus for such protests he would have to think again.

Prescott's anxiety about whether it was safe for politicians to continue talking to voters in the street or to go campaigning in shopping centres reflected an anguished debate which had gone on all day. At his morning news conference, Charles Kennedy said there was a danger that politicians and journalists were living in the same 'hermetically sealed media bubble' and were talking to each other rather than engaging with people outside the bubble who were really angry. Lord Razzall, the Liberal Democrats' campaign director, told The *World At One* they had to realise that electors were turning away from the political process. He doubted whether constituency visits by party leaders, and their attempts to talk to electors in high streets up and down the country, were the answer. 'Whenever Kennedy, Blair or Hague go out somewhere to meet the voters, it's as though the circus has hit town. They're immediately surrounded by a group of a hundred or so journalists, photographers and cameras crews and a real dialogue is impossible.' Most commentators agreed that Sharron Storer's courage in taking Blair on showed that voters could break through Labour's slick presentation, and that her words had been far deadlier in their aim than Craig Evans's egg. Mrs Storer told reporters she was amazed by all the fuss she had caused. 'I never thought I could do it by myself. I just wanted Blair to know he really does have to do something. He went to look at brand new places in that hospital when really he wants to go to the rest of the wards to see what's really happening.'

At Labour's news conference Jon Snow, presenter of *Channel Four News*, suggested the confrontation with Mrs Storer and the Prescott punch had been a 'refreshing insight' for politicians, and he asked whether the Prime Minister and his cabinet colleagues were partly to blame for attending too many stage-managed events at which they met only hand-picked people. Blair said it was 'nonsense' to claim Labour politicians were not meeting real people. 'Since the campaign began we have been out there answering questions. I am the person who is doing question and answer sessions with the public the whole time, interviews the entire time. The idea when you walk down a street and there is a gang of your own supporters on one side and Conservatives on the other, that you have a dialogue with people is far fetched.'

Nick Clarke, presenter of The *World At One*, asked whether Blair would take up Charles Kennedy's request and reconsider Labour's refusal to take part in a televised debate among the three party leaders. This was a touchy area. Programme planners at the BBC and ITV had put forward a joint proposal in November 2000 for two one-hour debates to be staged in the final fortnight of the campaign. Although Hague and Kennedy had both accepted, in January 2001 Labour rejected the invitation, stating that the two broadcasts would not 'significantly add to the public's interest in or understanding of the issues'. On Wednesday 9 May Michael Ancram, the Conservatives' chairman, had taken advantage of the final session of Prime Minister's questions to write to Blair to remind him that unless he changed his mind about the invitation from the BBC and ITV, voters would get no other chance until after polling day to see the three leaders on television debating the key issues of the campaign. 'Your refusal to participate in an independently produced series of debates is quite incredible and outrageous in this age of television . . . Outside the arrogant, sanitised and insulated formats so beloved of your spin doctors, you know only too well that your record on hospitals, crime, asylum, schools and taxes would soon be revealed in public debate for the cynical failures they are.' Blair had been reminded on regular occasions since the start of the campaign, by both the Conservatives and the Liberal Democrats, that it was Labour which had torpedoed plans for a leaders' debate in the 1997 election, and he was anxious to avoid further embarrassment at his news conference. 'Look, I'm not getting into the subject of the TV debate . . . I think I will probably do more genuine question and answer sessions with studio audiences than a party leader has ever done before. I think we are exposed to people's genuine concerns all the time.'

The point which was not put to Blair on this occasion was whether a leaders' debate might help avoid the low turnout which the opinion pollsters were predicting. Gallup's latest campaign survey for the *Daily Telegraph* showed an alarming fall in the level of enthusiasm among the electorate: only 66 per cent of eligible voters said they were definitely go to the polls on Thursday 7 June. If this forecast was accurate, turnout would almost certainly be the lowest since the 1918 general election, and the lowest in normal peacetime conditions since Gladstone beat Disraeli in 1874. Most newspaper columnists agreed with the Conservatives and the Liberal Democrats that a televised debate among the three leaders would increase voter interest. Donald Macintyre, writing in the *Independent*, appealed to Blair 'at this late hour' to think again, and in his column in *The Times* Peter Riddell condemned Labour's 'cynicism' and said their excuses were 'largely spurious'. In an attempt to eliminate any possible objections from the three parties, the broadcasters agreed to the same format for the two debates. Both would be shown in peak time, and in order to guarantee a mass audience the two channels had promised not to counter-schedule against each other by running highly popular programmes at the same time. David Dimbleby had been asked to chair the BBC's debate and his brother Jonathan was to preside at ITV. Other rival broadcasters would be given free access to the debates to ensure the widest news coverage.

On rereading the letter from Lance Price turning down the invitation, and looking at my notes of the lobby briefing given that day by Alastair Campbell, the reasons for Labour's refusal were obvious: the Prime Minister was so far ahead in the opinion polls that the risk was not worth taking, especially as Hague had demonstrated superior debating skills at the dispatch box. Blair wanted to have it both ways. His party invested an enormous amount of time and effort in securing the best possible television coverage, recognising that most people get most of the information which is likely to influence the way they vote from what they see and hear on the broadcast media; yet when the industry offered to co-operate with politicians from the three main parties in encouraging a public debate, Labour were prepared to frustrate it for blatant electoral advantage.

Price, Labour's director of communications – and, somewhat ironically, a former BBC political correspondent himself – argued in his letter that the reasons which justified televised debates between presidential candidates in the United States did not apply in the United Kingdom. A live audience of around one million for Prime Minister's questions saw the equivalent of a televised debate between the party leaders every week, and many millions more saw extracts from these exchanges on news bulletins. There was nothing comparable in the USA. When a sitting

President was challenged, it was not known who his opponent would be until a few months before the election, and when a President was retiring, neither candidate was well known. Price quoted the Bush–Gore debate of the 2000 presidential election as an example of the first substantive encounter between two candidates.

The obvious flaw in Price's argument, as Ancram and others pointed out, was that Parliament did not sit in the four weeks leading up to a general election. Campbell's briefing for lobby correspondents put forward an equally dubious argument. He said Blair had rejected the idea because he knew the news media would concentrate on the process of the debate rather than the policies being discussed. 'All we would get is endless discussion about the personalities of the leaders and flashbacks to key moments of the past like Richard Nixon sweating . . . There would be nothing but blah-blah about the ballyhoo of it all for days on end, both before and after each debate . . . We think you will have more discussion and more focus on policy without televised debates.'

Campbell was almost certainly correct in predicting that the tabloid press would see a televised debate in terms of a clash of personalities; but he seemed to have overlooked the interest and intelligence of viewers. I was convinced that many voters too busy to read newspapers, or having only a passing interest in politics, would find time to watch a much-publicised, peak-time debate on television, and in my view the failure of Labour's media strategists to recognise this showed a flagrant disregard for the modern democratic process and the danger posed by the appallingly low turnout predicted in the opinion polls.

Friday 18 May

John Prescott's split-second timing and the accuracy of his left jab had become a talking point in almost every pub and club in the country and, for the second morning running, his exploits dominated the front pages of the newspapers, although – to the chagrin of Millbank's media managers – the boxing commentators commandeered more space in the tabloids than the political correspondents. A sepia-coloured photograph of Prescott throwing 'a crushing right hook' in a boxing match in 1958 filled the front page of the *Mirror*, which said the Deputy Prime Minister had learnt to box as a teenage steward on cruise ships. His fights were in makeshift rings on deck and passengers were said to have bet huge sums on the outcome. In 1957, when he was nineteen, Prescott earned a silver cup for winning a final on the *Britannic* and he later won another tournament on the liner *Rangitata*. Not to be outdone, the *Sun* printed a mock poster showing Alastair Campbell, kitted out like the boxing promoter Don King, advertising an evening of sporting entertainment in which the top fight was to be between John 'Two Jabs' Prescott and William '14 Pints' Hague.

Almost every paper had a picture of Craig Evans, Prescott's opponent in Rhyl; but although he was shown posing with his girlfriend Gwen Edwards outside the cottage they rented in the hamlet of Fford-las, near Denbigh, he had added nothing to the statement which his solicitor made on his behalf and he would not comment on the accuracy of his aim when throwing eggs. Neighbours were quoted as saying that Evans, who kept several terriers and lurchers, was passionate about the country-side; according to Janice Walls, landlady of his regular, the Golden Lion at Llandyrnog, he was 'a mild-mannered giant who likes his pint after a hard day's work on the farm'. Evans's determination to keep out of the spotlight reduced some journalists to writing about his 1980s-style mullet haircut, described in scrupulous detail by the *Guardian* as 'a nostalgic short-on-top, but long-at-the-back look'.

William Hague dominated the day's political action after travelling to Dover, the 'asylum capital of Europe', to make a speech promoting the Conservatives' plans to curb bogus asylum seekers. 'A safe haven, not a soft touch' was the slogan for the party's policy. The aim was to reverse the chaos which, they alleged, had resulted from Labour's 'mismanagement': all new asylum applicants would be housed in secure reception centres until their cases were decided; the process to consider applications would be speeded up; applications from 'safe countries' would not normally be accepted; and those whose claims were rejected would be 'quickly deported by a new removals agency'. Hague said the British people were not bigoted, they were not ungenerous and they understood that Britain had responsibility to those displaced by war and persecution, but that there was now 'sustained and systematic abuse' of the asylum laws. 'Elect a Conservative government on the seventh of June and the process of ending the racketeering and human trafficking will begin on the eighth of June.' Hague quoted figures showing that in the last full year of a Conservative government 29,000 people had applied for asylum and that by 2000 this figure had risen to 76,000, the highest number of applicants to any European Union country.

Dover, a seat which the Conservatives lost in 1997, had not been chosen at random as the location for the speech: the channel port housed 500 asylum seekers who were living on benefit. Party workers who manned the Conservatives' call centre at Central Office, and who spent the day ringing up potential supporters in 180 target seats, insisted that although disquiet about bogus asylum seekers did not rank as high as health, education and tax in people's concerns, it was one of the issues raised by possible swing voters. This feedback reinforced the confidence of the party's policy strategists in their conviction that the problem of asylum and illegal immigration should be one of the key issues of the campaign. In an interview for the *Ten O'Clock News*, Hague denied that his speech in Dover had been insensitive. 'Not at all. The insensitive thing would be not to address this problem. Wherever I go around the country, people bring this up. They want it dealt with. They want it known that Britain is a hospitable and generous country, but that we won't have our rules abused. It's not too much to ask and it's an entirely legitimate subject of debate.'

Labour and the Liberal Democrats disagreed and accused their opponents of opportunism and racism. Charles Kennedy was scathing and succinct: 'All I would say about this latest lurch into populism by William Hague is that they are a political party that now contains all the instincts of Alf Garnett with the appeal of Michael Foot. This country is not a soft touch, it is a beacon of hope, which is why people want to come here. To play this card in the election is mad, bad and dangerous.' Barbara Roche, minister of state at the Home Office, insisted the problem had been sorting out the backlog and shambles left by the Conservatives. Holding asylum seekers in secure reception centres would not work and was 'quite possibly' illegal. Coverage of Hague's speech on the BBC's lunchtime news bulletins was criticised by Lance Price, Labour's director of communications, for 'effectively rewarding the Tories for refusing to face questions on their policies'. Millbank had been expressing increasing irritation over the Conservatives' failure to hold daily news conferences. In the first two weeks of the campaign, except for the manifesto launch, there were only two occasions when journalists had the chance to question Hague and other members of the Conservative front bench. Price argued that if Labour had refused to hold a daily news conference there would have been 'an outcry', and he issued a press release stating that broadcasters were supposed to 'cover events, not seek to shape them by helping a party get uncritical, unquestioning coverage and allowing a party leader to avoid any kind of questioning at all'.

Sky News had also incurred Labour's wrath for its election coverage on Wednesday 16 May, which had included a phone-in entitled 'Are the spin doctors spinning out of control?' Alastair Campbell complained by email, accusing the channel's political journalists of having become 'self-obsessed' for staging a discussion about spin and presentation. 'There are two elections going on. The media's election, focused on process, and the election the Labour Party and the public are interested in, focused on the economy and public services.' Another *bête noire* of Labour's spin doctors, the *Daily Mail*, tweaked Millbank's tail by sending a butler to Merseyside to serve champagne to Shaun Woodward, who had been 'shoehorned by Tony Blair' into the safe Labour seat of St Helens South. Photographs across a two-page spread illustrated the exploits of the paper's parliamentary sketchwriter, Quentin Letts, who reported that the former Tory frontbencher, who 'once remarked that "even my butler has a butler", had a severe sense of humour failure and ran away'. The picture sequence showed Letts walking through the town centre with Woodward, who was wearing a red and yellow Labour rosette. When he stopped to talk to a potential voter, the tailcoated butler, Ashley Powell, interrupted to offer the candidate a glass of champagne from a silver tray. Letts took up the story: 'Woodward, who took a moment or two to react, did a runner. With an "Oh, come off it!" he bolted, straight for the nearest shop.'

Woodward, like Peter Mandelson in Hartlepool, was finding that one downside of a high-profile contest was that it became a magnet for other fringe candidates attracted by the publicity that was on offer. The discontent which I had observed on Sunday 13 May, when local applicants were excluded from the shortlist for the St Helens South selection contest, had prompted the resignation of a former chairman of the constituency party, Neil Thompson, who decided to fight the seat as candidate for the Socialist Alliance. Helen Shaw, another party member, also resigned, to work for his campaign. She was one of those who voted against Woodward, claiming he had been imposed on them against the wishes of the constituency. Thompson announced his defection on Wednesday 17 May, the day the national chair of the Socialist Alliance, Dave Nellist, launched his party's manifesto in London. Later, after he was interviewed at the BBC's studios at Westminster, I met him again for the first time since I reported his expulsion from the Labour Party a decade earlier because of his membership of the Militant Tendency. Nellist told me the Socialist Alliance had no hope of winning a seat but that the manifesto was a campaigning document and their aim was to build up support for the local authority elections in 2002, when they hoped to add to their existing tally of twelve councillors. On *Newsnight* that evening, Nellist was equally sanguine when interviewed by Jeremy Paxman. 'We're not expecting to form the next government . . . We hope our work starts to build a much bigger socialist alternative than we've ever had before.'

Saturday 19 May

There could hardly have been a more telling demonstration of the strength of Labour's planning and organisation than the series of rallies which the party arranged for old-age pensioners across the country. Each event had a celebrity as compère, and the line-up illustrated the depth of Labour's support in the television and entertainment industries. One of the biggest events was held in Gloucester, where Tony Blair was joined by the singer and television presenter Jane McDonald, who led a pensioners' sing-song. The same combination of politician and personality was on hand in other towns and cities to welcome the pensioners; some of those who were invited said they were supporting Labour for the first time. The actor Richard Wilson from *One Foot in the Grave* backed up Cherie Blair and Andrew Smith at Ilford; the former *EastEnders* star Ross Kemp topped the bill at Clacton with Chris Smith; Sherrie Hewson from *Crossroads* shared the honours in Nottingham with Margaret Beckett; the children's television personality Floella Benjamin went to Hastings with Alistair Darling; David Blunkett was joined at the rally in Leeds by Tom Owen from *Last of the Summer Wine* and the test umpire Dicky Bird; *Emmerdale*'s vicar John Middleton assisted Stephen Byers at the Tynemouth rally; and the radio personality Dean Park was in Glasgow supporting Dr John Reid. I spent the morning and afternoon watching television pictures from the various locations being fed into the BBC's studios at Westminster, and I found it absorbing and impressive to see so many pensioners enjoying the company of celebrities like Richard Wilson and having a chance to talk to Cherie Blair and a host of cabinet ministers. To illustrate my report for *PM* I was listening out for some sound or noise which I thought might encapsulate the day, and I chose Jane McDonald's warm-up routine for the Prime Minister: 'Anybody fancy a bit of a sing-song? It's Saturday afternoon, what more could we want, eh?'

The scale of the effort which Labour was making to appeal to the eleven million pensioners in Britain reflected the damage which the party had suffered after the decision to increase the basic state pension by only 75p a week in April 2000. After a bruising time at the annual party conference in the autumn of that year, the Chancellor kept his promise to be more generous to the elderly, and in April 2001 introduced the biggest single increase for twenty-five years: £5 extra for single pensioners, taking their basic income to £72.50 a week, and £8 more for couples, giving them a basic state pension of £115.90 a week. Another hefty rise was promised for April 2002: £3 a week for single pensioners and £4.80 a week for couples. Repairing the harm which the 75p a week increase had done to Labour's standing with the elderly had been given the highest priority by Tony Blair, and from early on in the campaign, when asked at question and answer sessions to identify the single biggest mistake of his first four years in office, he said it was the government's failure to have been more generous to pensioners in April 2000.

The importance of the grey vote to Labour could not be overestimated: opinion polls had shown repeatedly that elderly voters were more likely to go to the polling stations than any other age group. On Tuesday 15 May the charity Age Concern published a survey by ICM which predicted that among those aged sixty-five and over the turnout would be 71 per cent, which was noticeably down on the estimated turnout by the same age group of 77 per cent in the 1997 general election. None the less, ICM's forecast turnout for this group was exceeded by only one other age group, those aged fifty-five to sixty-five, where the likely figure was put at 74 per cent. Against a background of repeated warnings about a catastrophic fall in the overall number of people who were likely to vote, Labour could not afford to take any risks with the elderly – not least because during the four previous general elections the Conservatives' share of the grey vote was comfortably ahead of their opponents'. In 1997 the estimated breakdown among those aged sixty-five and over was that 41 per cent voted Conservative and 36 per cent for Labour, a pattern which had remained pretty constant and which showed that even though there might be a low turnout across the country, the Conservatives were likely to gain the biggest share of an age group which was showing the second strongest intention to vote.

Unsurprisingly, competition for this crucial sector of the electorate was hotting up. In their attempt to appeal to pensioners, Labour's opponents were proposing higher upratings in April 2002 than those the government had announced. If the Conservatives won the election, pensioners who were seventy-five and over would do better: the increase for single pensioners in this age group would be increased to £4 a week and couples would receive an extra £6.80 a week. All pensioners would have also have the option of consolidating allowances like the winter fuel payment and free television licences into the basic pension. The Liberal Democrats proposed even larger increases from April 2002; they too would target more of the money on older pensioners, who they said were 'amongst the poorest and neediest people in the country'. There would be a basic increase of £5 a week for single pensioners and £8 a week for couples; this would rise to £10 and £18 a week for those aged seventy-five and over; and jump to an extra £15 and £28 a week for those who were eighty and over.

Labour's planning had left nothing to chance: Millbank's infamous grid setting out a timetable of events until the opening of polling stations had Pensioners' Day pencilled in for the second Saturday of the campaign. My report for the early morning news bulletins previewed the day ahead, and I outlined the efforts which the three main parties were making to woo elderly voters. Labour opened the proceedings with a news conference to promote the ten pledges included in the party's 'charter for pensioners' but, as Millbank had hoped, the focus soon switched to the celebrity line-up at the sing-songs and other events around the country. Blair told the rally at Gloucester that the basic pension was going up faster than the rate of inflation: 'We want pensioners to share in the rising prosperity of the nation. And it's only right as the country gets wealthier that pensioners share in that prosperity. I know we didn't get everything right these past four years, but I do believe we've made a start and laid the foundations.' Charles Kennedy, who was campaigning in the Isle of Skye with his girlfriend Sarah Gurling, defended the Liberal Democrats' proposal to fund their generous pension increases through the introduction of a top rate of income tax of 50p for people earning over £100,000 a year. 'It means the best-off are contributing to help the least well-off in the country, and I think that's the principle you need to bring a country together.' William Hague claimed Labour could not be trusted to defend the interests of the elderly. 'They've a cheek claiming to be the party of pensioners after the 75p increase that they gave and after the huge taxes they've levied on pension funds, to the tune of £5 billion a year taken out of pension funds by Gordon Brown.' But Millbank's carefully laid plans paid handsome dividends: neither Hague nor Kennedy had any chance of stealing Labour's thunder. Their invective might have been stronger, but Labour's images were far more appealing; and it was footage of the friendly faces of stars from some of the best-loved television soaps mixing it with pensioners and cabinet ministers that took pride of place in the evening news bulletins.

Sunday 20 May

Journalists were told on Saturday evening that Tony Blair would not be electioneering on Sunday as he intended to be with his family, celebrating the first birthday of his son Leo. We were in no danger of being short of any quotes we might need from the baby's doting father; Millbank had ensured that our every whim would be catered for. 'A remarkable interview' obtained by the *Sunday People* revealed 'the true extent of how his family shape and influence his life and every aspect of his job as Prime Minister'. Blair told the paper's political editor, Neil Wallis, that his family was the refuge to which he turned to escape the stress and pressures which he faced. 'The great thing when I see Leo is that I know that all he wants me for is me. Like my other three, he doesn't care whether I am Prime Minister or not, whether I'm famous and my picture is on the telly and in the papers, whether I'm at the top of the tree or the bottom of the heap. It's his first birthday on Sunday and, when I see him, all he'll want is his dad to play and talk with him. And that is very good for me, it keeps me in the real world when sometimes my world can seem very unreal indeed.' Blair also used the interview to reflect on his confrontation with Sharron Storer outside the Queen Elizabeth Hospital in Birmingham. He acknowledged that she was right to have challenged him about the length of time patients have to wait, and the pressure on nurses and other hospital staff. 'Frankly, in general I agree with her. It might not look comfortable for me, but I know despite the progress we've made there is a lot of frustration like hers out there when things go wrong.'

Much of the election coverage in the Sunday papers was similarly reflective, and an action-packed week provided plenty of material for background analysis. The *Sunday Times*' Focus team suggested that Gordon Brown and the media planners at Millbank had taken the blame for sending Blair to the hospital where he was ambushed by Mrs Storer. The campaign team had crammed too much into the election grid on the day of the manifesto launch, which did not need 'a follow-up event'. John

Prescott's biographer, the *Independent on Sunday*'s political editor Colin Brown, said there was 'panic' in Millbank when Brown was told that the Deputy Prime Minister had punched a protestor. Brown said Prescott 'stared in disbelief' when the police showed him the route he was expected to take through the countryside demonstration in Rhyl. 'When he was hit in the ear by the egg from a distance of two feet, he believed he had been struck a blow with a fist.' Craig Evans broke his silence about the incident by giving an exclusive interview to the *Mail on Sunday* in which he 'relived the drama' of what happened after he 'hurled the egg, from point blank range' and was then 'sensationally punched' by the Deputy Prime Minister. 'He looked at me with a glint of madness in his eyes, I could tell he was boiling with rage . . . It was pure anger.'

An insight into Blair's reaction to the events in Rhyl had appeared the day before in the *Guardian*, based on an interview which Alastair Campbell gave to Ewen MacAskill. On being told that Prescott had 'thumped someone' Blair's initial reaction was to laugh, thinking his press secretary was winding him up. MacAskill described what transpired the following morning, once Labour realised how the punch was playing in the news media, and the 'initial panic' at Millbank subsided. The two men relaxed again out on the road: 'Blair and Campbell were convulsed with laughter all the way down the motorway. They looked at other drivers and joked about which of them might want to punch the Prime Minister. They pointed at a lorry driver and speculated on whether he might want to take a swing because of fuel prices. Campbell said of the Prescott incident: "At least it shows we are not robotic. I would have punched him myself."' Campbell was credited by the *Financial Times* with having advised Blair to adopt 'a light tone' at the news conference the morning after and then abandon most of the events planned for the day on the Millbank grid.

Even though the manifesto launch was blown off the front pages, Labour's former head of advertising, Chris Powell, thought the events of the week had helped to refresh the campaign. Powell, chairman of the BMP DDB advertising agency, writing in the *Observer*, said there was a 'sense of relief' when Blair and Prescott in their different ways 'made contact with flesh-and-blood disgruntled voters'. Both incidents were difficult for William Hague to exploit: a sustained attack on Prescott would have gone against the grain of most news coverage, and the danger in trying to capitalise on Sharron Storer's outburst was that it might have rebounded and drawn attention to the Conservatives' record on health.

The Tories' mishandling of the Oliver Letwin saga produced a savage rebuke from usually sympathetic columnists. Peter Oborne, writing in *Sunday Express*, said Hague's 'biggest mistake' of the campaign was to have bustled Letwin away 'like a convict' for having suggested that the Conservatives' long-term aspiration was to cut spending by £20 billion. 'It made the Tories look like a party with something to hide when it should have been shouting from the rooftops that its ambition is to reduce the burden on the long-suffering taxpayer.' In his weekly media column in the *Spectator*, Stephen Glover blamed the 'largely instinctively pro-New Labour' media for having accepted the spin that the Tories had a guilty secret. 'Lewtin behaved like a chump in cutting and running. He should have defended his corner.'

One minor embarrassment for Millbank's famed spin doctors was the revelation that the former Spice Girl Geri Halliwell, who had featured in Labour's first election broadcast on Monday 14 May, would not be able to vote because she had taken a 'conscious decision' to keep her name off the electoral register for 'security reasons'. Ms Halliwell's conversion to Blairism sparked numerous features, including an account in the *Sunday Times* by Simon Sebag Montefiore of his interview with the Spice Girls for the *Spectator* the Christmas before the 1997 general election, when Ginger Spice linked 'girl power' to Thatcherism. 'The most articulate and the most Tory were Geri (Ginger) and Victoria (Posh) . . . Geri was the most fun, the sexiest and the most instinctive. She understood the potential of the idea, saying: "We Spices are true Thatcherites. Thatcher was the first Spice Girl.'"

Monday 21 May

Week three of the campaign opened with the three main parties battling it out over their rival economic policies. Labour tried to put William Hague on the spot by giving journalists copies of Michael Portillo's first 'Tory Boom and Bust Budget', printed in a blue booklet similar in style to the Treasury's yearly red book which sets out the annual estimates for tax revenue and spending. The Conservatives retaliated by unveiling a business manifesto promising tax breaks and reductions in business rates. The Liberal Democrats, intent on publicising their transport plan, refused to get dragged into the big political row of the day which revolved around claim and counter-claim over the possibility that Labour and the Conservatives might be forced to increase national insurance contributions.

For the first time in the campaign I had the chance of attending, in the correct sequence, all three early-morning news conferences, something I had previously been unable to accomplish owing to a run of late shifts. Having on the one hand no clout, and on the other no wish to become the tail-enders, the Liberal Democrats had no choice but to go first, at 8 a.m.; and their daily news conference was in a venue linked inextricably with the early days of the Labour Party. Bevin Hall, which they had hired for the campaign – their own headquarters building, a couple of blocks away in Cowley Street, does not have a room large enough for a televised news conference – is in what used to be called Transport House, the original headquarters of the Transport and General Workers' Union. Its first general secretary was Ernest Bevin, who joined the war cabinet as minister of labour in 1940 and became Foreign Secretary in the 1945

Labour government. Transport House, now renamed Local Government House, having become the new head office of the Local Government Association, doubled up for many years as the headquarters of the Labour Party. It faces on to Smith Square, just across the road from Conservative Central Office, and I have visited it regularly since 1968 when I started working at Westminster. In the 1970s I conducted frequent radio interviews there with Ron Hayward, the then Labour Party general secretary, and throughout the 1980s I spent countless hours in it reporting union meetings. So walking back into Bevin Hall for a Liberal Democrat news conference was quite an experience.

The party put the space to good use, providing live camera positions with a clear view of the conference platform where Charles Kennedy was introduced by his campaign director, Lord Razzall. Because he had to go first, and did not know what issues might arise at the Labour and Conservative news conferences, Kennedy's first task was to get in a soundbite on the economy, one of the likely topics of the day: 'We reject Tory stealth cuts or Labour stealth tax increases. We want honesty in terms of delivery of public services.' He then turned to the party's environment spokesman, Don Foster, to introduce the party's transport plan. Most of the follow-up questions related to the competing claims of Labour and the Conservatives to be the party of business, another issue which looked like being of interest because of the launch that morning of the Conservatives' business manifesto and the publication in the *Daily Telegraph* of a letter, signed by 140 business leaders, which attacked government policy and repudiated a statement put out the previous week by fifty-eight company chairmen and directors who supported Labour's re-election. Kennedy insisted he had the support of senior business leaders as well, but he did not think it influenced voters. 'Labour and the Conservatives are entitled to parade the support they have from the business community but it's something at the margins of the campaign.'

There was no time to linger, because Labour's news conference started at 8.30 a.m. at Millbank Tower, quite a step away. I was overtaken en route by ITN's chief political correspondent, Jo Andrews, who was speeding along on a shiny micro-scooter. She happily chortled away to me about how her colleague Elinor Goodman, political editor of *Channel Four News*, had been grounded because she could not get insurance for her power-assisted scooter. At that point we were both overtaken by Jon Snow, the bicycling presenter of *Channel Four News*, who was wearing a distinctive yellow crash helmet. I managed to catch up with him at the pedestrian crossing near Lambeth Bridge when he stopped to take a call on his mobile phone.

At Millbank Tower, Labour were continuing to do all they could to make the most of the Conservatives' discomfort over their disgraced frontbencher Oliver Letwin, who had still failed to re-emerge at Westminster. Copies of the 'Boom and Bust Budget' were handed out and we were told that it would be presented by Alistair Darling, who said that unlike Letwin, he would take questions. Darling, not known for his exciting delivery, mocked what he claimed would be Michael Portillo's first financial statement to the House of Commons: 'A Tory Budget for instability. A Tory Budget for in excess of £20 billion cuts. A Tory Budget that locks in irresponsibility year on year.' Darling's play-acting as 'Chancellor' only drew attention to the absence on the platform of Gordon Brown, who on GMTV the previous morning had refused to rule out the possibility of raising the ceiling on national insurance contributions, a step which Labour had proposed in 1992 in John Smith's ill-fated shadow Budget. Brown's answer to a question on this subject appeared to leave open the option of removing the upper limit: 'I'm not going to be drawn into every aspect of income tax or national insurance.' Darling, who was seen by Millbank as a safe pair of hands, fielded a barrage of hostile questions and did his best to hold the line by arguing that no political party could make such a pledge. 'The Conservatives are asking us to give commitments that they won't give themselves. And there are, I think, some 250 different tax rates and allowances throughout the system and no government or prospective government can deal with every single one of these allowances.' When Darling accused the journalists of raising a question planted by the Conservatives, Elinor Goodman denied doing the Tories' work: 'If Labour aren't giving a firm pledge on national insurance, you are free to put it up. Why won't you answer the question yourself?'

By the time we had all trooped back to Smith Square for the start of the Conservatives' news conference at 9.15 a.m., William Hague had the edge on his opponents, because the war room in Central Office had been monitoring the live television coverage of the two earlier news conferences and had seen Darling as he struggled to avoid giving a straight answer. Hague, who was joined on the platform by Michael Portillo for the launch of the business manifesto, wasted no time in exploiting Gordon Brown's failure to give a pledge on national insurance when Labour had given such an undertaking in their 1997 manifesto which explicitly ruled out abolishing the upper limit. People earning over £29,900, said Hague, would have to pay an extra £800 a year in tax. 'It means higher taxes for our senior nurses, doctors, police officers and teachers. If Gordon Brown does not intend to raise the national insurance ceiling and tax the income of middle earners more, I challenge him to rule it out now.'

If Hague had been hoping for an easy ride he was mistaken. This was only the third daily news conference to have been held by the Conservatives, and it was first chance for the Westminster media pack to hound the party leader over the continued absence of Oliver Letwin. In response to the inevitable questions, Hague denied the Conservatives had a specific plan to increase their spending cuts from £8 billion to £20 billion, and he stood by his Treasury spokesman. 'Oliver Letwin remains an extremely capable shadow chief secretary to the Treasury. There is no such arithmetic progression, there is only one figure, £8 billion . . . As far as I am concerned that matter is settled.' Pinned on the walls around the conference room were a selection of the party's election posters promising to lift the burden on harassed public service workers: 'Form Fillers? Teachers will be teachers with the Conservatives . . . Paper shufflers? Police will police with the Conservatives.'

As it was the final news conference of the morning, and as there had been so few chances to speak to Hague's team in Central Office, I hung around and waited for an opportunity to speak to the party's head of media, Amanda Platell. Was she enjoying the campaign? 'Yes,' she replied, 'I'm having a ball. A British general election is such fun.' I had just started to ask her what she thought of the way the Conservatives had responded to Prescott's left jab when we were interrupted by the *New Statesman*'s political editor, Jackie Ashley. Ms Platell immediately nudged her and asked if she had noticed one of the photographers who was there that morning. 'Did you see him? He had a mullet haircut. How do you do that, Jackie? Cut the top short and then leave the rest to go all yukky at the back?' At this point they both moved away to continue their conversation without me, and I was left high and dry.

I could only assume that Ms Platell's mind had been wandering while Michael Portillo was extolling the virtues of the Conservatives' business manifesto and that she had spent the news conference casting her eye over the assembled photographers, perhaps on the lookout for some characters or storylines for her next literary offering on the steamy sex life at the interface between journalism and politics. *Scandal*, Ms Platell's first novel, had been published in December 1999, eight months after Hague appointed her the party's head of media. Her fascination with the mullet haircut reflected the extensive coverage which Craig Evans' hairdo was continuing to provoke in the pages of the tabloid press. 'Egg chucker's mullet confirms hair revival is on,' said a headline in the *Sun* over a picture line-up of the celebrities who had been seen in 'the dreaded eighties hairdo'. Ms Platell had made her name in popular

journalism and she knew what made a good tabloid story. After gradu-
ating from the University of Western Australia, she mastered the latest
computerised production techniques during her training on the *Daily
News* in her home town of Perth; after working on the *Sun-Herald*,
Sydney, she arrived in London in 1986; and after working on *Today* rose
to become group managing editor for *Mirror* newspapers. She then had a
succession of jobs: managing director of the *Independent* and
Independent on Sunday, acting editor of the *Sunday Mirror* and finally
executive editor of the *Sunday Express* until her dismissal in January 1999.
On her appointment as the Conservatives' head of media the following
March, the party chairman, Michael Ancram, said that her fifteen years'
experience on national newspapers would help build 'an election-
winning political machine' at Central Office.

In an article she wrote for *The Times*, explaining why she had taken the
job, Ms Platell said a 45-minute interview she had with Hague, when she
was editing the *Sunday Express*, made a big impact. She was struck by his
uncompromising vision and determination in the face of daunting odds.
'Most people would have been crushed by the months of endless criticism, the polls, the lampooning, the personal attacks. He was undaunted.
I liked that.' Hague phoned her the day after she was sacked and 'simply
asked if I was OK', and then they met again before she was offered the
job. 'I only really began to understand the whole man when he and Ffion
invited me to their home . . . Over a couple of beers and a bottle of wine,
lounging around in big, soft chairs, I saw William the husband.' She said
she had become disillusioned with Tony Blair and felt the Labour government was leaving a 'nasty aftertaste . . . as though I had been force-fed the
line of a politically modified Prime Minister. I had witnessed at first hand
the unhealthy way some parts of the government are manipulating the
press. When you see the bullying, the tricks with mirrors, it's refreshing
to meet a man who is honest and straight, whether you like what he's
saying or not. There's nothing phoney about William.' Within weeks of

her appointment there were stories in the newspapers about her plans to improve Hague's image; to get him seen more frequently with his wife Ffion; and, as the *Daily Telegraph* put it, to persuade Conservative MPs to 'chuck out the chalk', which was how she described 'that stuffy old Tory look' of double-breasted suits with loud chalk stripes.

My first chance to observe her in action came after Hague's success in the elections to the European Parliament in June 1999, when the Conservatives took thirty-six seats, doubling their contingent of MEPs. At a celebratory news conference next morning at Central Office, she stood alongside Hague's chief of staff, Sebastian Coe, and his parliamentary private secretary, David Lidington, welcoming reporters with a broad smile. Just before Hague emerged on to the platform she walked to the rear of the conference room and stood in a strategic position next to the television cameras. Although the turnout in the United Kingdom was only 24 per cent, the lowest for a direct election to the European Parliament, the Conservatives had won their first national election since 1992, taking 36 per cent of the vote, well ahead of Labour on 28 per cent. Hague saw it as a vindication of the decision taken by the shadow cabinet in October 1997 to go into the next general election campaigning against British membership of the European single currency. 'Our policy is to keep the pound. That clearly has the support of people across the country. This is a winning policy. This is a solid victory.' Ms Platell smiled again when he explained to the media that it was up to the party's pro-European MPs to decide whether to support the campaign to keep the pound. 'I am not going to bargain with anyone. MPs are free to give their own views. Collective responsibility applies to the shadow cabinet.' Alan Duncan, who walked over to where I was standing, told me I should not underestimate the importance of what he believed was a significant personal victory for Hague over senior pro-Europeans. 'Michael Heseltine and Kenneth Clarke are now extinct.'

The success of the Conservatives' campaign to keep the pound made a deep impression on Ms Platell, and a few days later she told a BBC documentary, *How to be Leader of the Opposition*, about her strategy for promoting Hague: 'I am presenting him into situations which he feels completely natural with. I am pretty confident it will be a relatively easy task . . . the tide is turning for William.' The following month news leaked out of a vivid illustration of the strength of Miss Platell's support for the policy he was pursuing. She had secretly commissioned a diamond-encrusted gold pendant, made in the shape of a sterling pound sign, which Ffion Hague wore at the Conservatives' rally on the eve of the European Parliament elections. Reporters were told by Central Office that it was a 'thank you present' on the second anniversary of his election as leader and 'an emblem of her husband's most treasured beliefs'. Five weeks later, when the jeweller complained about late payment, it emerged that the necklace with its sterling-shaped pendant was not the 'love gift' from Hague to his wife which the newspapers had reported but a publicity stunt thought up by Ms Platell who had hurriedly paid the £1,400 bill herself before being finally reimbursed by an embarrassed party leader. Her dogged attempts to rebrand Hague and his wife had attracted the attention of Labour's spin doctors and a Millbank press officer, Mathew Doyle, told me that it was their tip-off to the *Financial Times* which got the story going. 'We heard that the jeweller had not been paid and we slipped this to the *Financial Times*, but we had no idea the *Evening Standard* would get such marvellous quotes or that the story would then get picked up by every national newspaper.'

Ms Platell was an easy target. In August 1999 the *Daily Telegraph* published a leaked copy of a memo, headed 'Project Hague', which she had drawn up with the help of his wife and which set out ideas for activities to show that he had a 'life beyond politics' and strong family roots in Yorkshire. Among the suggested photo-opportunities were: return to comprehensive school in Wath-on-Dearne, 'jacket off, talking to pupils'; holiday shot with Ffion, 'evening walk on beach?'; regular summer activity, 'judo with army'; and appear relaxed and confident before conference, 'pre-conference walk in Dales, country pub, colourful locals etc.'. Labour politicians had a field day ridiculing Ms Platell's attempts to give Hague yet another makeover, and she continued capturing the headlines throughout the autumn of 1999 in the build-up to the publication of her novel, *Scandal*, which the *Mail on Sunday* said was 'a bodice-ripper and truly blue bonkbuster' which would set Westminster alight.

Trouble was building up for Ms Platell on another front: the return of Michael Portillo, who won the Kensington and Chelsea by-election in November 1999, set in train a series of internal party feuds in which she became deeply implicated. The catalyst for one of the most serious splits was Hague's shadow cabinet reshuffle in February 2000. Portillo was appointed shadow Chancellor and Francis Maude moved sideways to become shadow Foreign Secretary. When Maude's chief of staff Robbie Gibb, an avid Portillo supporter, asked to continue his work on the economic brief and remain with the new shadow Chancellor, his application was vetoed. Within a few weeks Gibb had left the staff of Central Office, following in the path of several other disgruntled party workers who had departed in similar circumstances and whose grievances were being aired regularly in the newspapers. Maude and Portillo believed Ms Platell was to blame for blocking the appointment, and although both sides denied being responsible for giving hostile briefings, journalists found there was plenty to write about. The storyline had all the elements for a long-running Westminster saga: Hague's failure to improve the Conservatives' rating in the opinion polls was a source of continuing criticism and unease; he was backed by Ms Platell, whose fierce loyalty to the party leader and her unwillingness to compromise led to friction with her colleagues; and waiting in the wings were aggrieved Portillo supporters, known as the Portillistas, who were increasingly being portrayed as the group which was plotting and preparing for the inevitable leadership contest after Hague's expected defeat in the 2001 general election. Hague and his shadow cabinet colleagues tried repeatedly to smooth over these differences in order to present a united front and to get ready for the election campaign, but as the months dragged by and there was no sign of the much hoped-for upturn in the opinion polls, the tension persisted and backbiting stories continued to appear in print. Ms Platell became a handy scapegoat, and she took much of the blame whenever Hague's interviews or photo-opportunities went wrong. And yet, although the suggestions she had made in her 'Project Hague' memo had been ridiculed a year earlier, the Conservative Leader was still faithfully following her advice the following summer and doing all he could to promote his strong family roots in Yorkshire.

One of Ms Platell's aims had always been to reduce the number of briefings Hague gave to political correspondents so that he could spend more time talking to journalists on consumer and general interest magazines. In the summer of 2000 he was presented with what seemed like a perfect opportunity to connect with an upmarket audience when he was interviewed for the September edition of *GQ* by Nicholas Coleridge, the managing director of Condé Nast Publications. Hague was billed as the Tory leader whose 'scathing wit and shrewd appeals to populism have started to rattle the once untouchable Labour government'. Much of the interview focused on his early life in South Yorkshire during his late teens and early twenties and his holiday job with the family firm, Hague's Soft Drinks. Anyone who thought he spent his holidays 'reading political tracts' should have seen him helping to deliver crates of soft drinks and barrels of wholesale John Smith's bitter to working men's clubs around Barnsley and Rotherham. 'We used to have a pint at every stop – well, the driver's mate did, not the driver, thankfully – and we used to have about ten stops in a day . . . You worked so hard, you didn't feel you'd drunk ten pints by four o'clock . . . We used to do that, then go home for tea and then go out in the evening to the pub.' When

Coleridge put it to Hague that he must have been drinking fourteen pints a day, he did not disagree. 'I think when you're a teenager you can do that.'

The boast of being able to sink fourteen pints in one day made front-page news in the tabloids. Under the headline 'Billy Liar', the *Sun* quoted Terry Glossop, assistant manager at the Angel, one of Rotherham's oldest pubs, as saying it was 'laughable' to suggest he could drink so much. 'He was known as Billy Fizz and Billy the Pop. No one can remember him drinking as much as half a lager.' An already bruised and battered Ms Platell was slated again by commentators and columnists alike. Anne McElvoy, writing in the *Independent*, backed her decree that Hague should cease announcing 'endless and forgettable Opposition policy initiatives to sympathetic newspapers', but pronounced it a mistake to have allowed him to talk about his 'wild-child years' in a 'glossy magazine favoured by les lads', which did nothing to bridge the gap between 'his own natural political assets and the dodgy image of his party'.

Ms Platell took the only course of action which was open to her: she tried desperately to lower her profile and avoid contact with those journalists who could cause her trouble. Initially I met her quite frequently, accompanying Hague on his early morning interviews at the BBC's studios at Westminster or at the news centre in west London. If I tried to interview him inside the newsroom she often complained, saying she 'hated' the office as a backdrop, and would insist on finding a more appropriate location. I found her approachable and admired her assiduous attention to detail. I thought she was helping to create a friendlier environment, especially for broadcasters, who had long felt their needs were overlooked. As she retreated from front-line contact, I came to rely increasingly on her two most senior colleagues, her deputy Nick Wood, the chief spokesman, and the assistant head of media, Andrew Scadding, who had joined Central Office in June 1999, shortly after Ms Platell. Wood concentrated on briefing newspaper correspondents and

Scadding, formerly senior producer for the BBC's political programme *On the Record*, was the first point of contact for broadcasters.

Ms Platell's failure to establish a steady working relationship with political journalists in the lobby or to grasp the complexities of news coverage on radio and television put her at a considerable disadvantage and was in marked contrast to her opposite number Alastair Campbell. In many ways he was a one-off, and his devotion to the Labour Party had impelled him to do what most journalists would have hated doing: become a political propagandist. But Campbell, like Peter Mandelson before him, was a dedicated political strategist and he had drilled into his staff the importance of gathering all possible intelligence about the story-lines which the various journalists were pursuing. Press officers were there not only to impart news but also to collect information which might assist in the formation of the media strategies that Labour was to deploy. I got the impression that Ms Platell had no understanding or appreciation of this aspect of her work, and although I spoke to her on numerous occasions she never once tried to find out what I was up to or to discover what I thought was interesting or newsworthy.

The closest she got to being identified publicly as a possible source of the stories that Michael Portillo was plotting a leadership coup was in December 2000, in the troubled aftermath of a speech in which Hague blamed the Macpherson Report for a collapse in police morale and a rise in street crime. Sir William Macpherson had investigated the murder in south London of the black teenager Stephen Lawrence, and his report accused the Metropolitan Police of 'institutionalised racism'. Hague considered Labour ministers and the 'liberal elite' had made a mistake in supporting the report and that, in what he called the 'post-Macpherson collapse in police morale and the rise in street crime', it was the members of the ethnic communities who were suffering most. After the *Mail on Sunday* reported that Portillo had made a 'devastating' attack on Hague's decision to raise 'the explosive issue of race and policing', Francis Maude broke cover and denied the story on *The World This Weekend*. He believed the source of the story was inside Conservative Central Office and said Hague had given him a personal assurance that if identified, the culprit would be sacked. 'I find it breathtaking that some people think it helpful to spread poison in this way. Whoever is doing this is inflicting great damage.' Political journalists and MPs from the left of the party interpreted this as a clear, if coded, attack on Ms Platell.

As one of Hague's closest advisers, Amanda Platell remained an easily identifiable target for criticism of Hague's tactical mistake in not taking immediate disciplinary action against the Yorkshire East MP John Townend when he claimed that Britain's 'homogenous Anglo-Saxon society' had been seriously undermined by massive immigration. The black Conservative peer, Lord Taylor, who kept up the pressure which helped to force Hague's belated decision on Monday 30 April to demand an apology from Townend, believed his leader had been 'very badly advised' in failing to act sooner in publicly reprimanding both Townend and Laurence Robertson, who was seeking re-election in Tewkesbury. Furthermore, he singled out one adviser by name in an interview for the *Sunday Telegraph*: Ms Platell, whose novel *Scandal* had personally offended him. 'The Conservatives are the party of family values, of respect for decency, for law and order, and yet the leader of our party allows his press secretary to write a dirty porn book.'

Lord Taylor's interview, published on Sunday 6 May, was fresh in my mind as I walked out of Central Office and pondered on my brief conversation with Ms Platell and her chatter about mullet haircuts. On reflection I thought she had probably used small talk as a way of deflecting any more serious questions which I might have tried to ask. She seemed as cheerful as the rest of the leader's campaign team and that afternoon, when live pictures were fed back to London of Hague speaking in Northampton, I recalled her delight in June 1999 after the Conservatives' success in the European Parliament elections. Hague's determination to continue campaigning against Britain joining the euro had not dimmed, and as he spoke to a boisterous crowd in the town centre he was surrounded by party activists holding Conservative Keep the Pound placards. Hague had no difficulty firing himself up with the pantomime routine he used out on the stump, and the louder the boos from Labour supporters, the more he liked it and the better his repartee. 'Would you merge your currency with the euro? No, you wouldn't! [Cheers.] That's why we'll keep the pound! [Cheers.] Tony Blair daren't get out and meet real people. All he does is send out a few supporters to shout at me. Let me challenge Tony Blair again, today, to have a debate in front of the people. Let him debate with me, any time, any place.'

Tuesday 22 May

The ability of camera crews to obtain dramatic television footage of Tony Blair and John Prescott being ambushed the previous week on their final steps towards election events in Birmingham and Rhyl respectively was seen in far more menacing terms by the party's command structure in Millbank Tower than Labour's public pronouncements had suggested. News of the most ill-judged complaint of the campaign did not emerge for four days, but once it had been exposed in the newspapers, the party leadership beat a hasty retreat. After admiring Sharron Storer's tenacity in taking on Blair, marvelling at the precision of Prescott's left jab and then hearing about the irritation of Millbank's media managers, I did wonder if there would be a formal response to the coverage. Ever tighter restrictions were being imposed on the filming of arrivals at Labour's events, and I thought the party's propensity to fire off complaints to broadcasters at the slightest provocation made it unlikely these two high-profile incidents would be allowed to pass without comment. And sure enough: 'TV to blame for protests, says Labour' was the headline on the

Daily Telegraph's lead story about an official complaint which had been made by the party's general secretary, Margaret McDonagh. The paper reproduced a leaked copy of her letter, dated Friday 18 May, in which she accused BBC, ITN and *Sky News* of being implicated in disrupting the party's campaign events. Ms McDonagh did not refer directly to either Mrs Storer's tirade outside the Queen Elizabeth Hospital or to the countryside demonstration at Rhyl, both of which took place on Wednesday 16 May, but the wording of her letter, and the timescale she referred to, made it abundantly clear what was on her mind.

Her letter got straight to the point: 'Over the past forty-eight hours I have been provided with growing evidence that broadcasters have been inciting and colluding with protestors at campaign visits made by senior Labour politicians. I am sure that, like me, you will want to ensure that this behaviour ceases immediately. It crosses the line between creating and reporting the news. It also puts at risk the safety of Labour Party staff, politicians and the public. This matter is so serious I would like a meeting with you as soon as possible – preferably over the weekend or at least by no later than Monday. I am sure you share my concerns and will want to stop this situation escalating.' *The Times* and the *Guardian* followed the *Daily Telegraph*'s example in leading with Ms McDonagh's complaint; but Labour refused to supply any details of the 'growing evidence' to which she referred, and the newspapers were left to their own devices in trying to pinpoint the incidents which were to blame. The *Daily Telegraph* referred to a report in the *Independent on Sunday* which asserted that Prescott had told colleagues he was 'convinced *Sky News* was tipped off by hunt protestors' to be in Rhyl for his arrival, and it also reported a separate claim by Blair's advisers that the BBC had 'miked up a farmer to have a go at Tony'. *The Times* believed that it was the conduct of BBC and ITN crews during Blair's tour of East Anglia and his visit to a hospital in King's Lynn which finally prompted the complaint. At one point a Labour aide 'allegedly pulled the plug out of the back of a television camera' after the cameraman had attempted to film the Prime Minister inside the hospital, and Blair's special assistant Anji Hunter was seen having 'a heated conversation' with an ITN reporter.

All three broadcasting organisations issued statements denying there was any evidence of collusion; Labour had been informed in the clearest terms these concerns were not justified. After John Humphrys told listeners to *Today* that Labour and the BBC had both declined to be interviewed, he turned to one of the Conservatives' campaign spokesmen, Tim Collins, who claimed that Labour had 'crossed the line between wanting to spin events, into a position where they are saying people who disagree with them must be silenced'. He believed there were signs of a pattern of serious behaviour. 'We now have third world ethics from Labour, thuggery and intimidation to stop dissent and protest . . . Yes, it is intimidation. Demonstrators who tried to get close to the Prime Minister have been bundled away by Labour Party workers.' Reporters arriving for the morning news conference at Millbank Tower were told immediately that the dispute had been settled. There had been 'amicable' discussions and the party's concerns had been addressed in 'a serious, mature and constructive way'. Gordon Brown, who was chairing the news conference, insisted that Labour had never attempted to 'influence the broadcasters' agenda'; its only concern had been for the safety of the party's staff. Blair expressed his satisfaction with the discussions which had taken place and indicated his desire to put an end to the story: 'The matter is closed as far as we are concerned. I think it is right we are out there answering people's concerns, and that is what we will do.'

Later he told the *Jimmy Young Programme* that he accepted the assurances given by the television channels that they played no part in provoking either the egg-throwing in Rhyl or his unexpected encounter with Mrs Storer. He believed the public wanted to hear about jobs and living standards and get away from questions about 'the process of the election'. Blair followed the usual practice of his official spokesman and did not deign to acknowledge that it was Labour, rather the electronic news media, which had provoked and then publicised the story. Ms McDonagh's letter, marked 'private and confidential', was a typical example of the kind of complaint which Labour tends to send direct to the senior management of broadcasting organisations in the hope of exerting pressure behind the scenes. Once news of it leaked out, Blair and Brown had little alternative but to smooth over any differences with the broadcasters, fearing Labour could only be damaged if reporters kept asking for evidence of the 'inciting and colluding' of which Ms McDonagh had complained. Although the *Daily Telegraph* would not reveal the source of the leak, there were unconfirmed suggestions it came from *Sky News*, which was particularly forthright in its denial of the accusations. After the *Daily Telegraph* asked for Labour's response, the party's senior spokesman, David Hill, released the contents of the letter to both *The Times* and the *Guardian*, indicating that initially Labour were intent on publicising the complaint. However, the potential damage which a drawn-out confrontation with the broadcasters could have inflicted, unless Labour had backtracked, was evident at their opponents' news conferences. Michael Portillo said Blair's campaign was becoming the most 'shambolic' since Michael Foot led his party to defeat in 1983, and Charles Kennedy considered Labour were pathetic for being so thin-skinned.

The only possible example of 'colluding' which was uncovered by the BBC's media correspondent, Torin Douglas, involved a Norfolk farmer who was given a personal microphone by the BBC when he wanted to ask a question about organic farming during Blair's visit to Lincolnshire. A Labour Party press officer was informed of what was happening but in the event Blair moved on and did not answer the question. Richard Tait, editor-in-chief of ITN, told me Ms McDonagh's complaint was the height of hypocrisy because Labour were encouraging their own activists to attend demonstrations. As Blair was telling Jimmy Young that the public were fed up with the media talking about 'the process of the election', an ITN crew following William Hague's campaign tour in Devon filmed a group of protestors who were wearing Hague masks and carrying posters denouncing the Tories' £20 billion spending cuts. 'Our reporter John Gilbert, who was doing a report for the news on Channel Five and was dressed in a white suit, looked inside one of the Hague masks. It said they were produced by the Labour Party. That gives you an indication of whether it was ITN or the Labour Party which was colluding with demonstrators.'

The masked protestors reappeared later that evening when Hague's battle bus pulled into Plymouth, where a rally for the Conservatives was competing for an audience with a new action-packed special effects film. Lady Thatcher, who as Prime Minister was never slow to spot a possible news line, needed no prompting after being introduced on the platform. 'On my way here I passed the local cinema and it turns out that you were expecting me after all. For the billboards read *The Mummy Returns*.' Her appearance in the city was not intended to be simply a morale boost for the party leader; she also wanted to take the first opportunity to give her full endorsement to his strategy of making opposition to the euro the most important issue in the election campaign. 'Blair says he wants to lead in Europe. But the price of that is that he is expected to lead Britain by the nose into the single currency. He's prepared to do it. I would never be prepared to give up our own currency.' At the word 'never' Hague had no choice but to stand there smiling in support – although with this single word she had blown apart the Conservatives' delicate and carefully constructed policy position of saying 'no' to the euro for the duration of the next Parliament. Afterwards, Lady Thatcher told reporters she meant it when she said 'never' because the United Kingdom's sovereignty was at stake. 'A country which loses the power to issue its own currency is a country which has given up the power to govern itself. Such a country would no longer be free.' Lady Thatcher's intervention threatened to provoke unease among Conservative pro-Europeans and strengthen the hand of those Conservative candidates who were also intending to say 'never' to the euro. Labour and the Liberal Democrats could not believe their good fortune.

Labour had been in difficulty all day because Gordon Brown had found no way to silence the Conservatives' accusation that a re-elected Labour government might be tempted to scrap the upper limit on national insurance contributions. Hague claimed this could result in four million people paying tax at a rate equivalent to 50 per cent. Finally the Chancellor's patience snapped and, late in the afternoon, the political editors of BBC and ITN, Andrew Marr and John Sergeant, were called to Millbank Tower for what Labour said would be the 'definitive interview'. Brown was intent on demolishing two smears. The first was the Conservatives' charge, made originally on Saturday 12 May, that petrol could go up to £6 a gallon; and the second was the talk of a 50 per cent tax rate. 'These are smears which the Conservatives know are not true and I repudiate them. They are smears the Conservatives will live to regret.' I was dispatched immediately to Sloane Square tube station, where Michael Portillo planned a photo-opportunity and would give his response. When I arrived he was standing there rather forlornly holding a poster for a billboard. It said: 'Income tax up to 50p admits Brown.' A newspaper seller at the tube entrance told Portillo and his two assistants that he would 'bloody well' tear the Tories' poster up with his own hands if they dared to place it near his stand.

After talking with his assistants for a few moments, Portillo walked over and suggested I might like to try asking the newspaper seller for permission as a BBC journalist would probably be seen as impartial. I declined politely, noticing that I was being eyed intently not only by my own cameraman but also by ITN's news producer Lucy Manning and her camerawoman Marcia Hunte. In the end a party worker held the poster aloft as Portillo repeated his accusation about a possible 50 per cent tax rate. I shared a taxi back to the Millbank studios with the ITN duo, who teased me for nearly falling for Portillo's trick. I had realised just in time that Ms Hunte had a glint in her eye and was poised to catch me on camera. 'We'd have got you, Nick,' said Ms Manning. 'BBC hack caught red-handed colluding with the Tories.' We got talking about how Portillo always went out of his way to please the television crews. Ms Hunte asked me if I had noticed how, at news conferences, he always acknowledged the photographers and television crews in a calculated way. 'When Portillo is on the platform he looks in turn to the snappers and then at us. He knows what he's doing. He holds his pose, waits for the flashes and the clicks, and then lifts his chin. He then does the same for the crews. There's no doubt he's seeking us out. It's the same on doorsteps. When he arrives he always slows down, smiles, sometimes separately for snappers and crews, and then looks at us again to see if we've got our shot. We all think he's doing it because he's going to stand for the leadership if Hague goes.' I asked Ms Hunte if other politicians looked out for the cameras in such a purposeful way. 'Another one who seeks us out is Gordon Brown. When cameras are on him he makes a point of looking serious and studious. We often think he's just combed his hair.' Ms Hunte had time to give me only two more of her vivid descriptions: William Hague 'always looks over the heads of the crews into the far distance', and as for Ann Widdecombe, 'Well, she never responds to us at all, you can never catch her eye.' She hadn't seen the latest technique which some camera crews had observed when Tony Blair was being filmed on walkabouts. As he left a building or walked along a street, he sometimes raised his hand and looked up, as though acknowledging someone waving from the window of an upper storey. However, when the cameramen swung up to take a picture there was no one there. They assumed Blair had perfected the action in order to make himself look animated.

Back in the newsroom I had to concentrate on a story about a leaked document on European tax harmonisation which Conservative Central

Office was releasing under an embargo for use next morning. Andrew Scadding said the contents were 'explosive stuff' because the paper showed the European Commission intended to urge the Council of Ministers to agree to the harmonising of income tax and value added tax, a step which Labour had previously announced they would oppose. When I checked this out with Brown's special adviser, Ian Austin, he demanded that I immediately fax him the leaked document. I told him I could not possibly do so as it was under embargo. Austin was shameless in his persistence, and his zealous support for the Chancellor had already attracted comment. When Brown chaired Labour's manifesto launch on Wednesday 16 May, Austin suggested questions which reporters might like to ask. He was overheard by other journalists when he approached *News 24*'s chief correspondent, Nick Robinson, who told me Austin whispered a question which he suggested would be 'helpful' to the platform. Robinson protested and rejected Austin's invitation, which became the subject of a renewed attack by Tim Collins on *Today*, when he responded for the Conservatives to Labour's charge that broadcasters were 'colluding' with demonstrators. Collins said the newspaper reports about Labour 'planting' friendly question at news conference was an example of the double standards which would apply if 'Blair gets the second landslide Alastair Campbell has been boasting about'. Campbell's explanation for the approaches Austin made to broadcasters was that Labour was trying to ensure 'a number of different issues' were raised at the manifesto launch. 'It's quite normal for us to get a feel for where questions may be coming from . . . Nobody wants a soft, sympathetic question.'

5 Battle of the Patriots

Colour photographs of Lady Thatcher waving and smiling at the Conservatives' rally in Plymouth filled the front pages of the morning newspapers. Headlines picked out either the word 'never' or her quip about *The Mummy Returns*. Political editors were unanimous in their judgement: Lady Thatcher's dramatic declaration that she would 'never be prepared to give up our own currency' had finally thrust Europe to the centre of the election campaign. The *Daily Telegraph* said she had received a rapturous welcome when she went 'well beyond' the official Tory policy of ruling out membership of the euro only for the lifetime of the next Parliament.

When journalists had arrived to report the speech, party officials had dismissed any suggestion that the former Prime Minister might deviate from the stance to which Hague had stuck so steadfastly in an attempt to keep the party's pro-Europeans on board. But, as *The Times* pointed out under its headline 'Thatcher stretches Tory line on euro', although the advance text of her speech kept to the position of referring only to the 'next Parliament', she 'could not resist adding to the script' and breaching his policy. Most political commentators noted her praise for Hague's 'cool and gritty leadership', which they thought was far warmer than anything she offered to John Major in the 1997 election.

Hague, out on the campaign trail in Newark, tried to make light of Lady Thatcher's intervention: 'I think she was restrained compared with what she usually says.' His careful response reflected the heightened sense of concern within Central Office both about her speech and about an interview she had given in Monday's *Daily Mail*. Amanda Platell feared journalists would seize on comments about immigration and asylum seekers she had made to Simon Heffer: 'I want a society of opportunity for all, irrespective of colour or ethnic background. But I don't wish to have what they call a multi-cultural society . . . I hate these phrases. Multi-cultural society!' But the hostile and damaging questions which Ms Platell feared did not materialise, and for the second day running the interview was not raised at the morning news conference. Journalists were handed copies of the 'leaked' document which the party claimed to have obtained from the European Commission. Michael Portillo said it showed the United Kingdom 'would no longer have the power to set income tax rates itself'.

In Brussels, however, Portillo's warning that this document signalled that tax rates would be harmonised upwards was rejected out of hand by Frits Bolkestein, the Commissioner in charge of tax and the single market. 'There is no need for an across-the-board harmonisation of member states' tax systems . . . It's not on the agenda of the Commission. It will not happen.' Commissioner Bolkestein could not understand what the fuss was about. The discussion document which the Conservatives claimed was 'confidential' was already in the public domain. Confirmation of this came from the BBC's office in Brussels, which said the Commission's proposals were well reported at the time in both *The Times* and *Daily Telegraph*.

Labour refused to be deflected from their attempt to exploit Lady Thatcher's use of the word 'never' to expose the scale of the Tories' split on Europe. Gordon Brown called a second news conference in the afternoon to publicise information which Labour activists had collected in the constituencies. This showed that in campaign literature and speeches eighty Euro-sceptic Conservative candidates had broken away from Hague's official line on the euro and were sounding defiant. Twenty-three candidates were calling for renegotiation of British membership of the EU or complete withdrawal. Lady Thatcher's intervention provided a platform for the United Kingdom Independence Party to exacerbate Tory infighting over Europe. Nigel Farage, one of UKIP's three MEPs and its candidate in Bexhill and Battle, claimed the Conservatives were splitting into three parties. 'There's one Conservative Party led by Kenneth Clarke, another Conservative Party led by William Hague and the third Conservative Party is clearly led by Lady Thatcher, and I think that Lady Thatcher and her wing are actually in the wrong party and should be in the UK Independence Party.'

When Hague appeared that evening with David Dimbleby in the BBC's *Question Time* series for party leaders he went further than before in pushing his own policy to the absolute limit. He said he had not used the word 'never' because no Parliament could bind the next. 'When people say it's OK to join, I say prove it . . . I can't see circumstances in which in the coming Parliament I would say we should join the euro and I think it probably is the last chance to save the pound . . . Labour would choose the question. Labour have rigged the rules, so this is the last chance to save the pound . . . So yes, this election is a referendum on the euro.' Dimbleby asked Hague if he would accept the verdict of the British people. 'I think this election will decide it. I think if Blair is put back into No. 10 the pound is certainly lost. So if Labour wins this election, the pound is sunk.'

The *Financial Times* had a new angle on the euro and predicted that in a speech later in the week Blair would pave the way for a referendum on the single currency in the autumn of 2002. 'Blair to base euro case on patriotism' was the headline on the paper's front-page lead, which said the Prime Minister would argue that joining the euro was 'the patriotic thing to do if the conditions are right'. Journalists had been warned by Alastair Campbell early on in the campaign that Blair intended to make six major speeches, but this was the first time there had been a hint that he was about to use one of them to a give a signal on the likely timing of a referendum, and that one of the arguments for supporting the euro would be based on an appeal to patriotism.

Whenever Blair went out electioneering there usually seemed to be the right photo-opportunity in the offing, and today, whether by accident or design, the news media were not be disappointed: a picture emerged which fitted the patriotic storyline of the day and provided an opening shot for the evening news bulletins. Blair was on a visit to Itchen College in Southampton where, in a room next to the library, he talked to students about tuition fees. One of them, eighteen-year-old Jo Balchin, was wearing a light blue top which had a large union flag printed across the middle. As Blair stood in the middle of the room with one of the students, Ms Balchin got up to take their photograph. She then went over to join Blair, put her arm round him, turned to face the television crews and photographers and, in a blaze of flashlights, held her position for a few moments. It was a full frontal shot displaying the whole of the union flag.

After tapping the Prime Minister twice on the head and ruffling his hair, Ms Balchin sat down – to a chorus of 'give him a kiss' from her fellow students. Photographers and television cameramen, who had been corralled some distance away because Blair was wearing a personal microphone, immediately shouted out asking her age. Surrounded by laughing and cheering students and still looking rather taken aback, Blair was led out of the room by John Denham, the minister of state for health, who was also the candidate for Southampton Itchen. Carolyn Quinn, a BBC political correspondent, was one of the reporters listening on earphones to the sound feed. 'They were telling Blair there was a danger that because some students were so hard up, they might be forced into drug dealing or prostitution to pay for tuition fees, but he assured them there was no reason for that. Blair did look a bit embarrassed when Jo put her arm round him. She was young, attractive and in a tight T-shirt. It was calculated, but not that calculated.' John Denham told me the event was a complete surprise. 'She suddenly came up to Blair wearing a Union Jack T-shirt . . . No, we didn't arrange it. We might be good, but we're not that good.' Pictures of Jo Balchin giving the Prime Minister a hug led the *Ten O'Clock News* and provided BBC political correspondent Mark Mardell with a topical opening line: 'Meeting students, Tony Blair gave a whole new meaning to embracing patriotism. It was his lucky day in more ways than one.'

Thursday 24 May

There was no shortage of anecdotal corroboration from the constituencies to back up warnings in opinion surveys that the public were less interested than usual in the general election. Party workers were finding it extremely difficult to persuade people to put up candidates' posters in front windows and gardens. The first hard evidence of a knock-on effect from the disaffection and disillusion which the activists were reporting was a significant drop in the overall number of candidates. After the close of nominations on the evening of Tuesday 22 May journalists had a chance to look through all the constituency lists and write with some certainty about some of the more bizarre prospective MPs. First place in the list of exotic fringe candidates went to the glamour model Jordan, who was backed by the *Daily Star* and had no difficulty stumping up the necessary £500 deposit in order to stand in the Greater Manchester constituency of Stretford and Urmston. Her surgically enhanced breasts were featured regularly in the newspaper, and the *Star*'s front-page splash which declared she was seeking to become an MP ('that's Member of Parliament, not Massive Pair') claimed she had 'set Britain's most boring general election campaign ablaze'. Her top manifesto pledge was free 'boob jobs' for all. Jordan was to stand as an independent under her real name of Katie Price, and the confirmation of her inclusion in the list of nominated candidates proved to be the most popular story of the day on BBC *News Online*, attracting 59,000 page views, almost twice the number of hits for the main election campaign story on Europe.

Two fringe candidates who were seen as serious contenders were Martin Bell, the former Independent MP for Tatton, who was fighting the Essex seat of Brentwood and Ongar, and Dr Richard Taylor, a retired consultant physician, who was standing in the Worcestershire constituency of Wyre Forest in support of his campaign against the downgrading of Kidderminster Hospital. Bell, a former BBC war correspondent, had lived to regret his 1997 promise to the electors of Tatton that he would stand down after one parliamentary term if he succeeded in defeating the sitting Conservative MP Neil Hamilton, who had become engulfed in the allegations of sleaze which dogged John Major's government. As the 2001 general election got closer Bell's name was linked to a number of constituencies where he thought a high-profile independent might do well and he finally settled on the seat of a Conservative frontbench spokesman, Eric Pickles. Dr Taylor's decision to contest Wyre Forest was attracting considerable attention because the Liberal Democrats had decided not to fight the seat in order to give a clear run to what had become a popular local campaign against cuts in the National Health Service.

The main disappointment when the full nomination list was published by the Press Association news agency was that the total number of candidates stood at 3,294, well down on the 1997 figure of 3,715. Labour and the Conservatives were to contest 640 of the 641 constituencies on the Britain mainland, the one exception being the Glasgow Springburn seat of the Speaker, Michael Martin; the Liberal Democrats were fighting 639 seats; the United Kingdom Independence Party 428; the Green Party 145; the Scottish National Party seventy-two; and Plaid Cymru forty. One notable absentee from the list was the defunct Referendum Party, which in 1997 had fielded 547 candidates with the help of funding from the Eurosceptic billionaire financier, the late Sir James Goldsmith. His party had taken votes away from many Conservative candidates in that election; but although the United Kingdom Independence Party was mounting a significantly stronger challenge in terms of candidates, it was failing to attract anything like the same kind of publicity, except in some specific areas like the west country.

Tory party strategists had been convinced that William Hague's Keep the Pound campaign would have an effect once the constituencies started gearing up for polling day, and the failure by the halfway point in the campaign to see any improvement in the opinion polls was causing deep disappointment. A MORI survey for *The Times* showed Labour retaining their record lead: at 55 per cent, the highest share recorded for them by MORI for eighteen months, they were way ahead of the Conservatives on 30 per cent. The Liberal Democrats were down a point on 11 per cent. Nevertheless, despite the buoyancy of Labour's position in the polls, there was persistent speculation about the soul-searching which was said to be going on inside Millbank Tower. So far as I could tell, it all seemed to revolve around the direction the campaign was taking. Gordon Brown was treating it like a referendum on Labour's first term, fighting a defensive exercise while at the same time stoking up voters' fears about the Conservatives. Tony Blair had become frustrated by this approach and wanted to find ways to inspire and enthuse the electorate. His impatience with the tactics which the Millbank strategists were pursuing became public when he was interviewed by the *Independent*. He did not think Labour should be responding to the guerrilla tactics which the Conservatives were adopting simply to attract the interest of the news media and to avoid debating health, education and the economy. 'What I find frustrating is that I am longing for this dialogue with the public to be on a proper basis. I believe the public have a got a real hunger for that kind of debate. But the reality is, the way it is being covered by a lot of national radio and television is a long way off that.' Blair's frustration resurfaced at Labour's morning news conference, when rather than hear Brown defend Labour's record on health and attack the Conservatives £20 billion tax cuts, he took control of the proceedings and delivered an animated justification of the need to defeat the Conservatives and increase public spending. 'The truth is that we want to put this investment into public services and they want to take it out. Everybody knows that, you know that, you know what they want to do . . . Our choice is to carry on investment, their choice is to cut it back. That's the election in a nutshell.'

Friday 25 May

After being the first newspaper to report that Tony Blair was planning to use an appeal to patriotism in any future referendum on Britain joining the euro, the *Financial Times* followed up its own story with an exclusive interview previewing his much-heralded speech on Europe. 'Blair says he can win euro debate' was the headline over a report in which the Prime Minister 'asserted confidently' that he could persuade voters to back British membership of the single currency. When asked if Labour could win a euro referendum, Blair had no doubt: 'Of course, provided you mount the argument well, provided we are setting out why it is economically and politically in Britain's interest.' But his self-assured answer to the *Financial Times* about the outcome of a referendum was not repeated in his speech in Edinburgh. The main thrust of his remarks there was that support for close political ties with Europe required a forward-looking approach, 'a new modern patriotism', because that represented the true national interest. 'That patriotism demands that in a world moving ever closer together we do not turn our back on Europe, the key strategic alliance, right on our doorstep, on which millions of British jobs depend and sixty per cent of our trade depends.' In response to William Hague's claim that the election was 'the last chance to save the pound', Blair said he feared polling day was in danger of becoming a referendum on something of far greater consequence, Britain's place in Europe. 'The

Conservatives now confirm they plan two summits straight after an election to renegotiate existing European treaties which Britain has signed. I warn this country, that is a policy playing with fire. It is a step away from leaving Europe and that would be a disaster for Britain, British jobs, British industry and influence in the world.'

After spending so much time out on the road, promoting his Keep the Pound campaign, Hague at last had Blair in his sights at his morning news conference and he relished the opportunity to go head to head. 'It's a funny form of patriotism to say we can't run our own affairs in this country. We are the fourth largest economy in the world, the fourth military power in the world. We trade with countries all over the world who have no problems keeping their own currency.' Hague was prepared to wave the flag as fervently as Blair. 'When historians look back at the general election of 2001, they will be interested in one thing . . . They will remember whether we voted to remain an independent country. They will remember whether we preserved the freedoms we are privileged to inherit . . . To people in every party who believe in this country, we will say, lend us your vote this time so that your vote will still mean something next time and the time after that. Vote Conservative this time, so that we can carry on having meaningful elections in an independent Britain.'

If Hague was aiming to make Europe a key issue in the election, Labour could hardly have given him a better platform. The initial spin from Millbank Tower was that Blair had always accepted he would have to make a speech on Europe at some point in the campaign and he believed the political destiny of himself and his government lay in being an engaged and active partner in the European Union. None the less, the Prime Minister had helped energise Conservative Party workers who had been demoralised by the stubborn refusal of the opinion polls to move in their direction, and in a speech to an evening rally in Manchester, Hague ratcheted up his warning about the threat to the pound. 'If Labour and their Liberal Democrat sidekicks win on June the seventh, they will begin taking us into the euro on June the eighth. That process would begin immediately. We have two weeks to save the pound.' Michael Ancram, the party chairman, did a round of interviews that evening and told me afterwards Hague could not believe his good fortune. 'We were all concerned as to whether we really could fire up Europe as an issue and keep it running high in the campaign. So to Blair, we all want to say "Thank you very much," as we never thought we could get it going on our own.' An hour later, the Conservatives' assistant head of media, Andrew Scadding, was on the phone to tell me that the following day would be devoted to keeping up the pressure on Blair. 'We always planned to have our Keep the Pound day on the third Saturday of the campaign but now we're really going somewhere. Labour have made a big strategic error in starting this off for us. There's an arrogance in Blair which we can go for, him saying his future lies on the European stage and that this won't be complete unless Britain goes into the euro. Blair's got cocky and fallen into our hands.' Scadding set out the programme for Saturday: Hague would have a rally in Loughborough and speak from his Keep the Pound truck; there would be 500 street stalls in 170 constituencies handing out 850,000 Keep the Pound leaflets and giving away pens, car stickers, key rings, badges and mouse mats. The high spot of the day would be the unveiling of an advertising van with a digital clock counting down the days, hours, minutes and seconds left to save the pound.

I had rarely heard Scadding speak with such fervour. His eagerness to impart the details of their events was in sharp contrast to my conversation half an hour later with Labour's chief spokesman David Hill. After he had run through Millbank's plans for a series of 'upbeat' rallies on the NHS, I tried to elicit a response about the Conservatives' planned campaign on the pound. 'Look, as far as we're concerned, we're going nowhere on the euro. A lot of spin has been put on the *Financial Times* story and it is not what it seems. The Prime Minister gave an obvious answer to an obvious question and it hasn't moved the position one iota. His speech wasn't on the single currency but on the distinction between Labour's policy of being active and engaged in Europe and the Conservatives' lack of leadership. Our view is that the Conservatives' campaign on the pound will run out of steam. They can huff and puff as much as they like, we've nothing to say on the euro and we want to get back to health.'

As I prepared my overnight report for the morning news bulletins I was not sure who was right about the likely impact of the new-found vigour in the Conservatives' save-the-pound campaign. I was equally puzzled about the significance of the Prime Minister's comments on the euro. Brian Groom, political editor of the *Financial Times*, told me Blair was 'very engaged' when he said he would win a referendum. 'Instead of batting the question away, he spoke with real enthusiasm.' I listened in to the Prime Minister's speech in Edinburgh at the constituency headquarters of Kensington and Chelsea Conservatives. We were waiting for Blair to finish so that Michael Portillo could respond, and I did detect a heightened sense of anticipation among party workers, as if they thought the campaign against the euro was at last taking off. Portillo delayed his remarks until after the completion of the 5 p.m. news bulletins in the hope that his speech would be broadcast live on *News 24* and *Sky News*. As the minutes ticked by I sat chatting with Vanessa Ford, who until 1995 had been the party's head of news. She then moved to the chairman's office and afterwards became a fundraiser, working closely with the party's treasurer, Michael Ashcroft. During the campaign Ms Ford was helping in the call centre at Central Office, where sixty volunteers spent the day phoning voters in sixty marginal seats. 'We do get lots of information to feed back to the constituencies. If someone says they are Labour or Liberal Democrat that's fine, we know not to bother them. It's just the same if they're Conservative. What we're looking for are people who are undecided, who might swing our way.' She would not give anything away, but in reply to my direct question said the party did spend too much time on Europe in 1997.

Ms Ford had been a press officer in the 1992 election and had worked under the then director of communications, Shaun Woodward. I told her I had been to St Helens South and wondered if she could settle an unresolved question of the campaign: Did Woodward have a butler? 'Yes,' she replied, 'everyone knew Shaun had a butler. When he was my boss and I had to ring up him up at weekends with an urgent press query the butler always told me to hang on because Shaun was playing tennis.' Ms Ford had read with interest the *Daily Mail*'s story about the day it hired a butler to serve Woodward champagne when he was out campaigning in St Helens. 'I'm sorry, I don't have much sympathy for Shaun. On the night of the 1992 general election he made me and another press officer, Simon Brooke, stay downstairs at Central Office and deal with the press while he was hiding upstairs in his office. He was convinced we had lost and he only came down when it was clear from the results that we had done well.'

That Friday morning, Gordon Brown probably wished he had stayed upstairs in Millbank Tower rather than descend to the basement theatre and commit the worst faux pas on the news conference circuit. He failed to realise that men in the correspondents' corps were trying to hold back on purpose to let women have first go at putting questions and, when one of the two women on the platform tried to answer a question, he then put his foot in it again by interrupting her. Nick Clarke, presenter of The *World At One*, who asked the first question of the morning, later apologised on air for his gaffe, saying he seemed to have been the 'only journalist not told of the plot.' Jackie Ashley, political editor of the *New Statesman*, and Jo Andrews, chief political correspondent of ITN, were behind the intrigue; it was their way of protesting at Labour's failure to field more than a token woman at their news conferences. As there were two women on the platform with Brown that morning, Estelle Morris and Margaret Hodge, the women correspondents were encouraged by their colleagues to take the initiative. Brown should have got the message when *Radio Five Live*'s Fi Glover thanked him for letting her 'participate in ladies' day' when she suggested Labour might like to select another track from the Lighthouse Family's compact disc rather than keep playing 'Lifted', chosen as the party's campaign theme tune. When Jackie Ashley was called she complimented Brown on having more than one token woman on the platform for the first time in three weeks and then put her question about secondary education – but he still did not appreciate the point which the women were trying to make. As soon as the minister for school standards, Estelle Morris, tried to reply, he interrupted her saying: 'I am sorry [protests] . . . I am sorry, Estelle . . .' He then looked across to where Ms Ashley was sitting and said to her, 'I don't think you're right . . . ' At this point the Chancellor finally realised what was afoot and tried to cover up his embarrassment by joining in the laughter. Ms Ashley told The *World At One* there was a serious point to her protest. Labour's token woman had to sit on the platform looking pretty, but was not allowed to answer questions. 'This is a deep-seated problem in the Labour Party. Women don't have a place at the top table and four years into a Labour government women are going backwards.'

It was clear that anxieties about the likelihood of a low turnout had spread well beyond the core political worlds of Westminster and the constituency activists when the two most senior clergymen in the Church of England, the Archbishops of Canterbury and York, did their best to counteract apathy by encouraging worshippers to vote. In a joint open letter, Dr George Carey and Dr David Hope suggested that voters should assess the underlying moral beliefs and values of individual candidates as well as their parties' policies. Floating voters should inform themselves of a politician's attitude to strangers in their midst and to those on the margins of prosperity. The two archbishops ended their letter with an unprecedented warning to the political parties about the declamatory and disturbing nature of modern electioneering. 'We all sense how tempting it can be, especially in an election season, for the short-term, the negative and the self-serving to dominate the political stage . . . Not only is that wrong from a Christian perspective, it does not serve the best interests of the society which we all share.'

Saturday 26 May

If Keep the Pound day achieved nothing else, it at least provided William Hague with the platform he so desperately wanted to tell the British people of the appalling horrors which would flow from membership of the euro. After unveiling a digital clock counting down to polling day at the Conservatives' rally in Loughborough, he adopted the language of a street-corner preacher to talk in apocalyptical terms of the fate that awaited the country. He acknowledged that Tony Blair's confident prediction in the *Financial Times* was probably right: a Labour government would have 'a good chance' of winning a referendum, and that meant the future of the pound would be settled on polling day. Britain was on the eve of the 'single biggest decision' since the last world war. 'I am not choosing my words lightly when I say that this could be the last general election of its kind, the last time that the people of the United Kingdom are able to elect a Parliament which is supreme in this country . . . It will determine whether we live in a free and independent country . . . So there are now twelve days to save the pound, twelve days to secure our independence, twelve days to decide whether our children and grandchildren inherit the same freedoms were enjoy today. Think about it carefully. Thank you very much.'

At his Keep the Pound rally, Michael Portillo held up a pound coin to emphasise his warning that the British people could become 'frustrated, desperate and ugly' if they ever despaired of finding that their votes could no longer influence democratic change. 'I want to remind you that in the Bible there was that moment when Christ held up the coin and said: "Whose head and insignia is on that coin?" The answer was: "It is Caesar's, so rend unto Caesar that which is Caesar's." People understand the intimate connection between the person who held the currency and the person with the political power. If the euro was introduced to Britain, you would not see the Queen's head on the euro. When the people of this country say they want to keep the pound, they are not being ignorant or insular, they understand that what is significant to a country is having its own currency."

There were only two morning news conference and at my first stop, Bevin Hall, the Liberal Democrats' campaign director Chris Rennard smiled in wry amusement when I asked for his take on whether the Conservatives would get anywhere with their campaign to save the pound. He was surprised Tory strategists were continuing to ignore the lessons of their defeat in May 2000 in the Romsey by-election, when Sandra Gidley had won the seat for the Liberal Democrats with a majority of over 3,000. 'Hague fought that by-election on asylum seekers and the euro. He went down there with his Keep the Pound truck and yet the Tories couldn't hold a safe seat like that. If Hague is now saying the general election is a referendum on the euro, I am afraid it's going to become a referendum on Hague himself.'

For the sixth time in the campaign, saving the NHS was the theme of Labour's daily news conference. I did not get a chance myself to put a question about the euro because I had to stand at the live camera position for *News 24*; but, knowing of my interest, David Hill came up to me once the briefing was over to declare triumphantly that it had passed off without a single question being asked on either the pound or the euro, confirming his confident assertion of the previous evening that the Conservatives were going to end up talking to themselves. Because of my *News 24* commitments I missed the photo-opportunity taking place in the gardens at the rear of Millbank Tower. To dramatise Labour's warning about the Conservatives' plans for the health service, a large blue blanket was pulled off the back of a fifteen-foot-high wooden Trojan horse. Four party workers dropped out of its belly wearing T-shirts which proclaimed: 'Trojan horse health policy – Tories make you pay.' When I arrived Hill was still talking enthusiastically about the successful chore-ography of their stunt. 'You television lot should be thanking us. This was a very good photo-opportunity for a bank holiday weekend. We're really pleased with our Trojan horse.' I tried to cross-question Alan Milburn, the Secretary of State for Health, about what precisely the Trojan horse was meant to portray. Was Labour suggesting that Conservative policy would lead to the privatisation of hospital services? Wasn't that precisely what Tony Blair was proposing in Labour's manifesto, when he talked of encouraging private contractors to take on the delivery of public services? What was the difference? At this point I noticed I was beginning to attract attention. Standing slightly to one side, looking on intently, were Milburn's special adviser, Darren Murphy, and Ms Sally Morgan, Blair's political secretary. Milburn insisted it was obvious what the Trojan horse signified: the Conservatives would bring in a two-tier health service with 'fast-track treatment for those who could afford to pay and slower, second-rate services for those who could not'. What Thatcher could never get in through the front door, Hague was 'trying to get in through the back door with a Tory Trojan horse'.

Labour had used as their starting point a speech by the shadow health secretary, Dr Liam Fox, at a fringe meeting during the Conservatives' 1999 party conference. When describing his party's plan to introduce a guarantee for patients on hospital waiting times, he had said that what the Conservatives were starting was 'perhaps a Trojan horse' in the impact it would have on the NHS. The image was not a new one: Trojan horses get wheeled out regularly in general elections. In the 1992 campaign, when John Major tried to alert the country to the consequences of Neil Kinnock's flirtation with proportional representation, he claimed the Liberal Democrats might become the vehicle to get an unelectable Labour Party into power. Standing on his soapbox at Thornbury, near Bristol, he struck out at Liberal Democrats in the crowd and warned of the dangers to Britain of another Lib–Lab pact. 'There they are, the Trojan horse, the people who let in a Labour government in 1974.'

Sunday 27 May

Alastair Campbell was sitting behind the news conference set with his feet up on another chair, sipping tea from a Burnley Football Club mug, when journalists filed into the basement of Millbank Tower for an early showing of a Labour election broadcast to be transmitted that evening. Reports in the Sunday newspapers suggested it would be an emotional account by Tony Blair of his personal values and beliefs and would provide an insight into some of his most innermost thoughts. 'Blair: The Movie' was the *Sunday Mirror*'s headline over a picture sequence showing the Prime Minister reading to schoolchildren and enjoying a pint of beer in his Sedgefield constituency. We all settled back to watch what is traditionally one of the highlights of the campaign. Labour consider themselves masters of the genre. In 1987 Hugh Hudson directed 'Kinnock: The Movie', depicting Neil and Glenys walking along a cliff top to the strains of Brahms; 'John Major: The Journey' was the Conservatives' response in 1992, when John Schlesinger directed Major's trip back to the haunts of his political youth and the spot where he spoke from a soapbox in Brixton Market. Before the lights went down, Campbell gave us a thumbnail sketch of what we were to see this time. 'It's just under five minutes, by a young film-maker, Jack Price. He mainly does corporate stuff, like that one about a woman obsessed by Nike sportswear. That school scene mentioned in the Sundays is part of the volunteering the Prime Minister does; he reads to schoolchildren. Price spent a month with him, a lot in the constituency. We couldn't film in Downing Street because it's going out in the election.'

In one sequence Blair was filmed in a classroom talking about what motivated him as a politician. He described how, despite all the 'personality nonsense' in politics, he could visit a local primary school and find that things had changed because of 'a political decision' which did not happen before Labour were in office. 'I wouldn't stay in politics a day longer than I thought I had some useful purpose in it.' Asked why Blair was doing a highly personal broadcast when he had complained about the personalisation of politics, Campbell said Labour would be foolish not to make leadership an issue in the campaign and point out the 'weak leadership and opportunism' of Hague. 'I dispute the idea that the broadcast is personality-led . . . but people are conscious they are electing a leader and we will do more on that as we get into the last week.' Once prompted, Campbell was only too happy to compare and contrast. Hague was unable to give direction or heal the divisions in his party, and could not escape the shadow of Thatcher. Labour's focus groups were showing that her speech in Plymouth saying 'never' to the euro had been a complete disaster for Hague. 'Whatever people felt about Thatcher, good or bad, they cannot see any relevance she has to this campaign. Wheeling her out to support him reminds some of them they once had a strong leader and others that they were glad she went. It was a real no-brainer for Hague, a real low grader for the Tories.' By now the Prime Minister's official spokesman was in his stride. When asked to comment on the lead story in the *Sunday Times* suggesting Blair had overruled Gordon Brown in predicting he could win a referendum on the euro, he just let rip. 'What that story? The usual fictional voyage of discovery every Sunday . . . all it names is a source, a friend, an insider, blah, blah, blah . . . total one hundred per cent garbage.'

The Blair broadcast was to be transmitted at various times between 6 p.m. and 8.30 p.m., on six separate channels, and viewers would be invited to ring in afterwards and put questions direct to the Prime Minister and his cabinet colleagues. A call centre was being established in Millbank Tower for the evening, and through a conference call operated by a switchboard Blair would be able to speak to 500 callers at a time during six separate twenty-minute sessions. Overflow calls would go to ministers and MPs, and the system would be able to take 100,000 calls before it went to the engaged tone.

As we all packed up to leave the briefing and tried to get our heads round the idea of Blair, John Prescott, Robin Cook et al. doing the evening shift in a call centre, Campbell stopped us to say we would be getting a story that evening for use on Monday about plans which the Chancellor was announcing to direct more lottery money towards deprived areas. 'Don't leave it too late before telling us,' said David Wooding of the *Sun*. 'We're desperate for a page two lead.' I walked out of Millbank Tower marvelling at Labour's vast supremacy over the Conservatives. Campbell stood there saying Labour would be pumping out a statement on the lottery just as if he had been referring to a government announcement. The same thing tended to happen night after night, with fresh initiatives following one after another from various ministers. Blair's Cabinet could not start pulling the levers of power again until after the election; but they gave every impression by the way they were presenting themselves through the news media that they had not let go for an instant. I thought the co-ordination and expense which must have been involved in setting up a call centre of the kind Campbell described made Hague's Keep the Pound truck and his digital clock look like something out of *Dad's Army* by comparison. Walking back to Westminster along Millbank with John Hibbs, political editor of the *Scotsman*, I suggested witnessing the overpowering dominance of Labour's campaign felt like watching Manchester United take on

Wycombe Wanderers. Hibbs said Campbell had apparently cracked the same joke and had the scoreline settled already: Manchester United 33, Darlington 1.

We had found it rather unsettling spending so long at Millbank Tower, because the news bulletins had been dominated all morning by the aftermath of a night of rioting at Oldham in Greater Manchester. Asian youths armed with bricks and petrol bombs had fought pitched battles with police after trouble flared in the Glodwick area following reports that a gang of white men had attacked Asian properties. Politicians had been lining up to give their response. Simon Hughes, the Liberal Democrats' home affairs spokesman took the hardest line on GMTV's Sunday Programme, accusing the Conservatives of helping to fuel racial tensions. 'Some of us are critical of the language of William Hague and his colleagues. It doesn't help. It may not have a direct effect but, in some cases, it may encourage people to think they can get away with intolerant language, attitudes and sometimes intolerant behaviour.' Ann Widdecombe accused the Liberal Democrats of trying to make 'political capital' out of the riots. Hague was equally swift in denying he was to blame. 'It's an accusation made by parties trying to play the race card themselves. Asylum is an entirely different issue.' The Home Secretary, Jack Straw, sided with the Conservatives. He said it was 'stretching credibility' to suggest that any language used by Hague or Miss Widdecombe could be responsible for 'people throwing petrol bombs or attacking the police'.

Guests on the Sunday morning programmes were asked to give their assessment of the campaign so far. Neil Kinnock, interviewed on *Breakfast with Frost*, agreed that Blair was in an unusual position, going into an election with a such a substantial lead in the opinion polls. 'I think Labour's tactic must be not to cause excitement, so that things don't go wrong.' He complimented the Liberal Democrats on their campaign. Charles Kennedy was going well from a low start by being immensely energetic and putting himself around. 'His great strength is spontaneity and energy so it's sensible for him to exploit that.' Later in the programme, Kennedy told Sir David Frost of his concern that Blair might get back with a majority which would be too big for the health of Parliament and the country. 'If it looks inevitable Labour will win, the country will need an intelligent opposition with integrity . . . We know the Conservatives are likely to go into meltdown and will turn in on themselves. They will be off the field of combat and that's where Liberal Democrats come into play.'

My last task of the day was to monitor the pool pictures being fed from the Millbank Tower call centre. Blair told one caller: 'Thank you Catrina, we are allocating resources to improving children's education.' Prescott was shown responding to a caller who asked him about his famous punch. 'Don't talk to me about it, Bev. I'm overloaded with security now. I am walking around like I am with a platoon from *Good Morning Vietnam.*'

Monday 28 May

A well-trailed speech by the French Prime Minister Lionel Jospin, proposing an 'economic government' for countries within the euro-zone, provided yet another opportunity for the Conservatives to put saving the pound at the forefront of their campaign. Three shadow ministers were up bright and early on bank holiday morning to launch a new offensive which they hoped would add to the difficulties they expected Labour to encounter when trying fend off Jospin's ideas for closer co-operation among countries signed up to the euro and for moves towards the harmonisation of business taxes. The Tories' latest challenge to Labour was based on a report by the accountants Chantrey Vellacott which put the cost to Britain of converting to the euro at £36 billion. Iain Duncan

Smith, the shadow defence secretary, told listeners on *Today* that the bill the British people would have to pay would work out at around £2,000 per person. At their morning news conference Michael Portillo and Francis Maude called on Labour to reveal the Treasury's estimate for the amount the nation would have to spend on the changeover, because it looked like being twenty times as much as the cost of decimalisation. However, the omens for the Conservative assault looked inauspicious when, within an hour of Duncan Smith's interview on *Today*, Portillo slashed his calculation about the likely impact on the person in the street by 25 per cent and put the cost at £1,500 per household. And while Maude was having to admit on *Sky News* that £36 billion 'might not be the right figure' after all, William Hague was using this estimate for the cost of joining the euro to fire up the crowd at Keep the Pound rallies in Blackpool and Llandudno. 'That's £55 million for every constituency in the country, that's £1,500 for every family in the land, that's like paying for the Millennium Dome thirty-six times over. [Shouts of "Disgraceful."] Yes, it's like paying for a new Millennium Dome every month for the next three years.'

Labour ridiculed Hague's figures and Chantrey Vellacott's estimate began sinking rapidly down news bulletin running orders after the company's spokesman, Maurice Fitzpatrick, confirmed that the figure had been calculated the previous year for use by a leading anti-euro pressure group, Business for Sterling. 'We were commissioned to write this report for them fifteen months ago and it does seem strange it should have resurfaced now when it was widely commented on at the time.' I felt the attempt to hoodwink the news media by recycling a rather dated figure supplied by a pressure group and presenting this to journalists as a new announcement illustrated the haphazard performance of the media team at Central Office. If the Conservatives intended to make the cost of euro conversion a high point of their campaign, why hadn't they commissioned their own research? An up-to-date breakdown would have been much more authoritative, would have attracted far greater attention and might well have caused Labour real difficulty. Political journalists do not take kindly to finding they have been misled about the status of a document or the accuracy and authenticity of statistical information, and the Tories had already come unstuck in this way once, when the 'leaked' European Commission discussion paper on tax harmonisation was found to be neither new nor confidential and in fact already in wide circulation.

I had been trying for several days to put my finger on precisely what I thought was wrong with the media operation being run by Amanda Platell. Since the start of the campaign I had been unable to find another broadcaster or newspaper correspondent who had been briefed by her or who had even succeeded in obtaining any useful information from her about what the party planned to do. From what I could determine, her deputy Nick Wood was running the news operation in the war room and agreeing the line to take whenever the party's response was needed urgently. Broadcasters dealt with the assistant head of media, Andrew Scadding, but our briefings, especially on overnight stories, took place late in the evening, some hours after the same stories had been supplied to newspapers like the *Daily Telegraph* and the *Daily Mail* which had by far the best links with Central Office and were invariably fully abreast of what the party was planning to say. I had been expecting the Conservatives to be far more adventurous and assertive in their attempts to exploit the news media. I assumed they had spent the long run-up to the election preparing a hard-hitting critique of Blair's first four years in power and intended to use their news conferences to release new and challenging information about Labour's performance in the delivery of public services like health and education. The party's inability to provide journalists with a fresh, up-to-date estimate for something as contentious as the cost of Britain converting to the euro merely under-lined the apparent lack of planning in the war room and reinforced my reservations about Ms Platell's ability to direct the Conservatives' media operation.

I reflected on the inadequacies of the Conservatives' operation as I set off again for Millbank Tower for yet another briefing by Alastair Campbell. While I found the arrogance of Labour's media team off-putting, and although I never ceased to be amazed at their ability to manipulate friendly newspapers, I had no complaint about their efficiency at a technical level when supplying information. Campbell, David Hill and before them Peter Mandelson had all instilled into their staff the importance of careful preparation before news conferences. They understood that if journalists felt they had been duped, or if a story fell apart because basic facts or figures were incorrect or dubious, then all their earlier effort would be wasted. When Mandelson gave me his assessment of Labour's performance in the 1992 campaign after his election as MP for Hartlepool, he singled out the fiasco over the 'Jennifer's ear' election broadcast as an example of how the party had suffered through inadequate staff work.

Today Campbell had a surprise in store for us in the Millbank Tower briefing room: he was about to reveal the contents of Labour's private opinion polling. Usually party spokesmen tend to be offhand, even withering – at least in public – about the reliability of any opinion poll or survey, and none of us could remember an occasion when Labour had freely volunteered so much information from these sources. As was so often the case with Campbell, we began to wonder what his motive might be. He was obviously trying to unsettle the Conservatives, but I could not work out precisely what mischief was afoot. Campbell said that in addition to the regular focus groups held by Philip Gould, the party had commissioned four private opinion polls since the start of the campaign and they showed that Labour's 'relentless' focus on the economy and public services was the right strategy and that the Conservatives' 'single issue obsession' on Europe was not shifting public opinion. In their poll,

Labour began on a 44 per cent share which had risen to 46 per cent, while the Conservatives had remained where they started on 26 per cent. Campbell then gave a detailed breakdown. In the same poll in 1990 Labour and the Conservatives were level-pegging on 31 per cent on being trusted with the economy, but on this point the latest survey put Labour on 43 per cent and the Conservatives on 19 per cent: Labour's biggest lead on economic competence since the poll started. When it came to which party was to be trusted most in standing up for Britain, for example over Europe, Labour started the campaign on 43 per cent but had risen to 45 per cent, and the Conservatives' share had fallen from 35 to 33 per cent.

Journalists get used to being bombarded with opinion polls, and we have grown to be wary of them over the years. In trying to impress us with figures from Labour's internal polling, Campbell was preparing the ground for the message he wanted us to convey: 'It's beyond us at Millbank to know why the Conservatives ever thought Europe would work for them. It doesn't appear to be harming us and our poll shows it's now working against Hague, which all points back to a lack of leadership and that's what we'll be developing in a big way up to June the seventh.' Campbell seemed genuinely puzzled by the Conservatives' strategy. 'Obviously there are people who'll vote Conservative however bad their policies but our sense is that unless they start addressing the bigger picture, they'll end up talking to themselves on Europe, which takes you back to what happened to Labour in the 1983 election.' I found myself agreeing with Campbell's assessment. Throughout the 1970s and 1980s delegates at Labour and trade union conferences were obsessed by a long-running argument over nuclear disarmament. As I struggled to make sense of it, I remember slipping into the jargon of talking about splits between unilateralists and multilateralists, which I realise in hindsight was perhaps as annoying to many listeners as the constant reference in the 1990s to the split in the Conservatives between Euro-sceptics and Europhiles.

When we discussed what Campbell might be up to in releasing Labour's internal polling figures, I suggested he was probably hoping to take advantage of the low morale in Conservative Central Office by generating tension within Hague's high command about their campaign strategy and also perhaps provoke a backlash from the pro-Europeans. Some reporters thought Blair's spokesman was being rather more Machiavellian and was in fact pursuing a strategy designed to encourage Hague to stick doggedly to his Keep the Pound crusade. This theory was based on the likely reaction of Hague's advisers who, when hearing what Campbell had been up to, were more than likely to presume he was acting defensively and that in fact Labour's polling was revealing the opposite of what Blair's press secretary had said and that the save-the-pound campaign was beginning to work. Late that evening, after interviewing the Conservatives' chief election strategist Andrew Lansley, I was able to put this thesis to the test. He immediately smelt a rat: 'Campbell's done this because they're not hitting the news agenda. Our themes of saving the pound, asylum and tax have all led the bulletins. No political party briefs journalists on internal opinion polls. If they go against you, you are in trouble and if you live by the polls, you die by the polls. Why did Blair speak about Europe last Friday? Didn't they know we'd have Keep the Pound day on the Saturday? I can't believe they didn't know. We had 500 constituencies preparing for it.' Lansley was adamant there would be no change in the Conservatives' strategy on the euro. 'Elections are about differences and we've been dominating the news more than Labour. So far it's the opposition parties which have been setting around 70 per cent of the agenda and two-thirds of that has come from the Conservatives.'

Campbell's motives may sometimes have been obscure, but the greatest enigma of the campaign was William Hague's wife Ffion. When she was asked on Thursday 8 May, the day Blair called the election, if she was looking forward to it, Hague told a BBC correspondent, Laura

Trevelyan, that his wife was 'enjoying it already' – and that he would 'answer the questions'. Since that decisive rebuff Hague had continued to do all he could to protect Ffion whenever she found herself in a media scrum being bombarded by reporters' questions. None the less her passive role had become a talking point. Party press officers insisted that Hague's motives were completely genuine and that he was determined to ensure his wife did not get dragged into the campaign. Once her husband became leader of the Labour Party, Cherie Blair had refused to speak to reporters or comment on day-to-day political issues, and the wives of other politicians were said to admire her strength of purpose in sticking to the boundaries she had laid down. However, unlike Cherie, Ffion was constantly at Hague's side when he was out campaigning and this did provoke considerable press comment. Julia Langdon, writing in the *Mail on Sunday*, said the macho campaign which Hague was pursuing made Ffion look particularly uncomfortable and she had ended up playing the 'role of a mindless walk-on puppet in some sort of boys' own adventure'. In his account in the *Guardian* of a day's campaigning with the Hagues, Ewen MacAskill said 'Ffion feigns interest but totally gives herself away by occasionally smiling and clapping in the wrong places.'

Hague, whose humorous and good-natured responses to questioning won him many plaudits in the media, told reporters at Newark on Wednesday 23 May that he had not married Ffion to turn her into a political asset and she was not running for office. 'I think it is wrong for the spouses of politicians to be drawn into being interviewed.' After so many rebuffs there was consternation at the studios of BBC Westminster shortly before the *Six O'Clock News* when the cry went up that Ffion had done an interview but spoken in Welsh. Pictures being fed from Llandudno, where it had been a brilliantly sunny day, showed her being asked a question in Welsh and giving an animated reply. As John Pienaar put it in his report for the news bulletin, Ffion was the 'silent partner no longer' – but a rapid translation revealed she had been well trained by her husband and had avoided any political pitfalls: 'Yes, it's wonderful to be in Wales and to be back in Llandudno and I really am enjoying the weather.'

6 In the Bag,
or a Bubble About to Burst?

'Labour: it's in the bag' was the *Daily Mail*'s headline over its lead story on Alastair Campbell's 'crowing about Labour's thundering poll lead'. On the strength of some private opinion polls, the 'great spin master' was predicting Tony Blair was heading for an even bigger majority than in 1997. David Hughes, the paper's political editor, said he had never witnessed a similar briefing: 'It is unprecedented for a party to anticipate victory in this way, and risked accusations of massive arrogance and complacency in the Labour camp.' The *Daily Mail* claimed Campbell's intervention was a cynical move to distract attention from a speech by the French Prime Minister, Lionel Jospin, which set out his vision of the European Union as 'a socialist economic superpower'. The line taken by Hughes reflected the Conservative Central Office spin: that Labour were so worried about the issue of Europe they were desperate to say something positive. When I had put it to Andrew Scadding the previous evening that Labour's private opinion polling seemed to be in line with most published polls, he insisted I was failing to see the significance of Campbell's briefing. Labour needed a diversionary tactic to distract attention from Jospin's speech and the difficulties which ministers were facing in trying to counter the Conservatives' £36 billion estimate for the cost of Britain converting to the euro. My attempt to test the depth of the media team's support for the emphasis which William Hague was giving to Europe got nowhere because Scadding, like the party's election strategist, Andrew Lansley, just blocked my questions. He seemed wholly convinced that the scare tactics which the Conservatives were using to promote their save-the-pound campaign were succeeding in putting the government on the defensive. 'Labour never give an estimate for how much the changeover to the euro will cost because they're frightened to. They know if they ever get engaged in that argument they don't have the answers.'

After spending so much of my bank holiday weekend grappling with the intensity of the argument over the euro, and having to listen to the fervour with which the subject was addressed by the staff of Central Office, the unveiling of Labour's latest election poster held out the prospect of some light relief. The word was that Labour had come up with an image which would somehow encapsulate their attack on William Hague. I have to admit that, on first sight, it did take me a second or two to make the connection and realise that it was Margaret Thatcher's hairstyle which had been superimposed on Hague's face. The strength of the poster was its simplicity, yet it repaid a few moments study, and in the process it did hold my attention as I took in the slogan: 'Get out and vote. Or they get in.'

'No it's not Lady Thatcher, look closer,' said Mark Mardell in his opening script line for the *Six O'Clock News* over pictures of the poster, which was designed by Trevor Beattie, chairman of TBWA, Labour's advertising agency for the election campaign. Beattie told the *Independent* that in January 2001, when he first presented the idea of using a photograph of Hague's face with Thatcher's hair, he told Tony Blair he thought his agency had developed the icon for the whole of the election. 'The greatest moment of my career was presenting it to a Labour Prime Minister . . . Tony said, "That will run." That was a magic moment.' Party strategists always say the first test of a successful election poster is getting it reprinted in the newspapers and talked about on television, and Beattie's lampooning of Hague by giving him a Thatcher hairdo was so arresting that it provoked considerable discussion on the evening news programmes. The general conclusion was that it did get across the idea that Hague was incapable of forming his own policies and simply stood for reheated Thatcherism. The timing of the lady herself was as impeccable as ever, and most of the television news reports cut from shots of the poster to pictures of the former Prime Minister on a visit to Northampton, where she made her second appearance of the campaign. 'All is never lost. We are going to win,' was her firm prediction when she was asked in the market square about the Conservatives' failure to achieve a breakthrough in the opinion polls. Hague was not heading for defeat because 'he's got guts,' and she remained as resolute as the face beneath her hairdo in continuing to campaign against the euro: 'Let's keep the pound. That's right. Keep the pound and vote Tory.'

Depicting Hague trapped in a Thatcherite past gave a harsh edge to Labour's campaign, and it fell to her successor, John Major, to return the fire on Hague's behalf and trade insults in the opposite direction. In a speech at a party rally in Brighton, Major renewed his by now familiar attack on Blair for twisting the truth when presenting the government's achievements and for pushing spin 'far beyond gloss and towards bare-faced deception'. John Prescott, whose left jab had connected with the chin of the egg-throwing Craig Evans, was one of the principal targets in the sights of the former Prime Minister. 'Labour spun that famous punch brilliantly but am I alone in believing that Prescott's response was more that of a street-corner delinquent than a Deputy Prime Minister? "He acted by instinct," said Labour. Yes he did. But it was the sort of instinct that lands young football fans in trouble . . . And what did our Prime Minister say? "John is John," he said. "John is John." A pathetic line that will, no doubt, be favoured by the best friend of every punch-first, think-later hooligan around the country. And this of course from the Prime Minister who promised: "Trust me, I'll be tough on crime and tough on the causes of crime." But then, of course, Tony is Tony.'

Major's verbal assault on Blair and Prescott was of little comfort to Hague as he underwent an assault of his own from Jeremy Paxman during an interview for *Newsnight* which was prerecorded in a hotel on the Brighton seafront. Paxman ran through the succession of policy themes and slogans which Hague had adopted and then dropped during his leadership: fresh start, the British way, compassionate Conservatism, kitchen table Conservatism, the right way, the common sense revolution. Hague denied he had a 'flip-flop' approach to politics and insisted these ideas had all been brought together in the Conservatives' manifesto Time For Common Sense. 'Obviously it's a big challenge to take over the leadership after a huge election defeat . . . I accept that we went into this campaign as the underdog . . . but the reception for our candidates is extremely good and we are gaining support for the key issues of crime, tax, asylum and Europe . . . Most people expect Labour to win but that is not going to happen. Millions of people haven't even decided whether to vote.' When Paxman challenged Hague about his refusal to let his wife Ffion answer reporters' questions, the embattled party leader finally silenced his interrogator: 'Every man is entitled to be protective of his wife. My wife is a professional head hunter. I don't go head hunting for the afternoon. She is not a politician. It is a twenty-first-century thing to have different careers but when you are going through something very important as husband and wife, it's very important they show support for each other.'

Wednesday 30 May

William Hague's boundless energy and enthusiasm impressed friend and foe alike. Day after day he took the punishment and bounced back, ready to face another round of damning headlines and hostile questions. What we as reporters found so refreshing was that, unlike most politicians, he accepted that we had a role to play in an election campaign and he did not seek to take his frustrations out on the news media. However much he might have disliked what we were saying, he did not let it show publicly and he patently had no wish to blame us for his own misfortune. Knowing of his innate resilience and cheerfulness, I was stopped in my tracks when I saw a report on *Sky News* suggesting that Hague, who was in Scotland, was not showing much 'drive or energy'. Paul Bromley, who filed his report from Stirling, said the Tory leader had not been campaigning in his usual 'energetic way' and seemed to have fallen back on 'a safety first campaign'. A little later my brother, George Jones, political editor of the *Daily Telegraph*, confirmed that reporters on Hague's battle bus had been telephoning through to say that he was looking 'a bit down' as it had not been a good day for the Conservatives. Jones told *News 24* that Hague's great attribute was his 'inner strength', but that there had been setbacks that day and the Tory leadership was alarmed by the way their support seemed to be flattening out and they were being squeezed by the Liberal Democrats.

The morning newspapers must have been too much to bear. Trevor Beattie's prediction that his poster would probably become the icon of the campaign looked like being fulfilled. Hague's face, superimposed with Thatcher's hair, pearl earrings and a hint of pink lipstick, stared out from the front pages of *The Times*, *Daily Telegraph* and *Independent*. Far more worrying than the poster was the front-page headline in the *Guardian*, 'Tories face poll meltdown', over a report on the latest opinion poll by ICM which showed that Labour's advantage had 'soared to a spectacular nineteen-point lead'. ICM, which was Central Office's own private pollster and normally the kindest to the Conservatives, put them four points down on 28 per cent, their lowest share for two years, while Labour were two points up on 47 per cent. The extra six-point gap which had opened up in the space of seven days showed that Hague's week-long euro war had shunted the Conservatives into 'a campaign cul-de-sac'. The *Independent*'s front-page picture showed Alastair Campbell standing beside the reproduction of Hague's head and laughing and gesticulating at the crowd of photographers and reporters who turned up to see the actor Richard Wilson and the Secretary of State for Health, Alan Milburn, unveil the poster. Campbell was quoted as saying humorous posters were effective, especially among young people, and voters would get the message that the Tory leader had been bullied by his right wing and forced to retreat from his early liberal instincts, and had ended up trapped in Thatcher's shadow.

However, Hague would probably have been more concerned to read an adjoining story about the repercussions of Campbell's handiwork in giving reporters a breakdown on the way Labour's private polling was showing that the Keep the Pound campaign was damaging rather than helping the Conservatives. I had discovered subsequently that the briefing I attended on Monday 28 May was one of three at which Campbell supplied information about Millbank's internal opinion surveys: correspondents on Sunday newspapers were given the figures the previous Saturday and they had been mentioned again at a briefing the following Tuesday. If, as I suspected all along, the aim of Blair's official spokesman was to provoke a backlash among pro-European Conservatives, the *Independent*'s report provided the first confirmation that his ploy was proving highly effective. Two former Conservative ministers, Ian Taylor and Stephen Dorrell, were both quoted as saying it was folly to fight the election on a single issue. Taylor appealed to Hague to stop focusing on the concerns of the Tory euro-fanatics and give higher priority to health and education. Dorrell had found deep disenchantment with Labour on the doorstep and he thought the gap between expectation and delivery represented the biggest opportunity for the Conservatives. Almost as worrying as the reports in the *Guardian* and *Independent* was the front-page headline on *The Times*, 'Hague retreats on euro deadline', over an interview for the paper in which he admitted that the general election would not be the 'last chance to save the currency'. Although Hague had not said anything significantly different

from his previous explanations about it being harder to win a referendum if Labour were re-elected, he had not repeated his line about
there being only a few days left to save the pound, and *The Times* considered the change of emphasis reflected the internal criticism which he was
facing.

News bulletins led all day with reports of the attacks being made on
Hague from within his own party. On flying into Stirling by helicopter,
he tried manfully to dig his way out by denying there was any contradic-
tion in what he had said. 'No one will get a fair referendum from the
Labour Party. They've rigged the rules for funding, they would choose
the timing, so it is our case that this is the last fair vote about the pound.'
Here reporters had the first chance to ask for his reaction to Labour's
poster. How did he think he looked wearing a wig? His reply was not as
witty as some of his previous ripostes about having been satirised by his
opponents: 'Well, it would be nice to have all that hair; I wasn't sure
about the earrings. It's just trivia. We will continue to campaign on the
real issues in this election.'

Hague's discomfort over the outspokenness of Taylor and Dorrell, and
the claim by *The Times* that he had been forced to give ground, put a
spring in the step of Labour's chief spokesman, David Hill, as he went
round the House of Commons press gallery visiting the offices of the
various political correspondents. Hill seemed to be well abreast of the
Independent's efforts to canvass pro-European Conservatives for possible
dissent and said Labour was not expecting any other senior Tories to join
the two former ministers in denouncing Hague. 'We've been told the rest
of them will remain pretty disciplined and that it is Hague, Andrew
Lansley and Tim Collins who'll have to carry the can for the euro
campaign . . . We still can't understand why the Conservatives set up their
flag off the main battlefield and then chose to fight a campaign not
related to the rest of the election.' Did Hill accept the point Lansley had
made to me that the Conservatives' campaign was all about highlighting

differences and that on many days it had succeeded in dominating the news agenda? 'If the Conservatives are going to have any hope of winning they've got to recapture some of the ground which Blair has taken, but they've set up their camp well away from the public service battleground. The Tories have made the mistake of being separate and different; they aren't trying to show they're better than Labour on health, education and economic competence. We think the country understands what Blair is saying, that it's all about "work in progress" and "the work goes on" and we're ready for the final burst. It'll be schools and hospitals first.'

I was interested to hear Hill's assessment of the way the campaign had gone. Most of my time had been spent on late shifts, taking me through the afternoon and evening on to midnight and beyond. I told him I had been struck by a dearth of late-breaking stories. In previous elections much of the action had taken place late in the evening, after speeches or interviews, or when the broadcasters got wind of exclusive stories or disclosures in next day's newspapers. My experience of this election was that there were far fewer surprises and most of my evenings had been spent preparing rather predictable overnight reports on the campaign themes to be developed next day. Hill agreed that he could not remember an election when there had been less pressure late at night. 'We've had the same level of resources at Millbank and we've used up just about the same amount of energy but we've not been stretched. There hasn't been a run of surprise stories. The newspapers just haven't been dropping their usual bombshells.'

Thursday 31 May

After being outgunned for most of the campaign by the technical superiority of Labour's firepower, the Conservatives demonstrated they had not been outclassed completely and claimed they were a step ahead of their opponents by developing their website, www.conservatives.com.

Political correspondents were invited to Central Office to try out 'My Manifesto', a service which allowed internet users to get an individual printout of how they and their locality might benefit from the proposals contained in the party's manifesto, Time For Common Sense. Michael Ancram said it was an attempt to take election campaigning on the web to a whole new level of interactivity. 'We've already been giving information out on a day-to-day basis but now, with a week to go to polling day, we are trying to fit the manifesto directly to people who log on. With a few clicks of the a mouse they can get details of policy areas likely to be of greatest interest to them.' Gaby Hinsliff, a political correspondent for the *Observer*, was guinea-pig for the lobby and became the first journalist to press the button saying 'create my manifesto'.

Perhaps the Conservatives might have had a better day if they had redirected more of Central Office's resources to ensuring they kept in constant communication with William Hague, who was touring the west country. Journalists in London were supplied with a copy of a speech which it was said he would deliver when visiting a doctor's surgery in Weston-super-Mare. It set out the steps which Hague would take to tackle the problems at the 'heart of the crisis' in the National Health Service: the Conservatives would match Labour's plans for health spending; trust doctors and nurses, not politicians, to take medical decisions; scrap Labour's 'failed waiting list initiative' and replace it with a patients' guarantee on waiting times; and give general practitioners and their patients the right to choose which hospital to be treated in. As Hague had spent so little time campaigning on the NHS, correspondents and producers at BBC Westminster were lining up to see the television feed of what appeared to be his response to Labour's morning news conference, where Tony Blair had launched the party's campaign slogan for the final seven days: 'Schools and hospital first.'

During his visit to the surgery, the first he had been photographed in since the start of the campaign, Hague sympathised with the staff over the increase in paperwork, spoke briefly to reporters – and then left Weston-super-Mare without delivering the speech. In her report for the *Six O'Clock News*, Laura Trevelyan said that after travelling 'more than 5,000 miles before being pictured with nurses, this was only a fleeting visit and Hague was gone in twenty minutes.' Ms Trevelyan told me that party workers on the leader's coach insisted Hague never intended making a speech in the first place; it wasn't clear to her whether he failed to get the speech, whether there was insufficient time to deliver it or whether he simply decided not to make it. Andrew Scadding, who had alerted journalists to the advance text, suggested that instead of regarding it as a speech we should treat it as a statement of his intentions for the NHS.

If Hague had chosen on his visit to Weston-super-Mare to challenge Labour over which party had the best policies to deliver improvements in the NHS, he had an ideal opportunity. At his news conference Blair acknowledged there was 'a deep hunger' in the country for the renewal of the health service and education system, and that election was about more than which party won. 'It's about the country saying to its political leaders, "We are giving you an instruction, not just a mandate, an instruction. We want you to put that investment into schools and hospitals and put them first. That's what we're asking for."' Charles Kennedy, speaking at a rally in Southport, said most people in the country would have been taken aback on hearing Blair saying he needed not a mandate but an instruction to spend more on schools and hospitals. 'Prime Minister, where have you been for the last four years? Has it taken the last four weeks of the election to put you back in touch with the people's priorities?'

Later, in an interview with Andrew Marr, Hague caused another flurry of excitement when he acknowledged the possibility that he could be facing a spectacular defeat. Party leaders rarely if ever give sustenance to their opponents so close to polling day and are careful to avoid falling into the trap of repeating words put to them in questions. When asked by Marr if he thought another Labour landslide would be dangerous, Hague had no hesitation in replying: 'I think it could be dangerous. Obviously we're working on making sure there's no landslide . . . And so yes, it would be extremely dangerous for this country for a repetition of that majority. We are working on making sure there isn't a Labour majority at all.'

Friday 1 June

Within twenty-four hours of failing to exploit his visit to a doctor's surgery in Weston-super-Mare, William Hague had an opportunity to show his support for the medical profession and join it in urging the government to heed the threat of a mass resignation by general practitioners. A ballot conducted by the British Medical Association produced a big majority in favour of leaving the National Health Service within ten months unless new contracts were agreed. Two-thirds of the 36,000 family doctors responded and 86 per cent of those who voted favoured mass resignation. Alan Milburn, the Secretary of State for Health, offered a new timetable for negotiations on the doctors' contract and Tony Blair assured them the government was aware of their frustration. 'We know there is much more to do but the answer must surely be to keep that investment going in, to get the extra nurses and doctors that we need.'

The ballot result was published mid-morning, and although Hague's initial response was recorded in time for the *One O'Clock News*, journalists were told he intended to make a fuller statement that afternoon outside Central Office before departing to Bradford where he was to address an evening rally. Emerging to face the cameras with his wife Ffion, chief of staff Seb Coe and health spokesman Dr Liam Fox, he immediately launched into a lengthy attack on Labour for allowing too many public servants to vote with their feet because morale had 'never been so low'. If four out of five of the country's family doctors were prepared to consider leaving a service to which they had devoted their working lives because they could not get on with their work, it represented a 'very serious indictment' of government policy. 'We don't want the doctors to take action and everything must be done to prevent a collapse of the general practitioner service by carrying out sensible policies . . . We are not committed to Labour's fantasy numbers for doctor recruitment . . . The general practitioners I met yesterday talked about likely solutions such as abolishing the waiting list initiative and restoring freedom on consultant referrals, the things which are driving them out of the service . . . We believe the time has come to give the NHS back to the professionals.' When reporters shouted out that the health service needed more money, he insisted raising morale was the priority. 'We have the same spending plans as Labour. It's how we spend the money that matters.' Hague put forward a forceful case and seemed sure the Conservatives could find ways to stem the loss of NHS professionals.

As I stood listening to his statement and hearing the way he linked the low morale of family doctors to Labour's first term in office, I could not understand why it had taken him until mid-afternoon to realise the full potential of a story which was going to lead the news bulletins all day. If it had been Alastair Campbell and not Amanda Platell directing the media operation at Central Office, the Conservatives would have known in advance that publication of the BMA's ballot result was imminent and would have arranged photo-opportunities to ensure Hague and Fox were interviewed in settings which bore some relation to the medical profession. If Ms Platell's media team had been trying to take greater advantage of a breaking news story which had the potential to embarrass the government, then there was all the more reason for having ensured that Hague delivered his NHS speech in Weston-super-Mare which, with the kind of forward planning practised at Millbank Tower, could have looked ahead to the outcome of the family doctors' ballot and kept Blair and Milburn on the defensive for twenty-four hours or more. Yet at the Conservatives' morning news conference, only an hour or so before the ballot result was announced, Hague still appeared to have no inkling of the story which was about to emerge. In reply to Nick Robinson of *News 24*, who asked why the Conservatives had failed to hold a single news conference on health, he insisted he was using his speeches to address the crisis in the hospitals. Although he referred to the remarks the previous day by Dr Peter Hawker, leader of the BMA's consultants' group, who said the NHS was being forced to provide a standard of care which he would not wish on his own family, Hague did not relate his answer to the impending news about family doctors.

As I was leaving Smith Square I was joined by Simon Walters, political editor of the *Mail on Sunday*, who emerged from Central Office after interviewing Hague. He did not think he had much of a story. 'The trouble with Hague is he just bounces back. He doesn't crack, however bad it looks. If it was Neil Kinnock in there, he would have let fly by now and said something dramatic like "I don't give a sod about politics," and the air in there would have been blue. I'm having to push up my estimate for a Labour majority. I thought it would be eighty, now I'm revising upwards to over a hundred.'

Hague succeeded with some skill in extricating himself from any potential damage over the BBC interview in which he had admitted a second Labour landslide was a possibility and would be 'extremely dangerous' for the country. At his morning news conference, Blair portrayed Hague's remarks as part of a calculated strategy by the Conservatives to talk up the chances of a landslide and encourage Labour supporters to think there was no need to vote. 'We have the extraordinary spectacle of a Conservative Party and a Conservative leader either urging people not to vote or to vote Conservative to reduce the so-called Labour majority in an election that hasn't even happened. That is precisely what they want to do, to sneak in by the back door.' Hague retaliated by turning his warning into an attack on the way Labour's first landslide had allowed Blair to weaken the House of Commons by undermining the select committees and having only one session a week of Prime Minister's questions. 'They've been a government of spin, of arrogance, of sidelining and denigrating Parliament. Those habits will become ingrained in the Labour Party if they win again by any majority.'

Hague was following a line which Lady Thatcher had taken in a signed article in the *Daily Telegraph* in which she warned that if Blair were returned with a large majority Britain could get an 'overweening government sustained by cronies, ciphers and a personality cult'. She had already detected such tendencies in Blair and feared they would grow unchecked. 'At a time when our country's future as an independent nation lies in the balance, that is a risk too far. A quarter of a century ago, the great Lord Hailsham – a "force of conservatism" if ever there was one – warned of what he termed an "elective dictatorship". It is not too late to prevent that.' Lady Thatcher's third appearance of the campaign was a visit to Romsey, the constituency which the Conservatives had lost to the Liberal Democrats in a by-election in May 2000 and where a tactical vote against the Tories again seemed likely. She spoke to pensioners and shoppers, reminding them that she had been able to handle a big majority, but she was realistic about the challenge facing Hague. 'I know full well that it is very difficult to get down from 177 on one side to about seventy on the other, in one go. If we can that will be absolutely terrific.'

My last task of the day was to watch the television feed of the Prime Minister answering questions on the Merseyside set of the Channel Four soap *Brookside*. Dean Sullivan, who plays Jimmy Corkhill, escorted Blair into Bev's Bar which was packed with some of the actors and actresses, their friends and families and other party members. Blair took off his jacket – revealing a personal microphone pinned to his shirt – and sat on a bar stool with several children sitting close by, reinforcing the family atmosphere. Sullivan was an effective chairman, moving briskly through the questions and interrupting on occasion with his own supplementaries. One testing moment for Blair was his encounter with 23-year-old Suzanne Collins, who plays Nikki Shadwick, a struggling student in Brookside. She took him to task him over tuition fees and said many of her friends had been deterred from going to university by the prospect of having to pay back huge student loans; but Blair told her that it was only right that students who went on to gain a good job should make a contribution.

Labour's ability to call on such a large cast of supporters from the television and entertainment industries was the envy of their opponents. Shortly before the 1997 election, during a visit to the studios of Granada, I noticed the ease with which Blair talked to some of the leading characters in *Coronation Street* and I had to admire Labour's chutzpah in not simply being able to arrange for him to be seen mixing it with stars from popular soaps but also managing to get him filmed with them on sets which were so familiar to television viewers. The Liberal Democrats, who had already called on John Cleese of *Fawlty Towers* fame to deliver one of the party's election broadcasts, were determined not to be outdone, and Charles Kennedy basked for some days in the publicity which he attracted from his outing with the film and television star Honor Blackman. She joined him on Wednesday 30 May to campaign in Kingston and Surbiton, a seat which the Liberal Democrats took from the Conservatives in 1997. Ms Blackman was just as much at home on the hustings as she was on the set of *The Avengers*, and had great fun teasing Kennedy. At one point he blushed when she suggested he was sexier than Sir Sean Connery, with whom she appeared in the James Bond film *Goldfinger* and who was doing what he could north of the border to promote the interests of the Scottish National Party. In his column in the *Mirror* next day, Paul Routledge pointed out that Pussy Galore was a

Liberal 'back in the days of Jo Grimond, before Charlie could do up his own shoelaces'. When Kennedy was asked about her tease at his news conference next morning, it was obvious he had in fact enjoyed being given a higher rating as a sex symbol than Scotland's legendary Bond star.

However, the Liberal Democrat leader said he had to put an end to the fun: he had been told by his campaign team to stop doing impersonations and he advised the assembled media pack to call instead on the services of Rory Bremner who, complete with enhanced lips and a prominent quiff, was making a habit of turning up outside Conservative Central Office and passing himself off as Michael Portillo in order to promote his election special, Bremner Bird and Fortune's *Exit Poll*. Bremner's cameo appearances secured considerable publicity because of Labour's refusal to let him travel on Blair's battle bus. He had been commissioned to write an election column for the *Sunday Telegraph*, but Labour's campaign co-ordinator, Douglas Alexander, said that the only journalists who were being alowed to travel with the Prime Minister were those who wanted to report 'serious politics' and the party had no wish to provide a platform for Bremner's 'tittle tattle'.

From the moment the election was called Kennedy was careful to eschew the laid-back manner which he had cultivated on television chat shows in the years before he was elected party leader, and his general demeanour and style of campaigning was attracting considerable praise. Labour's election strategists would have liked a far shorter campaign, but four weeks on the hustings paid handsome dividends for the Liberal Democrats because it gave their party leader an unparalleled opportunity to get regular exposure in peak-time television and radio news bulletins. Broadcasters are duty bound by well-established guidelines on election coverage to allocate a fair share of time to the Liberal Democrats and, by convention, the party's voice is included automatically in most campaign reports. Kennedy's technique, like that of his predecessor Paddy Ashdown, was to contrast the good sense and moderation of his party with the extremes of Labour and the Conservatives. Amid the claim and counter-claim of the two biggest parties, viewers and listeners were assured the Liberal Democrats could be trusted and would always be honest in telling the nation what needed to be done. Kennedy was convinced his straight talking paid off, and when out and about with Honor Blackman in the shopping centre of Kingston upon Thames he had no hesitation in proclaiming why the Liberal Democrats were different: 'Honesty is the key issue we are presenting in this campaign.' Gavin Hewitt, who was reporting for the *Six O'Clock News*, challenged him immediately: 'Let's be cynical for a moment. You are selling honesty? Is there such a thing as an honest politician?' Kennedy was forthright in response: 'Yes, there is such a thing as an honest politician and I would hope to think you're looking at one.' Kennedy's answers on this occasion were short and to the point, allowing Hewitt to include his supplementary question. Often his replies were more complicated in construction and, like Neil Kinnock, he had a tendency to use sentences filled with so many sub-clauses they became too long for use in news reports, which usually had to limit an answer to not much more than fifteen to twenty seconds.

Once Blair declared the election, Kennedy embarked on an extensive regional tour, flying from one stop to the next, and in the space of three days he visited eleven major cities with, more to the point, eleven regional media centres. The aim was to cram in as many television and radio appearances as possible, and the party's campaign chairman, Lord Razzall, told *Radio Five Live* on Sunday 13 May that the trip had been an amazing success: Kennedy had managed to give 105 separate interviews. By the end of May, Kennedy's press secretary, Daisy Sampson, calculated he had done a total of 265 interviews, averaging ten a day after he finished his regional tour. 'It's gone brilliantly for Charles, he's just loved doing so many interviews.' Writing in her column in the *Sunday Telegraph*, Jane Bonham-Carter, who was the party's director of communications in the

1997 election, said she thought Kennedy had 'scored brilliantly' during his marathon trip round the country. 'Regional television and local newspapers have higher penetration and are more trusted than the nationals.' Her successor, David Walter, a former BBC political correspondent, told the *Evening Standard* that without so much television exposure the Liberal Democrats would find it harder to increase their support during an election campaign. 'Chat shows help in reaching the people who avoid the news, so we would happily agree to an appearance on mainstream daytime television . . . to be honest, we would not normally turn down any request to appear on a programme.'

Saturday 2 June

I could not resist the invitation to take part in a Channel Four programme which asked a studio audience to sit in judgement on whether the political parties were to blame for encouraging such cynicism among voters that the 2001 general election was in danger of becoming the 'great turn-off'. My role was to be one of the witnesses for the prosecution in *Campaign on Trial*, but to my discomfort I ended up on the wrong side because eventually it came down to an argument about whether it was even worth making the effort to go to a polling station. As I had already sent off my postal vote and considered journalists had a duty to encourage people to participate in the democratic process, I was gratified the motion was defeated.

Jon Snow, presenter of *Channel Four News*, read out the charge: 'This election has put presentation before principle as politicians have surrendered power to corporate interests and failed to offer genuine alternatives to the electorate.' In my testimony I argued that Labour had put spin before principle, and to illustrate my case I held up the *Sun* for Thursday 24 May, its front page filled with a picture of the Itchen

College student Jo Balchin in her union flag T-shirt with her arm around the Prime Minister. In an interview she gave to the *Daily Telegraph* on Thursday 31 May, Ms Balchin said it was entirely by chance she chose that top. She had wondered whether to go to her sixth-form college that morning wearing her 'Men Lie' T-shirt but thought that might 'scare poor Tony off'. My point in holding aloft the *Sun* was to explain how a fortuitous photo-opportunity could be used to help bolster the spin on an election speech by the Prime Minister on the importance of not overlooking patriotism in the argument about Britain's position in Europe. After Blair had delivered his address, the country still had no idea what the government intended to do about British membership of the euro.

Claire Fox, Director of the Institute of Ideas, who presented the prosecution case with the journalist and television presenter Janet Street-Porter, claimed the election was so 'utterly banal and uninspiring' she had decided on principle not to vote. As soon as Ms Fox revealed she intended to opt out of the election altogether the prosecution case was torn apart by the defence, led by Michael Gove, deputy editor of *The Times*, and Matthew Taylor, Director of the Institute for Public Policy Research and a former policy adviser to the Labour Party. Gove said that he and Taylor detested each other's politics but they were both on the side of democracy and believed every vote counted.

When the recording had finished I congratulated Taylor on winning the argument and for putting me through some astute cross-examination. His hunch about the election campaign was that the Liberal Democrats were in a far stronger position than the opinions polls suggested and he thought Charles Kennedy must be wishing he had the resources to increase their list of target seats. 'There's a real panic in Millbank about the strength of the Liberal Democrat vote. Labour and the Conservatives aren't worried so much about losing votes to each other but as for Labour, they really do think they could be hit in marginal constituencies which they won last time with a tactical vote from Liberal Democrats and which they desperately need to attract again.' Taylor told me he was busy canvassing for Iain Coleman, the Labour candidate in Hammersmith and Fulham, who took the seat from the Conservatives in 1997, and who needed to continue attracting Liberal Democrat votes if he was to get re-elected. 'Out canvassing we do get a lot of people saying, "We're not going to vote for you lot again." We have to mark them down as "against". They say they're not going to vote Tory but we don't know whether they might go Liberal Democrat or just not vote. The problem is that while there's a tactical vote working for the Liberal Democrats to keep the Conservatives out there's no sign of an equally strong tactical vote to keep Labour in.'

I assumed the anxiety in Millbank Tower which Taylor had spoken of was behind the decision to put more effort in the final days of the campaign into the party's traditional heartlands. Labour's morning news conference was held at Salford in Greater Manchester, where Blair tried to counter fears of a low turnout by repeating his warning that the Conservatives' talk of a Labour landslide should not discourage people from voting. 'Every vote for a Conservative is a vote for a policy of a return to boom and bust and cuts in schools and hospitals, because that is their policy. Every failure to vote helps that Conservative policy.'

William Hague's dire warnings about what might happen if Blair was re-elected were causing concern in Labour's ranks because the strategy seemed to mirror what was known as the 'Queensland effect' – the tactic of talking up the scale of an opponent's victory in the hope of swinging votes the other way. The Liberal–National coalition in Queensland, Australia, used the technique to good effect in an election in 1995 and came within a whisker of snatching victory. After appearing to concede defeat, the coalition called for a protest vote against the ruling Labor Party because of the dangers of a landslide. On election day, despite being way ahead in the opinion polls, Labor won by only one seat. Millbank's unease about Hague's talk of a Labour landslide meant the party could not afford to ignore the possibility that it might generate some protest votes and discourage normally loyal voters from turning out. The basis of Blair's appeal was that the Conservatives had lost the argument: 'It is the last desperate throw of the dice for the Tories because finally the agenda has come to the point where it is about the economy and schools and hospitals and they know they have nothing to say. Vote for us, and give us your strength. Give us our marching orders, give us the mandate to do the work. Because that's what we need.'

Sunday 3 June

'Go on, burst his bubble' was the slogan on the Conservatives' new poster; it summed up what William Hague had been saying about the danger of re-electing New Labour. On one side was a bubble containing the head of a grinning Tony Blair and perilously close to it was a pin held in the thumb and index finger of a large hand. But if Hague was working to the 1995 script of the Liberal–National coalition in Queensland, Australia, few of the pollsters and pundits who appeared on the Sunday morning breakfast programmes thought the 'Queensland effect' would work in Britain. The general consensus was that the Conservatives were heading for a huge defeat and, so far from being able to burst Blair's bubble, the worst they could do was wipe the smile off his face. Hague was a guest on *Breakfast with Frost*, and he denied that he was trying to dissuade people from turning out to vote as Labour had claimed. Talk of a landslide was started, he said, not by the Conservatives but by Blair's official spokesman, Alastair Campbell, when he gave journalists details of Millbank's opinion polls and told Labour's candidates they were going to get re-elected. 'If Labour win by the landslide which they have themselves predicted and arrogantly taken for granted, they would further marginalise Parliament, manipulate the media and seek to suppress dissent or disagreement with them.'

In other interviews, later in the day, he tried to take greater advantage of the interest which the 'burst his bubble' poster was generating in the news media. 'If you are among the many millions that want to clip Labour's wings or sling them out altogether, you can only wipe the smile off their face by voting Conservative.' Most political correspondents interpreted Hague's line of attack as further confirmation of the lack of confidence in Central Office and a recognition of the difficulties which the Conservatives faced in trying to limit Labour's majority. 'Tories: we know we're beaten', was the headline across the front page of the *Sunday Times*; but although it reflected the mood of the day and was backed up by an appeal to readers of the biggest-selling Sunday newspaper, the *News of the World*, to vote for Blair, the Labour leadership still feared Hague might succeed in stirring up a protest vote. Blair's response was to warn voters how they would feel if they woke up on Friday 8 June and found that Hague, Ann Widdecombe and Michael Portillo were running the country. Charles Kennedy's success in galvanising the Liberal Democrats was commended by his predecessor, Sir Paddy Ashdown, whose elevation to the House of Lords was announced in the pre-election honours list published the previous day. Sir Paddy, who was also one of Sir David Frost's guests, was convinced his party would get more seats. 'We have been offering a more honest form of politics, more truth to politics and I think Charles has fought a brilliant campaign.'

Kennedy began his tour of the studios at GMTV and told the Sunday Programme he could not remember a final weekend of an election campaign when his party had sensed such a surge in support. While he did not seek to criticise the co-operation there had been with Labour on constitutional reform, he believed the Liberal Democrats did better when they conducted themselves as a 'truly independent party'. Kennedy expanded on this theme when interviewed on *The World This Weekend*: 'I have had a clear game plan for this election. I am always much more comfortable if I tell it as it is. I didn't want there to be anything other than clear and unexaggerated claims . . . I am not leading this party on the *Waiting for Godot* basis . . . If you value good public services, you have to put your hands in your pocket as a society and fund that. The Labour leadership are no longer signed up to that and that creates a bit of turf in British politics, a gap for the Liberal Democrats.'

I watched the Sunday morning interviews at home, and what I found most arresting was the calm, matter-of-fact way in which Hague talked on *Breakfast with Frost* about his willingness to 'take responsibility whatever the outcome'. He was generous in thanking his party for the support which he had received during the campaign. He made no mention of the criticism which had been made by two pro-European former ministers, Ian Taylor and Stephen Dorrell, nor did he mention a subsequent report in the *Independent* on Friday 1 June of a speech given by the former Chancellor, Kenneth Clarke. A tape-recording of a meeting in Clarke's Rushcliffe constituency, obtained by the paper, revealed that he told electors he agreed with John Major that British membership of the euro should be decided by a referendum as it would be wrong to 'confuse it with a general election'. The *Independent*'s coverage vindicated Alastair Campbell's strategy of using Labour's polling figures to provoke Conservative pro-Europeans; but Hague told Sir David he had no complaint to make about their conduct. 'Everyone was saying we would have stories in the election about Ken Clarke saying this and Michael Heseltine saying that but the Conservatives are fighting together to win . . . I have enjoyed every day of the campaign so far. I enjoy politics and will go on enjoying it . . . Yes, of course, I accept responsibility for what happens. I get credit for success and blame for the failure. We fight to win on Thursday.'

Monday 4 June

In one of the cheekiest publicity stunts of the campaign, the bookmakers Ladbrokes upstaged the morning news conferences by running a one-horse race directly opposite the Houses of Parliament on College Green, the most famous stretch of turf in Westminster. New Labour was one of the tiniest mounts which the jockey had been asked to ride, but once it crossed the line, Ladbrokes started paying out winnings on all bets placed on a Labour victory.

Being the bookies' favourite was one thing, pre-empting the result was another, and at his morning news conference Tony Blair did not like being challenged by journalists about the dangers of another Labour landslide. 'Can I just say something to you very bluntly? The election hasn't happened. It is not for you to determine the result of the election before it has happened. The British people are the boss, they will determine this election, and I am asking them to vote for what they believe in.' Half an hour later in Smith Square, William Hague found he had no option but to row back from his repeated warnings of a landslide because of unease in Central Office about the impact of such a defeatist strategy. He outlined a plan of action for his first two weeks as Prime Minister and said his first trip abroad would be to go with the new Foreign Secretary, Francis Maude, to the European summit in Gothenburg on Friday 15 June with 'a mandate to begin a crusade for genuine reform of the European Union'. Hague did his best to rally party workers for the final push to polling day, insisting that Conservative candidates were buoyed up by the reaction they were finding on the doorstep. 'Over the coming four days, we will spare no efforts, hour or breath so that on Friday, you will be surprised, and we will be busy.' Hague could not shake off questions about his own fate if Blair were re-elected by another landslide, and he repeated the answer he had given on *Breakfast with Frost*: that the party leader always took the blame when 'things go wrong'. Michael Portillo, who was sharing the platform, paid his tribute to Hague's leadership: 'William has led a magnificent campaign. We have all enjoyed participating in the campaign. His energy has been boundless. He has set the agenda and we are privileged to have been part of it.' Earlier in the day Hague's stoicism in the face of adversity had provoked discussion on *Today*. Matthew Parris, sketchwriter on *The Times*, thought some voters might be put off by the 'never say die quality' of the Tory leader. 'If he would cry, would wince, or if we break him, he bleeds, then perhaps we might like him more.'

Once his news conference was over, Hague set off immediately by helicopter on a three-day, 900-mile trip around Tory marginals. Opinion polls and focus groups showed that floating voters often left it until the final week of the campaign to make up their minds, and Hague was anxious to avoid the criticism which the party leadership attracted in 1997 when the final days of John Major's campaign were said to have looked lacklustre. His first stop was at Newport on the Isle of Wight, where he added a new line to his stand-up routine: 'In the opening days of a Conservative government we will free the doctors, nurses and police to do their own jobs without interference.' By teatime, after calling at Cheltenham and the Wirral, he had reached Perth.

Hague would not have been amused if, on the first lap of his marathon tour, he found time to catch up with the lunchtime news, because an appeal which Blair had made at his morning press conference for 'decent, patriotic, one-nation Conservatives' to support Labour's policy of putting schools and hospitals first had produced a result by the time the bulletins went on air. With their customary flair for capturing the headlines, the media team at Millbank Tower knew precisely when to announce that Anthony Nelson, a former Conservative Treasury minister and prominent pro-European, had become a member of the Labour Party. Nelson, who was MP for Chichester until he stood down in 1997, said that as the election had got closer he decided that 'only Tony Blair offers the leadership and vision this country needs.'

Blair had a taxing time that evening in the face of Jeremy Paxman's questions on *Newsnight*. The sharpest exchanges followed the Prime Minister's assertion that if the government went after the 'few, most wealthy' people it would not help the poorest. On being challenged on his response, Blair was curt and forthright: 'I choose to answer it, in the way I'm answering it. The issue is not whether the richest person becomes richer, the question is whether the poorest person improves his position ... If you end up saying my task is to stop a person earning a lot of money, you waste all your time and energy taking some money off people who are very rich when in actual fact in today's world they probably move elsewhere.' Paxman tried again to find out whether it was acceptable for the gap between rich and poor to widen, and he had some robust advice for his interviewee: 'You want to be Prime Minister, I just want to be an interviewer; can we stick to that arrangement?' Blair refused to be drawn any further into possible tax rates. 'We are not sitting down, writing a Budget now ... It is not a burning ambition for me to make sure that David Beckham earns less money ... We have not clobbered higher tax earners and we have got no intention of doing so.'

Tuesday 5 June

An entire leader column was devoted to explaining why, for the first time in the newspaper's history, *The Times* was offering readers a 'cautious but clear endorsement' of Labour. After deciding in 1997 that it could not recommend any of the major parties to the electorate, it felt 'comfortable, as never before' with the case for Labour because the party had 'consolidated many elements of Thatcherism' and deserved the vote of the reformers. Winning the support of *The Times* gave Labour the backing of all four of Rupert Murdoch's national newspapers. The *Sun* was the first to declare, followed by the *News of the World*; then the *Sunday Times*, which was the least enthusiastic, concluded that Labour was the 'least worst party' but deserved to win with a significantly smaller majority. Renewed support for Labour was offered by the *Financial Times*, which backed Tony Blair in 1997 and thought the Prime Minister had 'earned his second chance' because of his government's competence on the three issues central to the election: Europe, economic management and public services.

The sting in the tail of the endorsement in *The Times* was that it believed Blair would go on blending 'Thatcherite means with social democratic ends', which was to prove an unwelcome reminder of the admiring way he had spoken earlier in his premiership about the achievements of the Thatcher years. At Labour's morning news conference he faced some pointed questions over the degree to which he was still in awe of the policies she introduced. While repeatedly acknowledging her influence, he insisted there were 'big failings' during her period in power. 'It is time we moved beyond Thatcherism. Not that we reject everything that happened then . . . By accepting those things that were right in the 1980s, it gives us a far greater power and authority to then say "Hang on, they got a lot of things wrong" . . . And what was wrong was clear: economic instability, gross underinvestment in public services, social division and an attitude to Europe that has no relevance to the modern world in which we live.'

Hanging over the final news conference at Conservative Central Office was not the glory of the Thatcher years but the spectre of defeat and the prospect of another divisive leadership contest. A grim sense of foreboding was broken only by the odd moment or two of gallows humour. The sound of construction work in another part of the building became distracting and Michael Portillo interrupted his opening remarks to appeal for help: 'Can someone from Central Office stop that drilling?' His irritation provided an opening for Nick Clarke, presenter of The *World At One*, who asked if the noise was coming from the sound of staff drilling their escape tunnels out of party headquarters. *Newsnight*'s correspondent, Martha Kearney, wondered if the commotion was something to do with the installation of extra telephone lines – a barbed reminder of the preparations which were made as part of Portillo's aborted bid to stand for the Conservative leadership in June 1995. 'That's complete drivel,' snapped the shadow Chancellor. 'At yesterday's press conference I set out how magnificently we had been led by William Hague and I said the rest of us would wish to be associated entirely with him in his campaign.' After Michael Ancram promised the 'most intensive campaign' the party had ever fought in the 180 seats which the Conservatives needed to get a majority, Francis Maude did his best to lighten the proceedings: 'Remember this election isn't over until the fat lady sings.' Andrew Scadding gave me a run-down of how, after making the fastest start to the campaign, the Conservatives planned the strongest finish. There would be a heavy street presence in towns in their battleground constituencies and Central Office had prepared separate leaflets for the four groups they were targeting. Known Conservative voters were to be told the party could win; people indicating they might vote Conservative were to be given details of the party's policies and a warning about Labour; potential Labour waverers would get information on the government's failure to deliver on public services; and supporters of the United Kingdom Independence Party would be told they could be sure of keeping the pound only by voting Conservative.

Scadding was anxious to hear my reaction to their latest photo-opportunities and posters. He thought the most imaginative idea in the Keep the Pound campaign was hanging a large poster from a barge which spent much of Sunday 3 June sailing up and down Thames past the Houses of Parliament. The poster bore an enormous £ sign followed by the words, 'Labour will sell it down the river.' I realised Scadding was anxious to keep talking about the technical highlights of the election almost as a defensive mechanism, to stop me asking about the overall direction of the campaign. 'Did you see the pictures of the barge poster? It was the opening shot for *On The Record* and on all the news bulletins. We're now going to send out emails which include the picture from our 'burst his bubble' poster and the pin actually goes across and bursts the bubble.' Scadding assured me that the poster to prick Blair's arrogance, Hague's warning of a Labour landslide and Lady Thatcher's alarm about the return of an 'elective dictatorship' were all part of a calculated policy. 'The BBC thought it had got an exclusive when Andrew Marr got Hague's warning about a landslide, but we knew what we were doing. He went ahead once we heard the *Daily Telegraph* was going to print Lady Thatcher's article on 'elective dictatorship' and we wanted to capitalise on the 'burst his bubble' poster to remind everyone how arrogant Blair could be.'

Scadding's insights were restricted solely to the mechanics of his work, and on previous visits to Central Office, during conversations with others in the media team, I had sensed the same reluctance to discuss strategy, as if somehow the whole subject was off limits. As Scadding went through the countdown to polling day I looked around in vain hoping to see Danny Finkelstein, the head of policy, who was fighting Harrow West, or perhaps Rick Nye, the head of research. The impression I had gained in the four weeks of the campaign was that while many of the long-serving Central Office insiders were proud of the technical success of their campaign, they were deeply disappointed at their failure to wipe the slate clean after the disaster of 1997 and to get across the idea that people should again feel comfortable voting Conservative. I thought there were a number of initiatives which, although they would have required additional expenditure, could easily have been used to outflank Blair and put Labour under pressure. For example, Hague could have promised to look at the decision of the Scottish Executive and Scottish Parliament to replace university tuition fees with a system requiring later, staged payments by students, or alternatively have given an undertaking to study the promise in Scotland to introduce free long-term care for the elderly. But, rather than searching out ideas which could have been paraded as one-nation Conservatism, the party's election planners had locked themselves into a campaign on Europe, tax and asylum – which certainly suited the approach of the party's two leading election strategists, Andrew Lansley and Tim Collins, and also the chief spokesman Nick Wood, who seemed to be at his happiest when the war room was issuing hard-line policy statements.

I found the atmosphere in Central Office oppressive after a light-hearted session at the Liberal Democrats' news conference in Bevin Hall. Charles Kennedy remained to be convinced that a Labour landslide was in the bag, and he was encouraged by the difficulty Blair was facing in presenting himself as the natural heir of Thatcherism. 'It wasn't until they hit this campaign that they woke up to the fact, as we've argued for years, that most people want quality public services and do know that does mean fair taxation to achieve it. So I think they are slightly twisting in the wind.' Fi Glover of *Radio Five Live* tried him out on the suggestion in the *Sun* that the phrase 'It's a Blair' was now being used by the bookies to describe a total wipeout at an election. What was his definition of a Kennedy? After a moment's thought he gave his answer: 'A Kennedy? Expect the unexpected.' His confidence about the Liberal Democrats' performance was based on reports from the constituencies that there were going to be some 'quirky results' in some part of the country. Chris Rennard, the party's campaign director, said the Conservatives still had not woken up to the danger they faced in constituencies near Liberal Democrat strongholds. Once a seat had been taken, it could provide the basis for establishing a cluster of Liberal Democrat seats from which it would then be possible to push out further into Tory territory. The party's three Hampshire seats, Eastleigh, Winchester and Romsey, provided a launch-pad for the nearby target seat of Mid Dorset and North Poole. Another Tory seat being targeted was Guildford, which was close to the Liberal Democrats' cluster of five seats in south-west London: Kingston and Surbiton, Sutton and Cheam, Carshalton and Wallington, Richmond Park, and Twickenham. 'Once we get a foothold we get more coverage on regional television and local radio and that helps raise our profile.'

Rennard agreed with the assessment given to me by Matthew Taylor of the IPPR on Saturday 2 June that the campaign to encourage tactical voting looked like working largely in favour of the Liberal Democrats rather than Labour. 'Liberal Democrats in Labour marginals who think Blair has not done enough on schools and hospitals are going to be less inclined now to switch to Labour, but it's still far easier for Labour voters to switch to Liberal Democrat if they think they can beat a Conservative, so I don't think tactical voting will be of much help to Labour.'

Wednesday 6 June

Party workers crowded into the South Bank studios of London Weekend Television for the Conservatives' eve-of-poll rally. William Hague's final appeal for support was a polished performance at an event which broke away from the usual cut and thrust of the hustings and allowed him to deliver a highly personal, upbeat message. The build-up to his speech was designed to demonstrate the Conservatives' commitment to the integrity of public life. One after another, four members of the shadow cabinet each gave an individual account of why they had entered politics. There was no hint of the triumphalism which marred Labour's much-criticised rally at Sheffield in 1992; but although the occasion was meant to galvanise the party faithful, it finished on a note of uncertainty. The studio had been arranged like the set of a television game show and the four speakers, each called from one or other side of the set to give his or her address from a separate lectern, looked as if they were contestants trying to win over an audience. The parallel was all too obvious. Should the testimonies we heard, which came across like a series of personal manifestos, be regarded by the news media as the opening round in the leadership contest which many of us suspected would follow an election defeat?

Michael Ancram, the party chairman, sat on what appeared to be a bar stool as he opened the proceedings. He believed they needed an opportunity to sum up the campaign and to explain that although their beliefs had different roots, they were all in politics for a purpose. Ancram remained a Conservative because he would never accept that it was 'politically incorrect to love my county' and he intended to use all his strength as a politician to stop the United Kingdom unravelling when it was under threat as never before from creeping nationalism and the regional and cultural divisions set in train by New Labour. Michael Portillo spoke without notes, away from his lectern, and admitted that in his youth he was attracted to the Labour Party, until he saw that Labour's way of using government to change society did not work. People brought about social improvement themselves. 'Labour have always believed in centralisation, but New Labour's control fetish has made it still more intolerant of diversity. Uniformity is the enemy of improvement. We passionately believe freedom and diversity deliver progress.' Ann Widdecombe said she entered politics in the 1960s from a sense of vocation. Although she had left the Church of England and embraced Roman Catholicism, she had never been tempted to change her party. She had not stopped thinking about her political values. 'I have tested them and challenged them and found Conservative values as relevant today as they have ever been.' Francis Maude was proud to have been 'almost literally born' into the party. His father, the late Angus Maude, was Conservative MP for Stratford-upon-Avon, and he grew up believing politics was a high calling, built on deep beliefs and high principles. 'In my family the idea that you went into politics for yourself was laughable . . . I grew up with the notion that a strong society is one bound together by the bonds of mutual obligation; that the strong have a duty to help the weak.' Portillo was the only one of the four shadow ministers who appeared comfortable with the format, seeming to be aware of the various camera positions and proceeding without hesitation towards his podium.

William Hague made his entrance from the middle, walking on like the compère of a celebrity contest. The principles which he joined the Conservative Party to defend, and which he stood up and spoke for from the conference floor when he was sixteen, were the same principles that he was proud to present as party leader. 'The people I went to school with are now doing many different things. They own their own homes, they save for pensions, they enjoy wider choice in their lives. Many now have families of their own . . . But the values we shared then are the same values we share now: pride, directness, generosity of spirit and, if I'm honest, a certain stubborn streak.' Hague recognised that many of his schoolmates voted Labour at the last election; but they now realised that Tony Blair had broken the promises he made in 1997 and shown that no belief was too important to be abandoned when circumstances dictated. One reason above all to vote Conservative was to challenge Blair's promise in his 1999 Labour conference speech to lead the 'progressive force that defeats the forces of conservatism'. Hague used the Prime Minister's declaration that he had embarked on an historic mission to 'liberate Britain from the old class divisions' as his rallying call to the nation. 'His attack on the forces of conservatism and his attempt to heap all the ills and evils of the twentieth century on the heads of decent people must rank as one of the most ill-judged political comments of all time. Tony Blair may have retreated in the face of the Women's Institutes and others, but they still remember, we still remember. And tomorrow the world will find out that the forces of conservatism are on the march.' Taking a swipe at the smirk on Blair's face was one sure way of cheering up the party faithful, and Hague got the biggest laugh from his studio audience when describing what happened on his first campaign stop of the morning, breakfast at 6 a.m. with traders at Smithfield market in London. As he went round the stalls, he said the shout went up: 'Whatever you do, William, win, go on William, wipe the smile from his face.'

Mingling with party workers before the speeches, I detected a mood of uncertainty, a feeling that there were so many undecided voters out there in the country at large that the activists were not sure what would happen and as a result were clinging to the hope that the result might be better than the opinion polls suggested. Many of those I spoke to praised Hague's resilience. He had not lost his cool, and they thought he had gained gravitas during the campaign. If Amanda Platell was concerned about the outcome, she did not show it as she busied herself with other members of the media team. Nick Wood told me Central Office was pleased they had managed to needle Blair with their warnings about the dangers of another Labour landslide. 'We planned it all a couple of months ago. When Andrew Marr put the question to William Hague we just went for it and Blair's been scratchy about it ever since.' Andrew Scadding butted in to give me a rundown of their success in using the 'burst his bubble' poster on the internet. Emails showing an animated pin pricking the bubble which contained a grinning Tony Blair had been sent to 100,000 party members and supporters who were on the mailing list of the Conservatives' Keep the Pound campaign.

Hague spent the rest of the day on a whistlestop tour of Tory marginals and, as the television pictures were being fed into the BBC's studios at Westminster, I noticed he got a pretty raucous reception in Hemel Hempstead. Seb Coe led the way with Ffion at the side of her husband. She was smiling and joking with people in the crowd. Hague shouted across to one woman: 'Yes, kick 'em out, you've got the idea.' Labour supporters shouted back when he set out the reasons for voting Conservative. 'We'll bring down taxes on your petrol. You've been robbed by Gordon Brown. ["Rubbish!"] . . . Labour are soft on crime. ["Rubbish!"] . . . Never have we had a government which has broken more promises in four years or more rapidly lost touch with the British people.'

Tony Blair's whirlwind tour struck a far more serious note as he appealed to the electorate to make their voices heard and to vote for what they believed in. One stop was in the Labour heartland constituency of Pontefract and Castleford, the seat of Yvette Cooper, the minister for public health. Ms Cooper, who was expecting her second child, was with her husband Ed Balls, chief economic adviser to Gordon Brown, and they greeted Blair as he arrived at the Magnet public house in Castleford to speak to well over a hundred supporters. After another reminder that it was not journalists but the British people who were 'the boss in this election', he said he hoped that with the strength and support of Labour voters, his government would be allowed to remain in office. 'If you are one of the millions of hard-working families in the country who depend on a stable economy, decent schools and decent hospitals, then this election matters and matters dramatically to you. So don't let the pundits tell you it doesn't matter, or the let the pollsters tell you it's over. If people come out and support us we can carry on with the work we have started.' He told his audience a general election was an important moment in the life of the nation. 'Remember, your vote is a precious thing. There are people, our ancestors, who lived and fought and sometimes died for the right to vote in this country. We honour their memory when we exercise our right to vote and we dishonour it when we fail to.' A pensioner in the audience, Reg Lavine, who was seventy-one, told the Press Association it was the first time a serving Prime Minister had visited Castleford and he was very proud to have witnessed it.

Before setting off on the last lap of his campaign, Charles Kennedy used his final news conference to reflect on his success in disproving the taunt of his detractors that he would turn out to be least energetic of the three party leaders. 'I have smiled ironically to myself and, because I am laid back, I do tell myself never to complain about all those caricatures, but people have rather overlooked the reality of the job I have been doing all these years.' Ross, Skye and Inverness West was bigger geographically than any other constituency in the country, and as his previous post was European spokesman for the Liberal Democrats, he had done his fair share of travelling. None the less the past four weeks had been pretty frenetic: he had covered more than 10,000 miles and been on at least sixty flights. Throughout the campaign his priority was always to do every possible interview for regional television and local radio. Peter Hunt, a BBC correspondent, told *PM* that frequently Kennedy had little time for a walkabout in the constituencies he was visiting. On Monday 4 June he travelled for three and a half hours from London to Teignbridge in Devon, but spent only eight minutes meeting local people because the interviews were piling up. On the following day, after visiting Cheltenham and Romsey, his patience finally snapped when he got to Folkestone: he refused to answer questions as he went along, saying there was not time to give 'a running commentary', and it was not until a gap between his interviews for Invicta Radio and Meridian Television that the journalists who were travelling on the Liberal Democrats' battle bus finally got the quote they were after.

Kennedy said the great difference from previous elections was that voters had got a clearer idea of the Liberal Democrats' commitment to quality public services following the initiatives they had taken in the Scottish Parliament in abolishing students' tuition fees and guaranteeing long-term free care for the elderly. He had been surprised by the defensiveness of the government. 'I would not have wanted to look so apologetic and have so few other ministers being seen with Tony Blair. I don't think a party which can only run on his fuel is sustainable in the long term. He's still saying he wants his marching orders, an instruction, but this guy is supposed to be Prime Minister. He doesn't strike me as being much of a leader.'

7 The Land Slides

No party leader can afford to miss the first engagement of the morning, the one compulsory photo-opportunity of polling day. Arriving to vote is just about the only picture which can be shown on television as the rules for broadcasters are strict: once the polling stations have opened there must be no more electioneering over the airwaves and the news bulletins have to be free of political argument until after the ballot boxes have been sealed at 10 p.m. ready for the count. By voting early the politicians hope to set an example which their supporters will follow, and if it were not for the party leaders, their partners and families adding a dash of colour and excitement to the coverage, the pictures in the lunchtime news summaries would probably be rather uninspiring, as a mid-morning tour of polling stations usually reveals just a trickle of voters and, more often than not, it seems to be only old-age pensioners who are bothering to vote.

The Prime Minister's photo-call provided a long tracking shot of a kind which television camera crews love to capture. Tony Blair, holding hands with his wife Cherie and daughter Kathryn, together with the couple's two eldest sons, Euan and Nicky, strolled across a playing field near their constituency home on the way to the polling station in Trimdon Colliery community centre. It was a sunny morning; Blair and his sons were in shirtsleeves and his wife and daughter in summery tops. The playing field was covered with buttercups and daisies and as they walked past the goalpost they waved to a group of boys playing football. Together as a family, with all but baby Leo who was asleep at home, they provided a lingering sequence of pictures which mirrored the same walk across the same playing field by the same family on polling day in 1997 – and once again it would not have looked out of place in *The Sound of Music*.

Twenty-five miles to the south in the adjoining constituency of Richmond in North Yorkshire, William and Ffion Hague were among the first to arrive at the Booth Memorial Institute in Catterick, the nearest polling station to their constituency home. The leader of the opposition joked and shook hands with the polling clerks and returning officers. 'I've even brought my polling card, in case they didn't know who we were.' Charles Kennedy, who had taken the precaution of voting by post and had started the morning by doing some gardening, was under strict instructions not to miss his slot on the news bulletins and, wearing a worn waxed jacket, he put in an appearance at a polling station in Fort Augustus at the southern end of Loch Ness.

The three final opinion polls of the campaign all put Labour comfortably in front and predicted a majority very similar to the landslide victory which Blair achieved in 1997. His historic second full term seemed assured. Gallup, in the *Daily Telegraph*, gave Labour the highest predicted score, a share of 47 per cent, way ahead of the Conservatives on 30 per cent, with the Liberal Democrats on 16 per cent. In a MORI poll in *The Times*, Labour had 45 per cent of the vote, the Conservatives 30 per cent and the Liberal Democrats 18 per cent. The final ICM poll, published the previous day in the *Guardian*, indicated a four-point fall in Labour's position, down to 43 per cent, and showed the Conservatives up by a similar margin on 32 per cent, giving the narrowest Labour lead recorded by ICM since March. The Liberal Democrats' share had also increased slightly to 19 per cent.

The all-important popular newspapers were equally favourable to the Prime Minister. Of the five tabloids, the *Express* provided the biggest surprise, devoting half its front page to explaining why it was recommending readers to vote Labour for the first time in the paper's history.

264 · *Campaign 2001*

After supporting the Conservatives in every general election since 1900, it said only Blair had proved capable of running the country and he needed 'a popular mandate big enough' to allow him to bring about the radical reform he had promised. 'Don't let us down Tony' was the headline on the *Sun*'s front page, next to a picture of the Prime Minister being kissed by a pensioner. The *Mirror*'s front page had the headline 'X marks the clot' under a picture of Hague, and a double spread inside, under the heading 'How to bury a Tory', gave advice on tactical voting. A short five-paragraph story on the front of the *Daily Mail* said Blair was apparently guaranteed 'an unprecedented second term' and the *Daily Star*, although it relegated election coverage to an inside page, said voters should give 'Tony another go'.

My role on election night was to work as a back-up television and radio reporter at Millbank Tower, ready to respond should Labour run into any unforeseen difficulties. On arriving at the usual entrance I found that access had been barred to newspaper reporters and that broadcasters were being redirected away from the media area and escorted to a remote corner high up in another wing of the Millbank Tower complex. As I walked past the ground floor of the main building, where we were told party workers would watch the results coming in, I saw that mirrored wallpaper had been stuck to the windows so that photographers and television crews would be unable to take pictures of the proceedings inside. From early on in the campaign, we had been informed there would be no repeat of the exuberant celebrations which Labour held at the Royal Festival Hall in the early hours after polling day in 1997. Party strategists were well aware of widespread disenchantment about the government's performance on public services, and they feared pictures or film of a victory party would be seized on by the news media and would contrast badly with the messages which the Prime Minister had been conveying that Labour needed a new mandate to continue with 'work in progress' and that 'the work goes on.' The last few hours before the first results are always tense, and the uneasy atmosphere I sensed at Labour's headquarters had not been helped by the repeated forecasts of an exceptionally low turnout. In Gallup's eve-of-poll survey for the *Daily Telegraph*, 73 per cent of those who were questioned said they definitely intended to vote, but the number who actually went to a polling station tended invariably to be lower, and the prediction for the likely turnout was adjusted downwards to 66 per cent: the lowest since 1918.

Once installed in our tightly controlled media enclosure we all settled down to watch live coverage on the rival television channels and wait for the exit polls. Released after the polling stations closed at 10 p.m., these confirmed another Labour landslide. MORI's exit poll for ITV's programme *Election 2001* predicted a majority for Blair of 175, four down on his 1997 victory. NOP's exit survey for the BBC's *Vote 2001: The Verdict* came in with a lower figure, suggesting that Labour would finish 157 seats ahead of the Conservatives.

The first minister to be sent along to the media enclosure was Lord Macdonald, the minister for transport, who unlike most of his government colleagues was not tied up at a count. He urged caution and reminded reporters they should not overlook the fallibility of such surveys; few in the party would forget the BBC exit poll which predicted mistakenly that Neil Kinnock was heading for victory in 1992. At 10.42 p.m. Sunderland South won the contest to be the first constituency to declare, beating its 1997 record by four minutes. Chris Mullin, a junior minister at the Department for International Development, was re-elected comfortably; but Labour's majority was cut by almost 6,000 votes and the turnout of 48.3 per cent was way down on the 58.8 per cent recorded in 1997. Lord Macdonald, who was standing by ready to respond for *Sky News*, said he was disappointed by the low turnout which he thought was the fault of the news media for having spent weeks predicting a landslide. I was tempted to remind him that Labour had done its utmost to encourage such coverage with the three briefings given by Alastair Campbell at which he released Millbank's internal opinion polls predicting a Conservative wipeout.

Our next diversion was seeing the first editions of the morning papers. 'Blair's back' was the *Sun*'s front-page headline, over a report by Trevor Kavanagh saying the Prime Minister's arrival at party headquarters after his count in Sedgefield promised to be 'a low-key affair compared to the near hysteria surrounding his 1997 conquest'. Having by this point already spent two hours corralled in our enclosure, denied any contact with the guests and party workers who were gathering downstairs, we hardly needed reminding that we had drawn the short straw. Millbank Tower was unlikely to see much of the action, and our freedom to work as journalists was being so tightly controlled that we could glean few insights and very little background information to offer the live programmes.

Soon the results started to settle into a pattern. In many seats there was a small swing to the Conservatives, like the 2.3 per cent recorded in Houghton and Washington East; and there were further signs of a sharp fall in the turnout, down to 45.8 per cent in Barnsley Central. However, Labour were holding seats won from the Conservatives in 1997, including Birmingham Edgbaston, scene of Sharron Storer's confrontation with Tony Blair. Gordon Brown was returned in Dunfermline East with a majority of 15,063. At 57 per cent, the turnout there was higher than in other seats in Labour's heartlands, but still way down on the 70.2 per cent achieved in the same constituency in 1997. Brown told *Vote 2001* that Britain was seeing a trend towards a disengagement from politics which was being witnessed in other Western industrialised countries and was even more marked in the USA. He denied voters had shown a of lack enthusiasm for the government. In a speech after the declaration of his result he promised Labour would obey the instruction given to them by the electorate to put schools and hospitals first. 'This mandate to put more into the public services is a mission we will pursue in government.'

Not all Brown's enthusiasm could hide Labour's difficulty: ministers were going to have find some way of explaining why so many voters had stayed at home. On the basis of the early results the pollsters and pundits were unanimous in concluding that the national turnout of 71.4 per cent in 1997 had almost certainly fallen to its lowest point since the 58.9 per cent recorded in the general election of 1918. Jack Straw was the next minister to pin the blame on the news media for having spent weeks discounting the result. He did not see why *Vote 2001* was making such an issue of it. 'Labour are clearly being returned with a stomping majority but you are trying to turn this into a story about turnout and not the story of the result.' John Prescott acknowledged the low poll was a setback. The real problem had been that the Conservatives lost the argument and then said people should not vote in order to deprive Labour of a big majority. David Blunkett accepted that the result posed 'very serious questions' about how politicians should engage with the public. 'People are switched off politics. They are disconnected with representative democracy and young people in particular don't see it as being relevant to their lives.'

Seeing the hard time Labour were having in putting together a convincing argument, we thought it would not be long before an emissary was sent along to our lonely outpost in Millbank Tower, and shortly after midnight we were told to gather round: David Hill, the chief spokesman, was about to give a briefing. 'If you are going to have a successful election you have to have a good opposition. In this campaign we have witnessed an element of contentment rather than conflict and that's why we've had the turnout we are hearing about tonight. The public believed the Conservatives had nothing to offer. They didn't put across the prospect of an alternative government. We can't help it if the Conservatives have made a complete and utter shambles of being the opposition. If there's no effective opposition, people make a judgement on how to vote.'

One moment of excitement just before Hill gave Millbank's assessment of the great stay-away was the news from Torbay that the Liberal Democrats' candidate, Adrian Sanders, had increased his majority over the Conservatives to 6,708. Sanders had won the seat in 1997 by just twelve votes and it was the most marginal in the country, topping the list of Tory targets. Out of the early declarations, Torbay was the one constituency which William Hague's advisers were confident he would retake, and as they waited for the first results to be announced it assumed a pivotal role, rather like the 1992 declaration at Basildon in Essex, which indicated that John Major had defeated the strong challenge mounted against him by Neil Kinnock. By delivering a 7 per cent swing from the Conservatives to the Liberal Democrats, Torbay sent Central Office into a tailspin. Nick Robinson, reporting there for *Vote 2001*, described the anguished faces of the Tory high command. Right from the start they had been assured Hague would secure twenty to thirty gains, and even after the release of the exit polls the Conservative leader in the House of Lords, Lord Strathclyde, told them to be patient and wait for the Torbay result. 'When Strathclyde saw the Conservatives had been beaten so badly in Torbay his face just dropped. He could not understand it. They all kept saying that people on the doorstep had been so much nicer to them than in 1997. They just couldn't fathom it.'

Steve Norris, the defeated Conservative candidate in the election for Mayor of London, said the results showed the scale of the task which the Tories faced in trying to rehabilitate themselves. Neil Kinnock, the next guest on *Vote 2001*, agreed. 'Tonight's result is a sensational dismissal of Hague's campaign about the euro, asylum and banging people up with the jock-strap vigour of the Conservatives. It's somewhere the British people don't live any more.' Kenneth Clarke, who was waiting patiently for his declaration in Rushcliffe, was only too happy to break his self-imposed purdah and explain why he feared Hague faced 'a difficult and disappointing night'. The public had not engaged with the Conservatives and his party would have to analyse the reasons. 'I campaigned on health, crime and the economy, which I felt people in my constituency were concerned about. I went into unaccustomed seclusion and I didn't give interviews because I knew most of them would be about Europe and the leadership and I didn't think that would be of any help to me in Rushcliffe.' Clarke said Hague fought 'a very courageous campaign' and the party would want to take time to regroup. 'My personal prediction is that William will continue in the job and it would be absurd of me to start talking about the leadership.'

Earlier in the evening another candidate who had spent the campaign trying to avoid the company of journalists was shown waiting expectantly for his declaration. Rewarded for his defection from the Conservatives by his last-minute selection to stand for Labour in St Helens South, Shaun Woodward was shown in one shot from the outside broadcast camera sitting at the count with the television presenter Esther Rantzen, with whom he had worked when he edited *That's Life* before leaving the BBC to become the Conservatives' director of communications in May 1991. No butler, of course, was to be seen. Reporters had enjoyed playing 'hunt the butler' when covering the attempts of Labour's wealthy and well-connected candidate to win over voters in one of the party's safest seats on Merseyside, and a front-page picture in the *Daily Telegraph* on the eve of polling day showed Woodward's wife Camilla, heiress to the billion-pound Sainsbury supermarket fortune, and Ben Limberg, the 'tall young man at her side, her faithful butler'. Mrs Woodward, the paper said, had 'broken cover' to support her husband's campaign and she and Limberg took 'turns to blow up red Labour balloons and distribute leaflets'.

Labour held St Helens South, but with its 1997 majority of 23,739 slashed to 8,985. The swing of 14.3 per cent was the largest against Labour to either the Liberal Democrats or the Conservatives. Brian Spencer, the Liberal Democrats' candidate, took second place with 7,814 votes. Neil

Thompson, who had resigned from Labour and stood for the Socialist Alliance in protest at the way Woodward had been imposed on the constituency, polled 2,325 votes and saved his deposit. In thanking his supporters, Woodward said it had been 'a very hard-fought campaign' but he felt a great sense of what needed to be done to help a deprived constituency. 'I am very proud to be the next MP for St Helens South and a member of the Labour Party which can truly claim to be the party of one nation and opportunity for all.' Interviewing Woodward on *Vote 2001*, Jeremy Paxman asked if the new MP's butler had voted Labour as well. Woodward insisted he had a loftier agenda: 'I enjoy your obsession, Jeremy, about the caricatures of the campaign but we won by talking about the real issues, jobs and schools . . . Yes, I spent some time in the Conservative Party and inevitably you must go along with the things they say but, as Winston Churchill said, I left the Conservatives to stop saying stupid things . . . I ended up with right-wing extremists and a bunch of people propelled by Hague to say outrageous things against asylum seekers and a ludicrous policy against Europe and they ended up with the result they deserved.'

At this point Steve Norris was brought into the discussion, and he declared Labour was welcome to its new MP. 'Shaun couldn't find his way up the motorway if he didn't have his chauffeur and butler with him.' But Woodward had the last word: 'Steve just resorts to personal attack . . . it's an illustration of why the Conservatives lost the plot.'

Scores were also being settled on the other side of the Pennines in Hartlepool, where Peter Mandelson faced an equally strong field of aggrieved candidates but where, unlike Woodward, he took full advantage of the publicity he had been attracting. On Mandelson's second resignation from Cabinet in January 2001 he had vowed to devote himself to getting re-elected, and in doing so he used every available opportunity to expound at length on his pleasure at leaving behind the Westminster media village. He told *Channel Four News* on Sunday 3 June that after being cast aside from the government his fightback in Hartlepool had not been easy. 'It was as if I had been turned into an international war criminal or child molester. Most of the town stood by me . . . I think people had expected something really serious to be revealed about me and when it wasn't, they began to wonder why their MP had to go through this, and then they began to think, "Why don't people stand by our MP?"' Jeremy Vine, who reported from Hartlepool for *Newsnight* on Wednesday 16 May, told me that he concluded that Mandelson wanted to give the impression that much of the local anger was directed personally against the Prime Minister for the way he had treated his friend and neighbouring north-east MP.

Mandelson was well rewarded for a hard-fought constituency campaign. Re-elected with a majority of 14,571, down by only 2,937 on 1997, he proceeded to deliver the most riveting acceptance speech of the night. He believed he had been revalidated by his constituents and would repay their vote of confidence by speaking up for everything they wanted. 'I am grateful to Hartlepool for putting me back on the political map. Before this campaign started it was said that I was facing political oblivion, my career in tatters, apparently never to be part of the political living again. They underestimated Hartlepool, and they underestimated me, because I am a fighter and not a quitter. My political opponents have their pound of flesh and they do, but they will never eat into the core of my beliefs of what I stand for and what remains today, that is the inner steel in me.'

The Prime Minister was said to have been stopped in his tracks by the unexpected fury of his friend and former colleague. Reporters who had been covering his declaration said Blair and Alastair Campbell were about to depart from Trimdon Labour Club for a flight south to London to attend Labour's muted celebration at Millbank Tower but stayed on for a few moments to watch the explosion of anger in Hartlepool. Mandelson had chosen his words with care, and his short speech constituted a point-by-point rebuttal of wounding remarks which were made about him in the days after he resigned as Secretary of State for Northern Ireland. Ministers who had served with him in Cabinet and had then been highly critical of his behaviour were all but identified by name: it was David Blunkett who told *Newsnight* that Mandelson's political career was 'in tatters'; Clare Short, interviewed on *The World This Weekend*, could hardly have put it any more clearly when she said 'Peter Mandelson's over' because he 'didn't speak the truth and let himself down'; and Geoff Hoon informed listeners on *Today* that Labour's election campaign supremo could no longer be allowed to play 'a prominent position' in the election and should limit himself to 'basic tasks such as knocking on doors and delivering leaflets'.

But Mandelson's ex-colleagues were not his only targets, and he expressed his delight that Arthur Scargill, president of the National Union of Mineworkers, who had stood against him as the candidate for Socialist Labour, gained only 912 votes and finished in fourth place. 'That great Titan of Old Labour, now Ex-Labour, came to bury New Labour in a traditional northern working town and he lost badly because the people have spoken very loudly and clearly in this constituency. New Labour can no longer be accused of being a metropolitan set. We are the popular, progressive choice for all the people of the United Kingdom.' Mandelson told Jonathan Dimbleby on *Election 2001* that his aim had been to re-establish himself in Hartlepool and he was not expecting to rejoin the government. 'I don't believe I will be back . . . I don't believe I will be offered another job.'

While waiting for Blair's result to be declared Campbell gave his assessment of the campaign, and then spoke for the first time about his own new role during Labour's second term. In an interview by Jon Sopel for *Vote 2001*, he said Labour had 'comprehensively beaten' the Conservatives on all the big issues and he believed their victory held lessons both for himself and for the way the government handled its relations with the news media. Previously Campbell had refused to answer questions about the planned shake-up inside No. 10 which was confirmed publicly on Thursday 12 April and which was expected to see him relinquish his duties as official spokesman in order to become Blair's first head of communications, taking overall control of the government's media strategy. Now he was happy to expand on the topic. 'The second term is going to be far more about strategic priorities and what this election has shown is that if you can win the big argument over time, it's far less important what the newspapers are saying day to day. I think the press will see much less of me from now on, which will be good for them and good for me. My role will change and will focus far more on strategic matters and far less on the day to day.'

The turnout in Sedgefield was 62 per cent, which was far higher than in many of Labour's safe seats but still down by 10 per cent on 1997, and Blair's majority was reduced from 25,143 to 17,713. He said the results coming in from across the country were showing that Labour were on the verge of accomplishing the extraordinary achievement of 'a second successful full term in office'. He acknowledged the mood in the country was 'more sober and more reasoned' than four years ago and that his government needed to show 'absolute humility' when referring to the amount that need to be done to meet their objective of reforming the public services. 'The message from the British people is clear. They agree with the direction we are taking this country but they want us to get on with that journey. It's a challenge I relish.'

The Conservatives' failure to retake Torbay was followed by their loss to the Liberal Democrats of Dorset Mid and Poole North by 384 votes and then of Cheadle by a mere thirty three votes. A chastened Michael Portillo, widely acknowledged to be the leading contender in a future leadership election, appealed for a calm and measured response. He was re-elected by a comfortable margin of 8,771 votes in Kensington and Chelsea and paid tribute to the campaign led 'so successfully' by William

Hague; but he accepted the party had to face up to another disappointing setback. 'I hope no one says anything in the coming days and weeks which we might regret later.' There was some encouraging news for Hague, who was still waiting for his count to finish in Richmond: Andrew Rosindell regained Romford in Essex on a 9.2 per cent swing from Labour to the Conservatives, and Angela Watkinson took back Upminister on a slightly smaller swing of 5.2 per cent; but there were no gains across the Thames estuary in Kent, despite the Conservatives' high-profile campaign calling for new controls on asylum seekers. Peter Duncan re-established a Conservative presence in Scotland by taking Galloway and Upper Nithsdale from the Scottish National Party, but in southern England and the south-west the Liberal Democrats continued their advance into Tory territory, capturing both Guildford and Teignbridge.

Just before 3 a.m. the live programmes reported that Hague would have to concede defeat: Labour had passed the target of 330 seats, the minimum necessary to form the next government, and Blair was on course for a massive victory with a majority bigger than any party had ever achieved for a second term. At his count in Devizes, Michael Ancram, who was re-elected with a majority of nearly 11,896, was swift with his praise for the leadership the Conservatives had been given. Hague had remained true to his beliefs and values. 'He led us in this campaign in the mainstream of the British nation which has always been our base.' Blair had faced a 4.7 per cent swing to the Conservatives in Sedgefield, but it was 8 per cent across the constituency boundary in Richmond, where Hague increased his majority from 10,051 in 1997 to 16,319. Being returned for the fourth time as Richmond's MP meant a great deal to himself and Ffion, he said, but his immediate concern was for Conservative candidates, activists and supporters who had worked so hard around the country for so little reward. He had already congratu-lated Blair on his victory and he believed the country should respect the wish of the voters and listen to what they had said, although it was 'a sobering lesson for all political parties' that millions had been reluctant or had refused to participate.' There was much for the Conservatives to reflect on. 'We, the opposition, have been elected to do a job: to hold Labour to account for the promises they have made and the trust placed in them. We in our party must renew, redouble and intensify our efforts to provide an alternative government for the country in the future.' He intended to make a statement about his own and his party's future later that morning.

Once the Richmond result was declared, one of the party's leading pro-Europeans, Ian Taylor, who was himself re-elected in Esher and Walton, felt free to express his criticism of the Tories' election tactics. 'Hague fought a brilliant, gutsy campaign but the strategy was wrong. It was clear this wasn't a referendum on the pound and I think the sceptics will regret that. Hague must realise that if we are going to regain power we must be careful about addressing public services. We talked about tax cuts which ruled us out.'

Praise for the leader is *de rigueur* on election night, especially among Liberal Democrats, who battled on for so many years against all the odds. Their dream for 2001 was to build on Paddy Ashdown's sensational success in 1997, when they more than doubled their number of seats and achieved the best result of any third party since 1929. By the time the votes had been collected from around Charles Kennedy's constituency in the Highlands and Islands and counted at the Dingwall Leisure Centre, he was well aware of the advances which the Liberal Democrats had made in traditional Conservative heartlands like Surrey, Dorset and Devon. Speaking after the discovery that he had increased his own majority in Ross, Skye and Inverness West from 4,019 to 12,952, he said he believed that the Liberal Democrats' success in winning extra seats and increasing their share of the vote in city after city was a verdict on the future direction of British politics. The country wanted 'a relevant and responsible' opposition in the next Parliament, and that was what Liberal Democrats would seek to deliver. 'It's an historic night for the Prime Minister, getting his second consecutive term, and it's a doubly historic night for us, because we have built on our amazing breakthrough of four years ago and we are very much the party of the future of British politics.' Lord McNally, one the party's home affairs spokesmen, told *Vote 2001* that Kennedy had been the star of the election. 'He joined battle with Labour on the public services and it was the Liberal Democrats who resonated with the public.'

Labour's vulnerability on schools and hospitals was underlined by the spectacular success of Dr Richard Taylor, who pulled off the most sensational personal victory of the night to romp home with a majority of 17,630 in the Worcestershire constituency of Wyre Forest. Dr Taylor, who stood as the Kidderminster Hospital Health Concern candidate, proved that it was possible to connect with the public on a single issue and demonstrated the kind of damage which the Conservatives might have been able to inflict if they had chosen to mount an effective campaign against the government's record on the National Health Service. David Lock, who was defending the seat for Labour, was a junior minister in the Lord Chancellor's department, but his majority of nearly 7,000, which he gained in 1997 on taking Wyre Forest from the Conservatives, had begun to look decidedly shaky when Dr Taylor began his campaign against the downgrading of Kidderminster Hospital, and the sitting MP's fate was sealed when Health Concern campaigners were given a clear run by the Liberal Democrats, who decided not to field a candidate. After the declaration of his result, Dr Taylor, a retired consultant physician, assured the voters of Wyre Forest that he still had plenty of energy to pursue his campaign at Westminster against cuts in the health service. 'This is a tremendous reaction from the people against a very powerful government, against a very powerful political system that overrides the will of the people.' He was only the second Independent to win a seat in

Parliament in almost sixty years, and the precarious existence of single-issue campaigners was reinforced by the defeat of Martin Bell, who must have rued the day he promised the electors of Tatton that he would represent them for only one term.

Bell had been invited by a group of disaffected Conservatives to fight the Essex seat of Brentwood and Ongar, but finished in second place behind the sitting Conservative MP, Eric Pickles – albeit reducing the latter's 1997 majority of 9,690 to 2,821. Bell had been attracted to Brentwood and Ongar because of unease about the alleged infiltration of the local Conservative association by a fundamental Christian group. Some newspaper columnists suggested he should have stood on an anti-sleaze platform against either Keith Vaz or Geoffrey Robinson, the two Labour MPs whose financial affairs were the subject of continuing scrutiny by the House of Commons Select Committee on Standards and Privileges. Both were comfortably re-elected. Vaz, the minister for Europe, held Leicester East with a majority of 13,442, down by just under 5,000; the turnout of 62.1 per cent was the highest in the three Leicester constituencies. In thanking his supporters at the count, he said he was pleased that the total number of votes he received and his share of the vote were higher than those achieved by the city's two other Labour MPs. Robinson, the former Paymaster-General, was returned by an equally respectable margin in Coventry North West, holding his seat with a majority of 10,874, down by just under 6,000 votes on his 1997 result. In Coventry North East Dave Nellist secured 2,638 votes for the Socialist Alliance, taking fourth place in a field of five but saving his deposit. Katie Price, the glamour model Jordan, failed to attract many admirers in the Greater Manchester constituency of Stretford and Urmston where she finished last with 713 votes.

The count which proved to be the most unsettling for the established political parties was on the other side of Greater Manchester at Oldham, where the returning officer, Andrew Kilburn, banned all candidates from making speeches in the civic centre, fearing they might incite racial conflict. Tension had remained high since the rioting on the night of Saturday 26 May when Asian youths fought pitched battles with the police in the Glodwick area after reports that a gang of white men had attacked Asian properties. Discontent within the white community had been seized on by the British National Party, which fielded candidates in Oldham's two constituencies and in other seats in Lancashire and Yorkshire where racial strains were evident. Nick Griffin, the BNP chairman, who stood in Oldham West and Royton, secured 6,552 votes and took third place ahead of the Liberal Democrats. His 16.4 per cent share of the vote was the BNP's best showing in a parliamentary election. His colleague Mick Treacy, who stood in Oldham East and Saddleworth, polled 5,091 votes, an 11.2 per cent share. As each result was declared, Griffin and Treacy stood in the line-up of candidates with gags across their mouths and wearing T-shirts emblazoned with the words 'Gagged for telling the truth'.

In addition to their unexpected loss of Wyre Forest, Labour suffered another embarrassing defeat in Chesterfield, which had been represented for the previous seventeen years by the veteran Labour MP Tony Benn, who was not seeking re-election following his retirement from the House of Commons. Labour's candidate was Reg Race, a former official of the National Union of Public Employees who had been MP for Wood Green in the London borough of Haringey from 1979 to 1983 and who was subsequently employed by the Greater London Council during the leadership of Ken Livingstone. Race was defeated by the Liberal Democrat candidate Paul Holmes, who overturned a Labour majority of 5,775 to take the seat by 2,586 votes. When asked for his reaction on *Vote 2001*, Benn said the result was a great disappointment. 'Chesterfield is a solid Labour seat, not New Labour . . . I joined the Labour Party not New Labour. It's Arthur Scargill and Tony Blair who both stood up their own party.'

Benn's reaction angered Labour's parliamentary press officer Don

Brind, who was on duty at Millbank Tower. He told me the former MP had been partly to blame for the defeat. 'He really lost us that seat. He hollowed out the local party and it just ossified under him. He was a hopeless constituency MP.' Brind was no stranger to the internal warfare of the Labour Party. I knew him in the 1980s when he was a reporter on *Labour Weekly*, and during the early 1990s, after he joined the BBC as a news producer, I worked alongside him when reporting the party's struggle to expel members of the Militant Tendency. Brind thought Blair's second landslide was far more catastrophic for the Conservatives than Michael Foot's defeat at the hands of Margaret Thatcher in 1983 was for Labour, because the Tories lacked the resources for a fightback. He described the gulf which had opened up in the finances of the two parties to highlight the point he was making: Labour had an income of £42 million in the two-year period 1998–9, double the amount received by the Conservatives. 'We invested in party organisation and in our key seats and it's obvious when you look at the results that the Conservatives don't have anything like the party machine they once had. Their great difficulty now is that they have got no one to turn to.'

I could not fault Brind's assessment. If it had not been for the money and encouragement of the trade unions, Labour might have found it harder to recover after Thatcher's landslide in 1983. Clive Jenkins, leader of the ASTMS union, told me at the time how he moved swiftly during the weekend following Foot's defeat to organise Neil Kinnock's campaign for the party leadership which he won in a ballot in October 1983. I was reminded again of Labour's long years in opposition when David Hill returned to the media enclosure in Millbank Tower to inform us that party workers had finally started their celebrations. Journalists were still being refused admission but he wanted us to know there was 'a great atmosphere' downstairs. Reporters and television crews would be allowed to stand in a pen by the main entrance so they could record the arrival of Blair and his cabinet colleagues. 'It always takes time for Labour to start celebrating. I have been at party headquarters for every election since 1974 and we have lost too many to be too euphoric too quickly . . . Yes, I think you could say we are loosening up a bit but we certainly aren't being triumphalist.' Hill was choosing his words with care because Labour was still searching for ways to reconcile its historic achievement with the depressing news that four out of every ten voters had stayed at home. Lord Falconer, minister of state at the Cabinet Office, toured the interview positions ready to offer Labour's latest explanation. 'When one political party abandons the argument and won't get engaged in discussing the issues which the electorate are interested in, of course you get a smaller turnout. We can't be blamed for that . . . No, we are not ignoring the 40 per cent of the electorate who didn't vote.'

Robin Cook, the Foreign Secretary, was the first cabinet minister to be sent to the media enclosure. I travelled up with him in the lift and I felt he looked edgy and ill at ease. Cook told the BBC World Service he thought the main reason for the low turnout was that so many people had regarded Labour's victory as a foregone conclusion. 'It's going to be very important if we are going to convince people who didn't vote this time, that we do carry out our mandate and that we do deliver better public services.' Cook and Gordon Brown had reached the front entrance to Millbank Tower within ten minutes of each other, and party workers had been encouraged to leave the privacy of their celebration and line up outside ready to cheer them in for the benefit of the cameras. John Prescott's coach was the next to arrive. He stood on the steps with his wife Pauline, waving to the photographers amid whoops of delight from the party activists who were filling up the concourse. A small stage had been erected at the rear of the building and we were told that was where Tony Blair would deliver a short speech to round off the proceedings. The slogan across the top had a familiar ring: 'The work goes on.'

It was clearly going to be a small, well-controlled affair, with none of the razzmatazz which had accompanied Blair's address at the 1997 victory party across the river at the Royal Festival Hall. At that event I was struck by the large number of young people, mostly in their early twenties, who crowded round the enormous brightly lit set from which he spoke. Labour's theme song for that election, 'Things can only get better', blared out from loudspeakers and the atmosphere was more like a pop festival than a political rally. Once Blair started his speech every sentence was punctuated by cheers and applause. The scene on the concourse of Millbank Tower now was much more restrained. There seemed to be far more young men than women, and they looked to be in their early thirties rather than their twenties. Most seemed to be dressed in suits rather than casual clothes and quite a few were busy talking enthusiastically on mobile phones. Free copies of the *Sun* were being handed to the revellers from an open-decked bus promoting the paper's three 'cleavage girls' who were wearing revealing blue, red and yellow outfits. I looked at my copy of the 4 a.m. election special. The front page was filled with a photograph of Blair being hugged by his father Leo. Below it was the headline: 'It's my son wot won it.'

My next assignment was looming already: I was to be the early reporter in Downing Street, and I had to be there no later than 5.30 a.m. ready for the Prime Minister's return to Downing Street after his speech to party workers. Word went round that Blair's car was about twenty minutes away and more of the revellers began to spill out on to the concourse. They all seemed to be drinking small bottles of champagne through straws and had been issued with 'Vote Labour' flags. As I set off for Parliament Square, I turned to take one last look at the stage erected by the car park. The sun was just rising above Lambeth Palace on the other side of the river, but the first rays did not reach the rear of Millbank Tower, which still looked dark and uninviting. When dawn broke over the Royal Festival Hall four years ago it felt rather special. The event that I was about to miss did not look like being a repeat of that unforgettable moment in the history of New Labour.

Friday 8 June

My rush to get back to Downing Street was hardly worth it. On completing his speech to party workers at Millbank Tower, Tony Blair made a swift return to No. 10 at 5.57 a.m. Downing Street was almost empty except for the television crews and photographers lined up on the other side of the road. He posed with Cherie for a few moments outside the front door and then turned to go inside. His body language implied it was going to be business as usual, and I thought the look on his face was saying a silent 'I told you so.' Blair had achieved what had always eluded previous Labour Prime Ministers: the chance to complete a second, full successive term in office. We were told he wanted to get some sleep before his appointment with the Queen at 11 a.m.

I managed to see most of the speech he gave at Millbank Tower on our television monitor in Downing Street. He thanked party workers for their 'wonderful work' and paid special tribute to Margaret McDonagh, Neil Kinnock, John Prescott and his 'brilliant' Chancellor, Gordon Brown, who had co-ordinated the election campaign and laid the foundations for the economic stability which would allow the government to implement their mandate to invest in schools, hospitals and transport. At long last Labour had the chance to offer the country a different political choice. 'For a hundred years we've been in office for short periods of time but never won a full second term of office. Now we have.'

News bulletins at 6 a.m. were my chance to get the latest round-up of the results. With fewer than thirty seats still to declare, Labour had taken 413, gaining four and losing ten; the Conservatives were on 164, having gained ten and lost seven; and the Liberal Democrats had gained seven, giving them forty-seven seats, although they were forecast to win another half-dozen. The average turnout was 59.4 per cent, only a fraction ahead of the 58.9 per cent recorded in 1918. Because a hundred MPs were unopposed in 1918, some political analysts considered 2001 had shown the lowest level of participation since the 1885 general election, which was the first time most adult males got the vote. Some constituencies in the big industrial conurbations of the north struggled to keep above the 40 per cent mark, and two seats slipped even lower: in Manchester Central only 39.1 per cent had voted, and the figure dropped to 34.1 per cent in Liverpool Riverside.

After reporting on Blair's arrival I headed back to BBC Westminster via Smith Square, missing by a few minutes William Hague's arrival at Central Office just before 7 a.m. A crowd of party workers had cheered him into the building and among those ready to welcome the party leader and his wife were Michael Ancram and Amanda Platell. Hague's announcement at the Richmond count in Northallerton that he intended to make a statement about his future had provoked considerable comment on the live programmes, but there was no consensus as to what he might do. Some commentators were convinced he would resign immediately rather than be forced to carry out a humiliating policy review knowing there would almost certainly be a challenge to his leadership, but other pundits pointed to the pressure there would be from senior figures in the shadow cabinet who feared that if Hague departed as rapidly as John Major had after the 1992 defeat, the party would be left rudderless during its worst crisis in the lifetime of most Conservative politicians.

The word from Central Office was that he would make his statement at about 7.30 a.m., and as I had half an hour to spare before returning to Downing Street I went back to Smith Square. There was a buzz of excitement in the media pack outside the Conservative headquarters: there had been some sort of meeting inside and Hague had been urged to carry on as leader. Apparently he had made up his mind and was about to announce his decision. On my way there I had seen two members of the shadow cabinet, Andrew Mackay and Iain Duncan Smith, hurrying away. Charlotte Kenyon, one of the party's broadcasting officers, was waiting round the corner, talking on her mobile phone, and she gave me the impression she was rather hesitant about choosing that moment to force her way into Central Office through the television crews and photographers.

By the time Hague eventually emerged at 7.50 a.m. I was back in Downing Street; so I was not present to hear him announce he was standing down. Reporters at the scene said he had seven handwritten pages in front of him and he went through his statement point by point, appealing to his party to recognise that the 'people have spoken' and to understand the lessons of the result. He said the Conservatives would start from a stronger base in the new Parliament than the last, and that the 'forces of Conservatism' were stronger and better organised than four years ago. 'Despite that stronger base and the diminishing enthusiasm for New Labour, we have not been able to persuade a majority, or anything approaching a majority, that we are yet the alternative government that they need. Nor have I been able to persuade sufficient numbers that I am their alternative Prime Minister.' He believed the result of the next general election would be much closer, and the Conservatives had an overriding duty not only to be effective in Parliament and rigorous in campaigning, but also to present a leadership with the strongest possible credibility and appeal. In achieving that objective 'no man or woman is indispensable and no individual is more important than the party.' He had led the Conservatives for four years and considered it a great privilege; he had 'actually enjoyed every single day' and believed 'strongly, passionately' in everything he had fought for. 'It's also vital for leaders to listen and parties to change. I believe it is vital the party be given the chance to choose a leader who can build on my work, but also take new initiatives and hopefully command a larger personal following in the country. I've therefore decided to step down as leader of the Conservative Party when a successor can be elected. I will continue until that time to carry out the parliamentary and other duties of the leader of the opposition.'

Hague said some of his colleagues had urged him to stay on for a period so that the party could reflect at greater length, but he believed a new leader had to be elected in time for the party conference in October. Selecting a successor would take some weeks because under new leadership election rules the process could not start until the House of Commons reassembled later that month and a new chairman had been elected for the 1922 committee, which represented Conservative MPs. After explaining the procedure to be followed, he paused for a moment, smiled and then pressed on with his conclusion, reaching out at one point to his wife: 'I'd like to express my heartfelt thanks for the untiring efforts of my colleagues across the party who made it possible to fight a coherent, vigorous and united, albeit unsuccessful, campaign. I'd like to express similar thanks to my staff . . . and to Ffion, without whom I would not have had the strength to carry the last four years, and above all to the many millions who voted Conservative yesterday. I wish I could have led you to victory, but now we must all work for our victories in the future.'

Hague's resignation was the top headline in the news bulletins at 8 a.m. and the way he terminated his leadership of the party so quickly and so decisively dominated discussion on the live programmes, taking precedence for a time over Blair's historic achievement. The sudden finality of his announcement, aborting a political career at the age of forty, caught many a friend and foe by surprise. Politics had been Hague's abiding interest since he was at school, and from the moment he addressed the Conservatives' annual conference at the age of sixteen he seemed destined for high office. His confidence and flair as a parliamentary debater meant Tony Blair could take no risks at the dispatch box, and he regularly had the better of their exchanges at question time. The internal restructuring of the party owed much to Hague's drive and energy, and the increased strength of the Conservatives in local authorities and the European Parliament provided tangible evidence that he was building the momentum for a sustained recovery. Seats which had just been lost in the general election were compensated for by other gains elsewhere, and although most newspapers, Labour and the Liberal Democrats had predicted with great glee that the Conservatives would fall apart once the election began, Hague had held the party together and marshalled a campaign which helped galvanise the constituencies and offered support to their candidates.

Despite his failure to achieve the breakthrough he had so dearly wanted, there were some strong arguments in favour of his continuing as leader. He could have offered another root-and-branch policy review and promised to redouble his efforts to assist the party to regroup and rebuild in preparation for the next general election in four or five years' time. Neil Kinnock, who was interviewed on *Today* within a few minutes of the announcement, was astonished to hear that Hague was quitting after only four years as party leader. 'I am speechless at the choice he has made. The gutsy thing to do would be to carry on and put everything into it. He is a young, fit man of obvious ability and I'm amazed that he didn't have the resolution, the fortitude – not the selfishness – to say, "I'm going to put everything I've got into it. If I have to go down fighting, I'll go down fighting, I'd rather do that, I'd rather die in the line of duty than take any other action."' Kinnock was speaking from the heart. His eight and a half years leading Labour had ended just as unhappily, but while he held office he dragged his party out of the pit of despair and took it a considerable way on the long, slow road back to government. After his first election defeat he pushed on, taking Labour's share of the vote from the 30.8 per cent he achieved in 1987 to 34.4 per cent in 1992, ready for Blair to make the final advance and win power in 1997 with 43.2 per cent of the vote. The Conservatives had taken the first, tentative step back to power under Hague, increasing their share of the vote from the 30.7 per cent they had achieved in 1997 to 31.7 per cent; when set alongside their advances in elections to local government and the European Parliament, it was a foundation on which to build. Kinnock was sure Hague had been totally sincere in reaching his decision, and he understood the pain of defeat, although his own resignation in 1992 was executed with none of Hague's cool precision and stark self-assessment. Kinnock gave the first hint of his imminent departure at his count in Islwyn when he promised to serve the British people in 'any capacity whatsoever'. A few hours later, at Labour headquarters, he spoke of his 'dismay and sorrow' that so many people did not share his own 'good fortune' in his personal life and then, late that evening, he finally faced up to the inescapable conclusion that it was all over and issued a statement saying he was consulting colleagues about the future leadership of the party.

But Kinnock had been blessed with more than personal 'good fortune' when he soldiered on as Labour leader. His party was hungry for office throughout the late 1980s and early 1990s, ready to set aside political and personal differences in the pursuit of power. Dumbfounded by Hague's decision, perhaps Kinnock did not comprehend the full strength of the forces which had been tearing the Conservative Party asunder for so long. Amid the shocked and disappointed voices of the newly re-elected Conservative MPs who were having to brace themselves for a divisive leadership contest, there were many expressions of regret, but few seemed to share Kinnock's perspective on the brutal end to such a brief political career. Alan Duncan, who had been Hague's campaign manager when he won the Conservatives' 1997 leadership contest, told *Radio Five Live* that he got a sense of what was about to happen immediately after the declaration of the Richmond result. 'Hague told me as soon as he got off the plane this morning that he had decided to stand down . . . This guy rebuilt the Conservative Party and I never once saw him snap in the path of the meteorite storms which hit him . . . I think people will look back on William and say that was a man of considerable calibre who held his party together at a critical time after the 1997 defeat.'

Stuart Wheeler, the betting tycoon and founder of IG Index who donated £5 million towards the Conservatives' election campaign, told *Today* he was convinced that if Hague had stayed he could have become Prime Minister in four or five years' time, but he 'failed to make the public believe it'. Wheeler insisted he had no regrets about helping to fund the Conservatives. 'I was very glad to do it. The party had the right leader and it would have been ghastly to have allowed them to fight the campaign with their hands tied behind their backs.' Steve Norris said he was staggered by the news. 'There is no blame attaching to William . . . He leaves with his head extremely high but we must accept his departure as a challenge. We must make this party more attractive. We are the ones who are out of touch and we must reconnect.'

Other prominent figures who had been silent during the campaign felt the rapid departure of their defeated leader allowed them the freedom at last to speak their mind; the forces which Hague feared would be unleashed were about to find expression. Michael Heseltine, who had stood down from the House of Commons and was made a life peer in the pre-election honours list, had his eye firmly on the looming leadership contest when he gave his critical assessment of the direction in which Hague had taken the party. In his first post-election interview, he told *Vote 2001* that the Conservatives had painted themselves into an extremist position by talking about tax cuts, asylum seekers and law and order. 'It all added up to an image of a right-wing xenophobic party talking to itself in an introspective way.' He accused the Euro-sceptics in the party of having undermined both Major and Hague. 'The Europhiles gave the leadership a clear run. What they did in return was leave Ken Clarke holed up in Rushcliffe. That can't go on. It's impossible to think Ken isn't in the shadow cabinet.' He thought the only way the party could unite was by allowing Conservative MPs to fight on either side of the argument over Europe, and pledged his support for Clarke in a forthcoming leadership election because the former Conservative Chancellor was 'the only person with the commanding stature to appeal to the country at large'. Heseltine used an interview on The *World At One* to set out what he believed was the biggest challenge to a new leader. The Conservatives had to match the aspirations of a new society which was different from the one they normally related to. It was no use looking to 'an elderly diminishing minority', thinking they held the key to No. 10, when that took no account of the growth in a multicultural society, increasing demands for gay rights and the reality of changing family relationships. Heseltine was beginning to sound rather exasperated by the time he was interviewed on *Radio Five Live*: 'Is the Conservative Party leadable? That is the question. Can anyone command the sense of unity we need?'

Chris Patten, one of Britain's European Commissioners and a former Conservative chairman, accused Hague of subcontracting Tory party policy to the *Daily Telegraph* and *Daily Mail* and of adopting a position on the euro which had not proved popular with the electorate. 'What we found great difficulty in doing was distinguishing between a bandwagon and a hearse.' Newly returned pro-European MPs added their voice to the demand for a fundamental policy rethink, expressing hopes that a leadership contest would allow the party to make a fresh start. Stephen Dorrell believed it was a strategic error to have mounted a campaign which was no more than a rerun of what the party had offered in 1997 and Ian Taylor feared that instead of just being 'marooned on the edges of the national debate' the Conservatives could end up drifting even further away from mainstream politics, in which case the Liberal Democrats would love to take their place.

Heseltine's pre-emptive strike in promoting Clarke as the pro-Europeans' choice for leader put pressure on other potential candidates to declare their positions. Ann Widdecombe told journalists she had no intention of speculating about the succession, and there was no word from any of the other possible contenders. None the less, Michael Portillo was already installed as the bookies' favourite, and the two other most likely runners were the shadow defence spokesman, Iain Duncan Smith, and David Davis, chairman of the House of Commons Public Accounts Committee. Clarke himself, while grateful for the pro-Europeans' support, demanded more time to reflect and declined to be drawn into discussing either his own plans or the future direction of the party. 'I am not going to join in the weekend's analysis. I'll spend my weekend deliberating on the last few years.' Many in the party hierarchy also kept their counsel, and of those who had campaigned so strongly in support of the Keep the Pound campaign, only Lady Thatcher struck a defiant note in her tribute to Hague for having worked tirelessly from start to finish. 'My friends, make no mistake. The Conservative Party will be back.'

As I stood in Downing Street listening on the radio to the torment and turmoil which was engulfing Labour's opponents, I found it difficult to focus on what lay ahead for the Prime Minister, who we knew was planning to start an extensive Cabinet reshuffle. A flurry of activity signalled Tony Blair's imminent departure for his 11 a.m. audience with the Queen, at which she would go through the constitutional formality of requesting him to form a government. In 1997 his drive to Buckingham Palace from his home in Islington was part of a punctiliously choreographed celebration which reached its climax when a newly anointed Prime Minister arrived at Downing Street to be greeted by a 'spontaneous outpouring' of congratulation from flag-waving supporters and party workers. Reporters who were outside the Palace this time said Blair's second post-election audience lasted for thirty-five minutes and they formed the impression it had been a low-key event. Back in Downing Street, the No. 10 staff were lining up ready for his return. I picked out Anji Hunter, the Prime Minister's special assistant; the Downing Street chief press officer, Anne Shevas; and another press officer, Hilary Coffman, who was also a special adviser and had spent the election organising Blair's campaign visits. Someone at the back of the group was holding Leo. Blair and his wife stopped to acknowledge the cheers of tourists at the gates to

Downing Street and then they started to walk up to No. 10, shaking hands with their staff and others who were crowding around.

Blair's remarks were far more measured than his first victory speech as Prime Minister. He began by commending his opponent. Even though he 'profoundly disagreed' with much of what the Conservatives said during the campaign, he thought Hague had shown 'extraordinary stoicism and resilience in very difficult circumstances'. Blair was in no doubt as to what Labour's 'remarkable and historic victory' meant for the country, and he gave a sombre assessment of the responsibilities which his government had to shoulder. 'It is a mandate for reform and investment in the future and it is also very clearly an instruction to deliver. I've learnt many things over the past four years as Prime Minister. I've learnt, I hope, from the mistakes as well as the good things, but above all else I've learnt of the importance of establishing the clear priorities of government, of setting them out clearly for people, and then focusing on them relentlessly whatever events may come and go. I believe there is an even greater obligation on us after re-election to tell people very clearly what are the choices and challenges we face and how we work our way through them.' He ran down a checklist of the tasks which faced his government: maintaining economic stability; keeping mortgages and inflation as low possible; investing in health, education and transport; reforming the welfare system; and remaining engaged with Europe and the wider world. 'I believe in the last four years we have laid foundations. I believe our victory in this election shows the British people understand that we have laid foundations, but now is the time to build on them.'

Blair then turned from the microphone and walked towards the No. 10 front door to join his wife and children. He was handed Leo; he kissed him on the cheek, and then held him up in his arms. Flanked by Cherie, his sons Euan and Nicky and daughter Kathryn, he posed with all of them for another historic family photograph. We were told the Cabinet reshuffle would begin after lunch.

John Prescott was the first to arrive and shouted back cheerfully to reporters when asked if he was happy about his new job. 'Of course I'm pleased. It's been a good two days.' Prescott had been widely tipped to take charge of an enlarged Cabinet Office following the disappearance of his previous post heading up the sprawling Department of the Environment, Transport and the Regions, which was to be split in half as part of a much-trailed shake-up in Whitehall. Jack Straw, the Home Secretary, came and went; there was speculation that he was going to be the lead minister in a strengthened environment department. There was no doubt about the intended new posting for David Blunkett, the Secretary of State for Education and Employment: his promotion to Home Secretary seemed a mere formality, and indeed the Home Office confirmed before the election that there had been some internal alterations to accommodate Blunkett and his guide dog. So confident was Blunkett about his new posting that he stopped off on his way to see Blair to be interviewed by the *Jimmy Young Programme*. The arrival of Estelle Morris, the minister for school standards, confirmed another widely expected promotion. She had been singled out in the newspapers as Blunkett's successor. The minister who had the longest meeting with Blair was the Foreign Secretary, Robin Cook He was still there when I set off for BBC Westminster, although he was seen later returning to the Foreign Office.

My final task after my lengthy stint covering election night and the aftermath was to prepare a series of radio reports for the early evening news bulletins. I had been anxious to hear the final tally, following the completion of the remaining counts. Labour had 413 seats, a net loss of six, and an overall majority of 167; the Conservatives had finished on 166 seats, having gained one extra seat following their success in retaking the Isle of Wight; the Liberal Democrats had increased their overall strength by six and ended up with fifty-two seats; the Scottish National Party had five seats; and Plaid Cymru four. Labour's share of the vote had dropped slightly to 40.7 per cent; the Conservatives were up marginally on 31.7 per cent; and the Liberal Democrats fared best of all, pushing up their share from 16.8 per cent in 1997 to 18.3 per cent. Results from thirty-four county council elections in England provided further evidence of the Conservatives' resurgence in local government. They retained control of eleven shire authorities and took power in another six: Cheshire, Dorset, East Sussex, Essex, Leicestershire and Norfolk.

Of the three main parties, only the Liberal Democrats were in a mood to celebrate, and Charles Kennedy was greeted with champagne toasts when he arrived at a reception at his party headquarters. Wider acceptance of tactical voting had produced spectacular results, and gains like Guildford, Norfolk North, Ludlow, Chesterfield and Cheadle meant that for the first time the Liberal Democrats had seats in every region of the country. After the best results for a Liberal party since 1923, Kennedy was confident he could exploit the Conservatives' disarray and become the de facto opposition. 'The public have made their view clear on that in the vote of confidence they have given us. We must not let them down. Having fought a campaign rooted in honesty, being straightforward with people, and in putting fairly funded, quality public services at the centre of our appeal, we must make sure that message is taken to the floor of the House of Commons.'

When details of the Cabinet reshuffle were finally released late in the evening, the reason for the delay was explained: Robin Cook had been holding out against being moved from the Foreign Office. Instead of going to environment as the newspapers had suggested, Jack Straw was appointed Foreign Secretary, and Cook became Leader of the House. Cook moved quickly to deny suggestions that he was disappointed at being moved from the Foreign Office, telling the *Ten O'Clock News* he was 'delighted' when the Prime Minister asked him to 'come back home to Parliament' and become Leader of the House: 'I look forward to playing a central role in overseeing the passage of a big programme of domestic legislation.' Three other top jobs were filled as predicted: John Prescott was to head the Cabinet Office and would have the title Deputy Prime Minister and First Secretary of State. David Blunkett's appointment as Home Secretary was confirmed, and he was replaced by Estelle Morris, who took the new title of Secretary of State for Education and Skills. The government shake-up which had been promised by Blair resulted in the reallocation of responsibilities across a total of ten Whitehall departments, and several cabinet ministers had entirely new briefs. Margaret Beckett was appointed Secretary of State for Environment, Food and Rural Affairs; Stephen Byers was made Secretary of State at the new Department of Transport, Local Government and the Regions; Alistair Darling retained control over social security but was given the new title of Secretary of State for Work and Pensions, as his department had taken on some responsibilities from the Department of Education and Employment; Patricia Hewitt was made the new Secretary of State for Trade and Industry; Tessa Jowell was appointed Secretary of State for Culture, Media and Sport; and Hilary Armstrong, who replaced Ann Taylor as Chief Whip, became the seventh of a record-breaking number of women in the Cabinet. Another newcomer was Charles Clarke, who was appointed Labour Party chairman and given cabinet ranking as minister without portfolio.

The list of appointments was rounded off by Alastair Campbell's promotion to Downing Street's director of communications and strategy. His responsibility for briefing lobby correspondents was to be shared between his deputy Godric Smith and Tom Kelly, hitherto director of communications for the Northern Ireland Office. They would divide up the task of representing the government and answering journalists' questions. Campbell would have overall control of the government's media strategy and consider how ministers' objectives could best be communicated to the public. When Smith described the new structure of the Downing Street press office he said Campbell would no longer brief the media but would still 'talk to the press from time to time'. Removing Campbell from constant conflict with reporters had been Blair's aim for well over a year, and by asking two civil servants to be responsible for holding the twice-daily lobby briefings rather than giving the task to another political appointee he hoped to stem the damaging publicity which his official spokesman had attracted and which on occasion had undermined his own authority and credibility as Prime Minister.

Saturday 9 June

One post-reshuffle initiation ceremony which ministers usually relish is a photo-opportunity at their new department. Some prefer to be photographed in formal surroundings, sitting behind a desk or at a table in the minister's suite of offices. David Blunkett was happy to take on all-comers at a photo-call outside the Home Office. He had a ready line in repartee and cracked jokes with the photographers and television crews: 'One of the things I was going to do was hold a truncheon, but I was advised this wasn't a good idea.' His priority as Home Secretary, he said, apart from listening and learning, would be to tackle violent crime and crack down on criminals who trafficked in drugs, people and weaponry. The new Secretary of State for Education and Skills, Estelle Morris, herself a former teacher, promised to support the profession, but there were limits on the co-operation she could offer. She wanted a partnership with teachers but the bottom line was that Britain had to do better in terms of education. Margaret Beckett, the first Secretary of State for Environment, Food and Rural Affairs, inherited the continuing task of controlling the foot and mouth outbreak which had been taken on by her new department following the disbanding of the old Ministry of Agriculture, Fisheries and Food. She promised to do what she could to revive farming and reform the agricultural policies of the European

Union. Farmers were feeling 'very bruised and unhappy' and deserved a fresh start. 'We need to try and create a new stroke of confidence . . . a new and better future for the countryside. If we all work together we can certainly achieve it.' When Tessa Jowell, the new Secretary of State for Culture, Media and Sport, welcomed television crews to her department she said she wanted to remember her first day as a cabinet minister for the rest of her life. She had taken on several responsibilities from the Home Office, including licensing, gambling, censorship and horseracing, and was in no doubt about her objective. 'My goal is to ensure that everyone, at every stage of their life, gets the chances to enjoy the best of what our rich culture and heritage have to offer.'

Jack Straw, the new Foreign Secretary, was the one cabinet minister who could not afford to come across sounding too upbeat, for fear of exacerbating the injured feelings of Robin Cook, who – for all his protestations the previous day – was not happy at having been removed from the Foreign Office. The morning newspapers were unanimous in their assessment: he had been axed because he was more expendable than Straw. 'Cook is goosed' was the *Mirror*'s headline over a report which claimed Straw pushed for the Foreign Secretary's job and Blair 'caved in and shunted' Cook to the House of Commons. Tony Lloyd, a former minister of state at the Foreign Office, told *Today* that Cook was 'a diplomats' Foreign Secretary' and loved his job. 'Being the politician he is, he is no doubt feeling slightly bruised, thinking slightly, "Why me? Why now? I could have soldiered on." But he'll wake up on Monday morning and say there is a job to be done.' Some newspapers made much of the fact that the reshuffled Cabinet contained a record number of seven women. The *Independent* said appointing the most 'female-friendly' government in history should silence those who had criticised Blair in his first Parliament for confining Labour's women MPs to the sidelines, and the *Guardian* noted that several of them had high-profile jobs in big spending departments.

But the story which dominated the coverage was the prospect of another divisive Conservative leadership election. 'Portillo gains early momentum in race to succeed Hague' was the front-page headline in the *Financial Times*; but the *Sun* revealed that within hours of Hague's standing down the shadow Chancellor had left the country, flying to Morocco for a weekend break. In his column in *The Times*, Portillo's biographer Michael Gove claimed the favourite was wary of standing for the leadership. 'Will the man who temporised in 1995, and was robbed of the chance to run when he lost his seat in 1997, take his chance now? . . . This weekend, as he contemplates his future, he is deeply uncertain whether to trim his sails for battle.' Gove said Portillo had been wounded by the continual speculation in Tory ranks that 'his main motivation was to destabilise' Hague, and he was taken aback that the party's head of media, Amanda Platell, 'should brief against him'. Gove said Portillo had also underestimated the impact of his own decision, just before he returned to the Commons, to acknowledge homosexual experiences in his youth. 'After all he has been through, is another eight years in the arid plains of Opposition to be relished?' Ms Platell was pictured in some newspapers making 'a swift departure' from Central Office, but according to Andrew Pierce, writing in *The Times*, she intended to stay on until a new party leader was elected.

The *Financial Times* and *Daily Mail* both suggested Hague would be remembered as the first Tory leader not to become Prime Minister since Austen Chamberlain in the early 1920s. Michael Heseltine, who was interviewed by the *Daily Telegraph*, said the Euro-sceptics had brought the party to its knees; Lady Thatcher's intervention was the 'final nail in the coffin' for Hague and he had already written off the Conservatives chances of winning the next election. Chris Patten renewed his support for Ken Clarke in an interview in the *Independent*, suggesting it was 'a spectacular example of self-denial' to run a party which excluded the former Chancellor from any leadership role. In a letter to *The Times*,

Michael Latham, a former Conservative pro-European MP and a Clarke supporter, urged the party to return to 'compassionate, domestic Toryism' and start a total policy rethink. 'Thatcherism was necessary in the 1980s. Mrs Thatcher remains a superstar, but in a vanished galaxy. Unless the party rebuilds from scratch, I will not live to see another Tory government. I am 58.'

Sunday 10 June

Tony Blair spent the weekend at Chequers recovering from the election campaign and deciding how best to reshape the rest of his ministerial team. Sweeping changes were being predicted among the ministers of state and parliamentary secretaries, and a fair number of young MPs from the 1997 intake were hoping to get their first jobs in government. Keith Vaz, the Minister of Europe, was widely tipped for the sack, and speculation about his imminent political demise increased when Leicester Royal Infirmary confirmed that the Leicester East MP had been admitted for overnight observation on Saturday afternoon. He had an infection and would be undergoing tests. Vaz's continuing ill-health after his collapse during a television interview in March provided Blair with an opportunity to drop the embattled minister, who was facing a renewed investigation into his financial affairs by the Commissioner for Parliamentary Standards, Elizabeth Filkin.

Robin Cook's demotion from Foreign Secretary to Leader of the House provoked considerable comment in the Sunday papers. The most popular theory was that his strong support for British entry into the euro had caused tension within the Cabinet and that Jack Straw was seen as an ideal replacement because he was less enthusiastic about the single currency. But again, most attention focused on the likely line-up for the Conservatives' leadership contest; and the first shadow cabinet member to break cover and talk about her prospects was Ann Widdecombe. She told the *Sunday Telegraph* that she did not want her interview to be seen as a declaration of intent to stand for the leadership, but she was taking soundings and would then decide what to do. Miss Widdecombe said the failure of the Conservatives' campaign was not that they talked too much about Europe, crime and asylum seekers but that they did not talk enough about other issues like schools and hospitals. In an interview for *Breakfast with Frost*, she confirmed that if she stood for the leadership she would want to include pro-Europeans like Ken Clarke in her shadow cabinet. 'Lots of people would like me to run, but that doesn't mean I can just jump in. I've got to see how wide the support is.'

Chris Patten, another of Sir David Frost's guests, renewed his warning that unless the anti-Europeans moderated their stance Clarke could never be part of the Conservative mainstream. Europe was only sixth on the list of most voters' concerns but it had totally distorted the campaign and was in danger of finishing off the party. 'We must be a broad church, not a narrow sect, or the core vote just gets smaller and smaller.' The *Mail on Sunday* claimed that William Hague was going to give his backing to the party's defence spokesman, Iain Duncan Smith, who was emerging as the 'stop Portillo' candidate. Hague was said to think that a 'family man' like Duncan Smith, who was the father of four children, offered the best hope of widening the Conservatives' appeal. He was known for his tough stance on Europe and law and order, and could count on the support of Lord Tebbit, his predecessor as MP for Chingford. Both the *Mail on Sunday* and the *Sunday Telegraph* had photographs of Michael Portillo in an open-necked shirt visiting Roman ruins near Fez in northern Morocco, but he declined to answer questions about whether he was preparing for stand for the leadership. His closest ally in the shadow cabinet, the foreign affairs spokesman Francis Maude, confirmed on *The World This Weekend* that the shadow Chancellor, like Miss Widdecombe, was thinking through his position. 'There is no question of Michael dithering, he is just taking his time. We must now define what modern Conservatism is and he is giving thought about how we do this . . . The party will have to change. We can't duck this after two massive defeats.'

Appeals by Maude and Patten on behalf of Portillo and Clarke for a period of sober reflection were welcomed by Nick St Aubyn, who lost his seat in Guildford to the Liberal Democrats. St Aubyn gave several interviews explaining why the 'thousands of aspiring young professionals' who lived in his constituency and who were natural Conservatives had stayed at home: because, he said, the party sounded out of touch by not talking, or appearing to care, about hospitals and schools. 'The people of this country do want to talk about the euro when a referendum is called but they're not going to allow the timing of that debate to be dictated by the Conservatives.'

St Aubyn's disappointment was in sharp contrast to the success on the other side of London of Andrew Rosindell, who regained Romford in Essex on a swing of 9.2 per cent from Labour and who believed the Keep the Pound campaign was the foundation of his success. Rosindell's election leaflets promised he would 'always put Britain first' and he had attracted considerable local publicity because he frequently campaigned with his Staffordshire bull terrier Spike which wore a union flag on its waistcoat. Rosindell, like St Aubyn, was in great demand in the television and radio studios, and he was uncompromising in his defence of the Conservatives' campaign to stop Britain going 'further and further' into Europe. 'We fought on a true Conservative message and Chris Patten should look at what happened in Romford before he says we could be out of office for ever. If we had all done what we did in Romford, William Hague would be in Downing Street now.'

Another ardent Euro-sceptic, Bill Cash, spent much of the weekend telephoning journalists to remind them that he secured a 3 per cent swing to the Conservatives in his constituency of Stone in Staffordshire and increased his majority from 3,818 in 1997 to 6,036. When interviewed on GMTV's Sunday Programme he was adamant that the next Tory leader must have the will to renegotiate with the European Union and retrieve the government and democracy of Britain. 'What we have to say is "never" to the single currency and we must also have a full and proper referendum on our place in Europe. You must be clear about our democracy. We are being taken over by a European government and the people of Europe don't trust either their governments or their political elites.'

Monday 11 June

Tony Blair's reshuffle of his junior ministers proceeded at a fast and furious pace. I spent the day in Downing Street reporting the comings and goings for *Radio Five Live*, and interest quickened when the minister for sport, Kate Hoey, confirmed she had been telephoned by the Prime Minister and told she had been sacked. When we heard that Peter Hain had been appointed the new minister for Europe we knew that Keith Vaz must also have been dropped from the government. Another early visitor to No. 10 was the minister for transport, Lord Macdonald, who was going to continue working for the Deputy Prime Minister John Prescott and had been appointed minister for the Cabinet Office. When we saw three former ministers making their way up Downing Street, we began to realise that Blair's reorganisation of the middle and junior ranks was likely to contain as many surprises as his Cabinet reshuffle. The most unexpected comeback was by Harriet Harman, who was appointed the new Solicitor-General. She had been sacked from the government in July 1998 amid much criticism of her failure, as Secretary of State for Social Security, to deliver effective reform of the welfare system. Alun Michael, who resigned from his position as First Secretary in the Wales Office shortly before a vote of no confidence in the Welsh Assembly in February 2000, rejoined the government as minister of state for rural affairs. Jeff

Rooker, former minister of state for social security, who was given a peerage in the pre-election honours, returned to the government as a minister of state at the Home Office.

Blair was equally adventurous in providing openings for the next generation of ministers, and well over a dozen Labour MPs from the 1997 intake were found jobs. Stephen Twigg, whose defeat of Michael Portillo at Enfield Southgate had given him celebrity status, was appointed a parliamentary secretary and assigned to assist Robin Cook as Leader of the House. Douglas Alexander's work as general election co-ordinator under Gordon Brown at Millbank Tower was rewarded with a job at the Department of Trade and Industry, where he was made minister for e-commerce and competitiveness. Ben Bradshaw, Labour MP for Exeter and a former BBC reporter, was appointed parliamentary secretary at the Foreign and Commonwealth Office.

The need to keep pace with the changes meant it was half an hour before I was able to return a call to Chris Mullin, who had been junior minister at the Department for International Development and whose constituency Sunderland South was the first to declare on election night. He told me that he had decided to leave the government and I should believe the spin: his departure was at his own request. Mullin, a former chairman of the House of Commons Select Committee on Home Affairs, said he had come to the conclusion he would rather return to the task of conducting parliamentary scrutiny than continue in the lower ranks of government.

The last appointment of the day was the one *Radio Five Live* had been waiting for: Richard Caborn had been switched from minister for trade to minister for sport. 'It's the job I've always wanted!' he shouted across to me as he got back into his ministerial car on re-emerging through the No. 10 front door.

At the post-reshuffle briefing for lobby correspondents the chair was taken jointly by Godric Smith and Tom Kelly, who between them had taken over Alastair Campbell's job of speaking to journalists. We were told that a total of twenty-two ministers and whips had left the government, which created the space for 'a wide array of new talent'. One appointment we had not caught up with was that of Blair's political secretary, Sally Morgan, who had been given a peerage and made a minister of state at the Cabinet Office. Correspondents were given copies of the Prime Minister's letter to Keith Vaz thanking him for his work in the Lord Chancellor's department and at the Foreign Office. Although journalists were not shown Vaz's letter of resignation, Blair said he hoped the former minister would make a full recovery. 'You have been put under intolerable pressure recently, which can only have aggravated your illness. I hope you will now have the chance for a proper rest.' In order to strengthen the Prime Minister's office and its focus on delivering Labour's manifesto commitments, Blair had reorganised his own staff in No. 10. They would be divided into three clear groups: Jonathan Powell, the Downing Street chief of staff, would oversee work on government policy; Campbell would control communications and strategy; and Anji Hunter would head up the section responsible for relations between ministers and the devolved administrations, and would also maintain contact with the party.

Downing Street used the completion of the reshuffle to slip out the news that Blair and his colleagues were to take the full pay increases recommended by the senior salaries review board. A cabinet minister's annual salary was to increase from £99,793 to £117,979 and the Prime Minister's annual income would increase from £116,339 to £163,418. Godric Smith said ministers had not taken their full increases during Labour's first four years in government: Blair had waived 41 per cent of his salary and cabinet ministers 27 per cent.

Arriving hot-foot back at BBC Westminster with the complete list of ministerial appointments and details of the pay rises, I found that the bulletins were leading with the news that Michael Portillo had decided to run for the Tory leadership and would make his formal declaration on Wednesday. Most national newspapers published photographs of the shadow Chancellor enjoying his weekend break in Morocco. He was pictured sightseeing in Fez or relaxing at his hotel. The *Daily Mail*'s photo spread showed the 'pretender to the Tory throne' enjoying a concert by the American gospel group The Edwin Hawkins Singers, where he began 'gyrating his body and singing along enthusiastically to the group's hit "Oh, Happy Day!"' In an article on the leader page, headed 'Oh, please let the Tories be normal again', the paper's columnist, Stephen Glover, said there seemed to be something wounded about Portillo, as though having 'renounced long-held beliefs, he is no longer absolutely sure of who he is'. Lord Tebbit took up the *Daily Mail*'s theme in an interview for the *Ten O'Clock News*. He had never been convinced that the shadow Chancellor was 'an arch-Thatcherite right-winger'; and, when asked to give his own preference for party leader, he then alluded to other doubts which the Tory right harboured about Portillo: 'Well, we have got Iain Duncan Smith, a man who is remarkably normal. He is married with children. He is a very normal sort of chap and he has done something outside politics. He has had a career in the armed services.'

Tuesday 12 June

When broadcasters gathered at the London School of Economics for a debate on television and radio coverage of the general election, we knew we could not escape our share of responsibility for the dramatic fall in turnout. Television remains the most powerful medium through which politicians communicate to the electorate and therefore we could not avoid some soul-searching of our own. I felt none of the major parties could really complain about a lack of coverage because they were able to take advantage of a massive expansion in the output of the electronic news media. In addition to regular bulletins on the main channels, BBC *News 24* and ITN's rolling news service were both covering a general election for the first time, and they joined *Sky News* and *Radio Five Live* in providing 24-hour news coverage. Numerous websites on the internet offered unprecedented access and supplied another quantum leap in the amount of information which was available to the public.

The general consensus in the LSE debate was that the catastrophic fall in voter participation should probably be blamed on a variety of factors. From the beginning, the result was considered to be a foregone conclusion, and this was borne out during the four weeks leading up to polling day because there was no real movement in the opinion polls, which suggested the campaigns being waged by the main parties were not changing many minds. Low unemployment and falling interest rates generated a widespread sense of well-being, and voters did not feel threatened either by the prospect of radical change in economic policy or by a great ideological divide between the two main parties.

A growing sense of disenchantment with the political process was identified as a significant consideration, and much of the discussion focused on ideas for stimulating greater interest and participation. A televised debate among the three main party leaders was identified as the one innovation which might have caught the public's imagination and perhaps encouraged more people to vote. Labour's refusal to participate in the two one-hour debates proposed for the final fortnight of the campaign, when the Conservatives and Liberal Democrats had both given their agreement, was roundly condemned by three leading broadcasting executives: Mark Damazer, deputy director of BBC News, Richard Tait, editor-in-chief of ITN, and David Lloyd, head of news and current affairs at Channel Four. They all felt Labour lacked any credibility in arguing that as British television viewers could see Prime Minister's questions, there was no need for the kind of televised debates which were staged between presidential candidates in the USA. Lloyd hoped that Sam

Younger, chairman of the newly-established Electoral Commission, would help the broadcasters develop a common front in putting pressure on Labour ahead of the next election. Tait doubted whether the commission would be able to assist, because a sitting Prime Minister would always have the last word. Tony Blair's refusal to participate was considered to have been all the more disappointing because since Labour had turned down a similar invitation during the 1997 campaign, both BBC and ITV had agreed not to counter-schedule against each other's debates and the two channels would have been able to deliver a mass audience, something which Tait thought would be harder to promise in the future because of an expanding multi-channel environment.

Adam Boulton, political editor for *Sky News*, appealed to the broadcasting organisations to arrange non-branded debates among the party leaders which could be offered for use on all channels and which would counter fears about the fragmentation of the television audience. Boulton believed the growth in continuous news services was forcing the political parties to rethink the way they campaigned. 'Whistlestop tours by party leaders in their battle buses don't work any more because the twenty-four-hour news services are exposing what they're up to. If you get a party leader repeating the same message all day at twenty live locations around the country everyone can see they're being totally repetitive and that they've got nothing new to say.' Boulton claimed that Alastair Campbell agreed with him that a growing capacity for live television coverage would change the way Labour fought the next general election. 'For all Labour's criticism of television and radio, there was much less direct intimidation of broadcasters in this election than in 1997 and I think Campbell accepts that the political parties trust the role that broadcasters play in a way they don't trust the press.' I thought Boulton's prediction that the growth of continuous news services would alter the way the political parties campaigned was wrong because it took no account of the strength of regional broadcasting. Charles Kennedy had shown that the great merit of a leader's tour was that it allowed his party to target the areas he was visiting and arrange countless interviews with regional television channels and local radio stations.

Richard Tait and David Lloyd remained dubious about the audience potential of 24-hour news services and were confident the main news programmes would continue to attract mass viewing figures. During the election campaign the 10 p.m. bulletins on BBC and ITV regularly pulled in a combined audience of around nine million and *Channel Four News* had a million viewers, while audiences for the news channels were numbered in tens of thousands. Tait said that on election night 42 per cent of viewers were watching entertainment on television rather the live election coverage – just about the same proportion as the number of people who did not bother to vote. Mark Damazer said the BBC's election night programme had an audience of over eighteen million between 10 p.m. and 6 a.m. which was better than ITN's overnight audience of fourteen million. On *Sky News*, the election night audience rose to a million over a three-hour period. Boulton was not sure what to make of the Liberal Democrats' reaction to the growth in continuous news services: the party's director of communications, David Walter, had advised his press officers not to look at *Sky News* or *News 24* because 'that is not what real people are watching.' He was even more perplexed about the role performed by the Conservatives' head of media, Amanda Platell. 'The Conservatives really do need to look at the way they communicate with broadcasters rather than clone people New Labour have hired without understanding how the industry works ... If anyone has any idea what Amanda Platell did during the campaign I would be interested to know. The Conservatives' operation was incompetent and it let down people working hard at Central Office.'

I was not surprised to hear Boulton's gripe about Ms Platell's failure to develop an effective working relationship with leading broadcasters; it was difficult to find correspondents who had had much contact with her or been impressed by her management of the Conservatives' campaign. Most radio and television journalists dealt almost exclusively with the assistant head of media, Andrew Scadding, and complimented him on his perseverance and dedication. Once the election was over I found some newspaper correspondents were prepared to speak a little more openly about their contact with Central Office and the strategy it adopted. One criticism was that Ms Platell and the party's chief spokesman, Nick Wood, had developed a 'bunker mentality' and seemed interested only in giving right-wing stories to the *Daily Telegraph*, *Daily Mail* and *Mail on Sunday*. Their overall conclusion was that William Hague got the media campaign he wanted and that much of it was directed by Wood, who had considerable influence because of his long experience as a political correspondent on *The Times* and *Daily Express*. But journalists who did have contact with Ms Platell said she talked proudly of the way she, Wood and Hague's chief of staff, Seb Coe, jointly thrashed out the line to take in conjunction with the two leading policy strategists, Andrew Lansley and Tim Collins. Ms Platell was said to have called her group the 'closed door set' because they would close the office door and work out the media strategy themselves.

8   Exit Portillo – Again

Michael Portillo selected the newest location in Westminster to launch his bid for the Conservative leadership and to start the race to succeed William Hague. Standing on the granite paving slabs in front of the imposing entrance to Portcullis House on the Thames Embankment, he declared that he wanted to offer the party a 'thoughtful and moderate' future which got away from the 'yah-boo politics' of the past. His choice of backdrop, the bronze and stone cladding of the new office block for MPs, was a symbolic gesture, a conscious break from the flamboyant neo-Gothic architecture of the Palace of Westminster. Unfortunately, the noise of the traffic thundering across Westminster Bridge and along the Embankment was so loud that some of the journalists who were crowding around failed to catch what he was saying and had to wait until they heard his declaration on the radio or saw it on television.

In putting his name forward, Portillo was in no doubt about the challenge he faced: 'Our party has suffered two catastrophic results and the responsibility for those results is shared by all of us who have been at the top of the party. Unless the party makes major changes in its style, and in the issues on which it chooses to focus, there is a danger we will go further down in public respect.' The Conservatives needed to adopt a 'moderate and understanding' tone which showed that the people's concerns were their concerns; and they had to broaden their outlook. 'Our party has to appeal to the whole range of people who now live in the United Kingdom; to people of all ages; to people of both sexes; and to people whose family origin is outside Britain. The key challenge for us in the next four years will be to attract to the party the broadest range of talented people from that whole diversity of people who make up today's United Kingdom.' They had to develop a much better understanding of the problems facing education, health and transport; and if he became leader, his shadow cabinet would be bound together by 'a common purpose and a sense of collegiate spirit'. Even though a majority of Conservatives were against the euro, their strong conviction about the danger of joining the single currency would carry more weight if it were seen to come from a party that was internationalist and involved in 'friendly debate' with Britain's neighbours, a stance which would make 'life more comfortable' for their pro-European members and supporters.

The build-up to Portillo's launch had been well orchestrated and he commanded considerable support, having obtained the backing of eleven members of the eighteen-strong shadow cabinet. His campaign manager, the shadow Foreign Secretary Francis Maude, told *Radio Five Live* they needed a big figure to pull the party round. 'I have been talking to Michael since Friday, from the moment we woke up to our second defeat. We came to a mutual agreement on the way to proceed.' By being the first candidate to make a public declaration, Portillo hoped to build up the momentum he needed to tackle the various hurdles that lay ahead in the new and untested procedure for electing a leader. In one of the first internal reforms pushed through after Hague took over, Conservative MPs relinquished their right to decide the leadership and agreed to open up the contest to the party's 350,000 members. Only two names would go forward to a ballot which would start in mid-August and that shortlist would be arrived at by MPs by means of a series of primaries to be conducted in July. The process could not start until after Wednesday 27 June, when a new executive would be elected to the 1922 backbench committee which represented the 166 MPs in the parliamentary party.

Portillo's head start put other potential contenders at a disadvantage. Kenneth Clarke, who on Monday 11 June denied reports that he was about to reach some kind of pact with the shadow Chancellor, thought it would be at least a week before he decided whether to stand. Nor was there any word from another likely candidate, David Davis. However, Iain Duncan Smith gave the strongest possible hint on *Channel Four News* saying that he was 'listening to a lot of people'. He went further in an interview for the *Ten O'Clock News*, declaring that the party wanted a leader who had 'the steel to take them through difficult moments' and who could encourage the public to start saying about the Conservatives, 'Ah, they're back, there is some choice at last.' Duncan Smith told me afterwards that it was important to remember that the candidate who came second in the MPs' final primary still reached the ballot among the wider membership, and he did not feel disadvantaged by Portillo's early start. 'Once this goes out to party members, it's going to be a wholly different game. I can be more sanguine about this, like Ken Clarke, because being the fastest out of the trap doesn't necessarily make a difference. Firecrackers do have a habit of exploding at the top of their run.'

One potential contender who seemed to be on the point of ruling herself out was Ann Widdecombe. She indicated she might back Clarke, whom she regarded as 'a formidable and very significant' candidate. Miss Widdecombe was scathing in her criticism of Portillo. She was not expecting to serve in his shadow cabinet and would not do so if asked. 'I cannot, simply cannot, serve Michael Portillo. It is as simple as that. I simply could not go through another four years of the sort of destabilisation and backbiting that has gone on among our supporters.' Miss Widdecombe mentioned one incident involving a Portillo aide who was alleged to have been caught out attempting to smear Hague. She did not identify the aide by name but the shadow Chancellor's press officer Malcolm Gooderham was quoted by the *Mirror* early on in the election as having urged the paper to find photographs of Hague 'being ambushed by protestors in lookalike masks'. Gooderham told me at the time the story was untrue and that whole incident had been engineered by a Labour-supporting newspaper to damage the Conservatives.

'Everyone knew I had been set up by the *Mirror*.' Miss Widdecombe must have realised her outburst was damaging the party, because after launching her assault on the shadow Chancellor's 'little band of backbiters' in an interview on *Today* she moderated her attack as the day wore on, and by mid-afternoon had absolved Portillo of any personal responsibility for the behaviour of some of his supporters. She had been encouraged by his assurance that if he became leader he would be guided by elected members rather than his advisers.

With Portillo being supported by two-thirds of the shadow cabinet there was no shortage of senior MPs to tour the studios and speak up for the leading candidate. After being interviewed by *News 24* the Conservatives' agriculture spokesman, Tim Yeo, said the leadership contest would be decided in sitting rooms across Britain and the 'friendly face' of the shadow Chancellor would help him fight a campaign fit for the twenty-first century rather than harking back to the 1980s. Yeo was convinced that Duncan Smith would stand and get support from the right of the party. 'We are ready for him, of course. Ken Clarke is just dithering and his support is slipping away.' I agreed with Yeo's assessment that Portillo would find it easier than any of the other likely contenders to project a new image. I thought he was the candidate feared most by the New Labour modernisers because, just as Tony Blair had abandoned Old Labour, Portillo had already thrown off much of his Thatcherite past and was busily reinventing himself. His appeal to a multicultural Britain seemed well founded; but his move away from the traditional family structures held so dear by so many Conservatives was bound to cause him grief. Julian Brazier was the first Tory MP to speak his mind, in an interview for the *One O'Clock News*: 'I am concerned that Michael Portillo wants to go beyond tolerance. In his speeches outside Parliament he suggested we should treat all lifestyles the same. I feel the Conservative Party should be committed to marriage.'

Tuesday 19 June

After taking longer than Michael Portillo to organise their campaign teams, Iain Duncan Smith and David Davis announced their respective bids for the leadership, each declaring himself best equipped to steer the party on a path which would reconnect with the British people while remaining true to Conservative principles. Their separate launches followed the wounded retreat the day before of Ann Widdecombe, who took a posse of journalists to see a neglected housing estate at Hackney in east London. Once she had reminded them of the plight of the 'forgotten decents' who lived on run-down estates up and down the country, she confirmed that she had finally relinquished all hope of becoming only the second woman to lead her party. 'It is not due to any lack of will on my part or to any lack of encouragement from the voluntary party that I cannot embark on that candidature, but to a lack of support from parliamentary colleagues.' Miss Widdecombe said she had decided to return to the back benches rather than seek to continue serving in the shadow cabinet.

Duncan Smith and Davis reaffirmed their opposition to Britain joining the euro, and both gave a pledge to stop the issue of Europe blighting the party. Duncan Smith believed the mature way to manage their differences was to allow frontbenchers to serve on the understanding that if they disagreed with the party line they could temporarily stand down during a referendum and campaign for the single currency. At the next election he wanted the Conservatives to have more candidates who were women and from the ethnic minorities, and their ambition as a party should be to secure a transformation in public services.

Davis said he had no intention of making the majority view against joining the single currency a 'test of party loyalty', and Conservatives must respect the public's verdict, delivered at the election, that the euro was a unique issue which would ultimately be settled in a referendum. He urged the party to have the courage to look at radical solutions in the public services rather than follow Labour's approach of holding a Dutch auction of ever higher spending promises. 'Only when we begin to talk about these issues that matter to people, and offer the hope of genuine change, will we win back the trust of a lost generation of voters.'

Michael Portillo's bid for the leadership had been strengthened by an endorsement from John Major on *Breakfast with Frost* on Sunday 17 June. The broad political posture which Portillo was offering, said the former Prime Minister, was the ground from which the Conservatives could stage a comeback, and after losing his seat at Enfield Southgate and having a 'brush with the real world', the shadow Chancellor seemed to have pushed aside the old certainties and ideological bent of his earlier years in government. Major welcomed Portillo's conversion: 'Michael seems to have gone on a long journey from where he was to where I was and I thoroughly welcome that. I think it is a good idea to reinhabit the centre ground. And I think the things that Michael is saying are an indication that he has learnt that, learnt a lot . . . And I have no reason to believe that Michael is not sincere.'

When Major gave his interview, Iain Duncan Smith and David Davis had not yet declared themselves as candidates, but it was obvious they were about to run and the former Prime Minister thought this was a mistake. 'I personally hope that some of the marginal candidates, some of the more inexperienced candidates, will decide that this is not the time for them to throw their hats into the ring. They should sit out this election and let more senior members of the party contest it.' Major believed the changing nature of society was a factor both in the low turnout in the general election and in his party's second defeat. Conservatives had to show greater understanding of the way people wished to live their lives. 'People are much more tolerant than before and people expect government to serve their needs. Political parties are too bound up in their traditional thinking, so some good could come out of the defeat if we think from the bottom on social policy and the social agenda.'

Major's appeal for a radical rethink was in marked contrast to a forthright defence of the party's election tactics by the two leading strategists for the campaign, Andrew Lansley and Tim Collins. In a joint article published by the *Daily Telegraph* on Thursday 14 June they said some 'dangerous myths' about their strategy needed to be dispelled before the Conservatives headed off in 'completely the wrong direction'. Although a total of 166 seats was fewer than Labour's low-point of 209 in 1983, the Conservatives' share of the vote was better than Labour had managed in either 1983 or 1987. The euro remained a powerful issue for the Conservatives because there were not many other policies where the party was supported by over 70 per cent of the public. 'The Conservative Party faces a situation which is both more challenging and more optimistic than is commonly assumed. We cannot move forward simply by doing the opposite of whatever has been done in the last four years.'

Thursday 21 June

Michael Ancram's resignation as party chairman in order to enter the race for the leadership was a further indication of the strength of feeling which was building up against Michael Portillo, who appeared to have entrenched his position as the clear favourite. A groundswell against him had been evident for some days, and the more the shadow Chancellor talked of the need to embrace change, the louder grew the voices of those calling for the Conservatives to revisit their basic principles. Ancram was joined by his wife Jane and daughters Clare and Mary when he made his announcement in gardens beside the Thames on a glorious sunny afternoon. He wanted to offer the membership the chance to choose the path of unity, and he believed he could lead the party in a spirit of harmony and reconciliation. Ancram viewed with alarm the radical future which was being suggested and said it was time the Conservatives re-established in their hearts and minds who they were rather than trying to follow the 'fickle winds' of political fads and fashions. 'We don't need to invent a new Conservative Party. We must start by reminding ourselves and the British people what we really stand for. This is no time to seek to match spin with spin, stardust with stardust. It is no time to strike out against the grain of our party and its traditions.'

When Ancram warned of the dangers of chasing New Labour into a new and enticing political environment he did not need to name the candidate he was referring to, because Portillo had that very morning given a vivid demonstration of the glamorous and audacious approach which the old guard so abhorred. Journalists and supporters were served champagne, orange juice and coffee at the Avenue restaurant in St James's Street, which had been chosen by the shadow Chancellor as the venue for a breakfast briefing to launch his personal manifesto. He believed the party was in grave peril and needed to be rebuilt. Conservatives had to be passionate about public services, and the ultimate challenge was to translate the party's enduring principles into the age in which they found themselves. All he could offer MPs and party members were his failures, and particularly his failure to hold his seat in 1997. 'It did mean I was forced to re-enter the real world. We must be, the Conservative Party must be, a party of ideas. I would intend to initiate the greatest and the most dynamic policy debate the party has seen since 1975, and that policy debate will involve not only all of the shadow cabinet but all of the parliamentary party.'

Tuesday 26 June

Delaying his entry into the contest by two weeks did nothing to lessen Kenneth Clarke's defiance of mainstream Conservative opinion, and he launched his bid for the leadership by issuing an unashamedly pro-

European manifesto. He was uncompromising in his criticism of 'four wasted years' under William Hague and of the strategy which had led to the Tories' 'worst election result for at least a hundred years'. Winning power had to be put ahead of the party's divisions over Europe, and he believed he was best able to carry the fight against the government and win back voters lost to Labour and the Liberal Democrats. He had eighteen years experience in government reforming health, education and welfare, which were the areas the party needed to address if it was 'remotely serious about wanting to return to office again'. A more balanced position on Europe would free the party to address in depth the domestic and social agenda which the Conservatives had neglected throughout the last Parliament. 'The issue of Britain's relations with Europe has poisoned the internal politics of the party for a decade, destroying both John Major's and William Hague's leadership. If we are to win, this has to stop.' Clarke's intention if he became leader was to allow all Conservative MPs, including the shadow cabinet, a free vote and freedom in debate when considering the euro. He remained a 'conviction politician' and had no intention of hiding his views on the euro; he would campaign in a referendum for a 'yes' vote. 'I believe it will be in Britain's interests to join when the conditions arise, including a sensible exchange rate.' Clarke was taking a high-risk route in taking on his critics head-on over Europe and soon risked looking rather like a loner, losing the support of several leading pro-Europeans who feared he would find it impossible to unite the party. Stephen Dorrell, a Clarke supporter in the 1997 leadership contest, was among those switched to Michael Portillo because the shadow Chancellor was offering to lead a party in which the pro-Europeans could feel at home.

Once he had finished his news conference, Clarke enjoyed posing for photographers on the steps of the Institute of Directors in Pall Mall and then set off for a round of radio and television interviews. When reminded by Carolyn Quinn on *PM* that he had passed his sixtieth birthday the year before, he insisted that he would still be among the youngest Prime Ministers if he led the Conservatives to victory at the next election. 'There is more life and vigour and creative thinking in me than some of my colleagues.' In his interview on *Channel Four News* he was tackled by Jon Snow about his refusal to serve in a shadow cabinet formed by any of the other leadership contenders. After twenty-five years on the front bench he felt he would be bored shadowing a job he had done before. 'My enthusiasm for politics would best be served by not taking a post in the shadow cabinet.' In each of his interviews he insisted he was a 'social liberal', a phrase on which he was challenged by Jeremy Paxman on *Newsnight*. 'Yes, I am a social liberal on lifestyles and cultural diversity. I am talking about tolerance. I welcome diversity.' Clarke approved of the speech which Portillo gave at the 2000 party conference in which he said the Conservatives were 'for people whatever their sexual orientation', and he was on the shadow Chancellor's side over his complaints about homophobia.

Portillo himself had used an interview on *Breakfast with Frost* on Sunday 24 June to reassure his supporters they had no need to fear further disclosures about his private life. Shortly before being returning to Parliament in 1999 he acknowledged homosexual experiences in his youth, and when he was asked whether these had continued after his marriage in 1982, he insisted no more details would emerge either during or after the campaign. 'I've been completely straightforward about this and I don't think any politician has been as straightforward as I have been. And I've nothing to add to that.'

Thursday 12 July

Michael Ancram was eliminated after securing the backing of only seventeen MPs when a rerun of the opening round of voting in the

Conservatives' leadership ballot finally delivered a decisive result. At the first attempt, on Tuesday 10 July, there was a tie for last place between Ancram and David Davis, who each polled twenty-one votes. Sir Michael Spicer, the new chairman of the 1922 Committee of Conservative MPs, ordered the vote to be taken again because the eventuality of a tie for last place was not mentioned in the rules. 'They can't even agree who comes last' was the *Mirror*'s headline on a farce which had failed initially to eliminate a single candidate. The *Daily Telegraph* said the joke doing the rounds at Westminster was that the Tories had devised a voting procedure which 'could not even pick a loser, let alone a winner'. Mocking headlines provided some light relief in a leadership race which had turned into a brutal display of the feuding and hatred which had become deeply ingrained in the party. Promises to behave graciously towards one another had been shattered in rancorous back-biting among the supporters of the five candidates who had taken full advantage of the long lead-up to the first round of voting to vilify their opponents. After Sir Michael was elected chairman of the 1922 Committee on Wednesday 27 June, he set out the timetable for a series of ballots and agreed to allow an extra week's campaigning, a move which was viewed as a setback by Michael Portillo's team. He remained the front-runner among MPs and members of the shadow cabinet, but Iain Duncan Smith was gaining ground and the first opinion poll put Kenneth Clarke way out in front as the favourite in the country at large. A survey by MORI for *The Times* on Thursday 28 June showed that Clarke had the support of 29 per cent of party members and was preferred by 32 per cent of the public, comfortably ahead of Portillo's ratings of 25 per cent and 17 per cent.

The quickening pace of the contest did not deter Portillo from putting down fresh markers for the kind of Conservative Party he wanted to lead. He announced he would take a tough line against MPs who made racist remarks and said that if he had been leader he would have expelled John Townend, the former MP for Yorkshire East, who had lamented the extent of 'Commonwealth immigration' and suggested that the British people were in danger of becoming a 'mongrel race'. Townend's remarks, he said, had cost the party 'very dearly' in the general election, and years of 'arrogance and bigotry' had lost the Conservatives millions of votes.

Michael Ancram began another round of recriminations on *Breakfast with Frost* on Sunday 1 July when he accused Clarke of demeaning the efforts of party workers who had carried the Conservative standard at the last election and fought to save the pound. 'To talk blandly about four wasted years is a real insult.' Earlier in the programme, Clarke had accused the Tory right of trying to thwart his chances of being included on the final shortlist. 'The danger is that the party membership are going to be offered two right-wing candidates, which is wrong . . . Once I get to the membership at large I do have a chance of winning.' Newspapers had been casting doubt on the accuracy of the party's claim to have as many as 350,000 members and 300,000 was regarded by most correspondents as a more likely figure. Ancram refused to comment when Sir David Frost asked him to give an accurate age profile for the membership. Was the average age sixty-two, sixty-four or, as some reports had suggested, sixty-eight? The party chairman looked nonplussed and waited for the next question.

Any hint of abuse was, however, avoided when the five candidates appeared on a special edition of *Question Time* on Thursday 5 July and protested their innocence in respect of the back-biting being reported by the newspapers. Portillo denied he had been disloyal during the election: 'William knows I was completely loyal to him.' When Ancram was asked if he was aware of any backstabbing by Portillo during the campaign, he cleared the shadow Chancellor of any such complaint. 'No, I don't think he was guilty of that . . . I think this suggestion is very destructive to the process of choosing a leader.' Ancram was similarly firm in seeking to distance the candidates from Lord Tebbit's slight against Portillo on Monday 11 June for suggesting that Duncan Smith would be preferable as leader because he was married with children and 'remarkably normal'. Duncan Smith joined the party chairman in regretting what had been said: 'My qualifications don't depend on being a family man.' The main newsworthy point in the programme was the request that the five candidates give their opinion on legalising the sale of cannabis. Ancram, Clarke, Davis and Duncan Smith said they were against such a move; only Portillo put the case for considering whether the law should be changed. He believed the argument was finely balanced and he felt it was an issue on which the party should have a 'most stimulating' debate and be ready to welcome new thinking.

Next morning the confirmation that Portillo was keeping an open mind about the possibility of adopting a softer stance on the use of cannabis became headline news because of an article in the *Daily Telegraph* by Peter Lilley, a former deputy Conservative leader. He went much further than Portillo and called unambiguously for the sale of cannabis to be legalised, on the grounds that the continued criminalisation of its use was forcing the users of soft drugs into the arms of the pushers of hard drugs. Lilley proposed that licensing justices should be granted the power to 'give premises off-licences to sell retail amounts' of cannabis to persons over eighteen. On *Newsnight* that evening Lilley, who was a declared supporter of Portillo, admitted that his call for legalising cannabis had been timed purposely to coincide with the leadership contest because he knew it would require the candidates to give their response.

Competing for space on the news pages with the drugs story were the first reports of another potential setback for the Portillo campaign. 'Platell's video nasty' was the *Daily Mail*'s headline over an account of the dramatic departure from Conservative Central Office of the party's head of media, Amanda Platell. She left the building the previous day soon after telling William Hague that she had been secretly recording her thoughts about the conduct of the election campaign for a television documentary. Her account of what happened had been edited into a 45-minute programme, *Unspun: Amanda Platell's Secret Diary*, and was to be broadcast on Channel Four on Sunday 15 July. Both the *Daily Telegraph* and *Guardian* said Portillo's supporters feared Ms Platell would use her video diary to attack the shadow Chancellor, of whom she was a known adversary.

Ms Platell denied that her video diary amounted to 'a hatchet job' and said in a press statement that it was intended to reflect her admiration for the way William Hague had conducted the campaign. 'So much was being written about the election and it was all secondhand. I wanted to set the record straight and tell it as it really was – it charts all the highs and lows of the day – and tells the story of William's courageous, almost heroic, battle against the odds.' She had recorded her daily insight into the month-long campaign on returning each night to her room in a Knightsbridge hotel, talking directly to a camera operated by her friend Zad Rogers, the son of the architect and Labour peer Lord Rogers of Riverside and managing director of Ideal World, an independent television company. Once it leaked out that she had recorded her account of each day's campaigning without informing Hague or any of her colleagues at Central Office, she had no alternative but to quit immediately, two months earlier than she had previously planned. Speculation about the contents of the video diary provided a fresh twist to the leadership story for the newspapers on Sunday 8 July, two days ahead of the first run-off in the leadership contest. In an interview for the *Observer*, Zad Rogers said Ms Platell called him at all hours of the night and he would cycle over to her hotel. 'I would ask what had happened during the day and what had pissed her off, and she would answer.' Although the contents of the programme were still secret, the *Observer*'s political editor, Kamal Ahmed, said he understood she had been critical of leading figures in the party who had not been 'pulling their weight'.

Portillo's supporters accused her of a breach of trust. Nicholas Soames said her conduct had been outrageous. 'It amounts to a grotesque betrayal to do this behind William Hague's back during the election campaign.' Francis Maude told *The Westminster Hour* that the extent to which Ms Platell was willing to betray the trust and confidence of a party leader confirmed his suspicion that she was responsible for damaging his own reputation and that of the shadow Chancellor. 'We know she has been treacherous to Michael and myself. We have been reading poisonous stuff about ourselves in the newspapers for the last eighteen months. I have no reason to believe it comes from any other source . . . William Hague does not believe we have been disloyal. It is complete rubbish and this illustrates that Amanda Platell was a thoroughly untrustworthy person and not fit to hold high office.' Another senior Conservative who felt his suspicions had been vindicated was Lord Taylor, who had criticised Hague for allowing Ms Platell to keep her job after the publication of her first novel, *Scandal*, which he considered pornographic. 'I told William at the time she was the wrong woman for the job . . . She was always going to use the situation for her own ends and with this television documentary of hers, how right I have been proved. It's nonsense to say she's done it for William. It's all about Amanda Platell and what she can get out of it.'

When the first round of voting finally took place on Tuesday 10 July, almost a month after Portillo declared he was standing, he remained the front-runner and there were predictions he could be supported by as many as fifty of the 166 Conservative MPs. Much of the interest focused on the likely level of support for Clarke and Duncan Smith, as this would indicate which of them was most likely to join the shadow Chancellor on the final shortlist. Sir Michael Spicer announced the result: Portillo obtained forty-nine votes; Duncan Smith thirty-nine; Clarke thirty-six; and Ancram and Davis each had twenty one votes. The result contained a number of surprises: Portillo's lead was not as strong as suggested; Clarke and Duncan Smith had done better than expected; and the forty-two votes split between Ancram and Davis showed there was plenty to play for once they had been eliminated. However, because there had been a tie for last place, Sir Michael ordered that a rerun should take place two days later on Thursday 12 July, triggering a hectic round of arm-twisting by the various campaign teams.

Most newspapers concluded that the result of the first round was a setback for the shadow Chancellor. The *Daily Mail*'s coverage was perhaps the most ominous for him, because it highlighted growing opposition to another aspect of the liberalising approach he had adopted. Portillo had confirmed that he favoured a review of the Conservative Party's continuing support for Section 28 of the 1986 Local Government Act, which banned schools and local authorities from promoting homosexuality. 'Does Mr Touchy-Feely believe in anything?' asked the *Mail*'s columnist Stephen Glover, who said forty-nine votes out of 166 hardly represented a triumph. 'Portillo has got to the point of out-parodying himself. To talk now about cannabis and Section 28 shows such a warped sense of priorities one wonders whether he has quite literally taken leave of his senses.' The hostility being shown to Portillo by a Conservative newspaper alarmed his campaign team, and the shadow Chancellor used an interview on *Today* to try to lessen the impact of the *Mail*'s coverage. He said his backing for a review of the law on cannabis and the Conservatives' stance on Section 28 did not form a central part of his campaign. They were issues on which he had made his position clear but were not matters he had sought to raise.

As his supporters had feared all along, the result of the rerun of the first ballot was hardly any more encouraging. The result showed that there had been some movement in the way the 166 MPs were voting, and Portillo's two closest rivals had gained most ground. Portillo received fifty votes; Duncan Smith forty-two; Clarke thirty-nine; Davis eighteen; and Ancram seventeen. Six of the seven votes which had been lost by Davis and Ancram had been shared equally between Duncan Smith and Clarke, and the seventeen votes freed up by Ancram's elimination as last-placed candidate offered plenty of scope for a fresh round of arm-twisting in the four days that were to elapse before the next ballot on Tuesday 17 July.

Portillo's campaign team knew they faced a difficult weekend: some of the newspapers were thought likely to print more stories hostile to the shadow Chancellor, and they also had to brace themselves for some potentially damaging revelations in Amanda Platell's video diary, scheduled for broadcast at prime time on Sunday evening.

Sunday 15 July

If political journalists harboured doubts about Amanda Platell's ability to run the Conservatives' media department during the general election campaign, they certainly could not question her talent for self-promotion. Alastair Campbell and Charlie Whelan, two of Labour's most calculated self-publicists, had both been similarly self-indulgent in allowing themselves to become the focus of television documentaries; but Ms Platell had upstaged them both by having herself filmed in secret and then arranging for her programme to be broadcast at a critical moment in the history of her political paymasters. If the advance publicity was to be believed, *Unspun: Amanda Platell's Secret Diary* was about to play a pivotal role in the outcome of a leadership contest which had plunged the Conservative Party into another round of vengeful bloodletting. From the moment she made her dramatic exit from Central Office on Thursday 5 July, Ms Platell's video diary was hot property. She had excited political journalists because she was offering a tantalising storyline: not only was her insider account of the 'highs and lows' of William Hague's defeat of great interest in itself, but it could contain some killer facts about the conduct of Michael Portillo, whose faltering bid to replace him was the top political story of the day.

Zad Rogers, whose idea it had been to film her daily diary and turn it into a documentary, wrote a trailer for his programme in the *Guardian* in which he described the double life which had been led by the Conservatives' head of media. He said she was 'smart enough' to realise the potential news value of 'stripping politics of its false mystique' by revealing how politicians were managing and manipulating the media. She had imposed tight conditions from the start: only Rogers would be allowed to do the filming each night, in her 'very modest' hotel room; no other broadcaster or television crew could be involved; and she would keep the tapes and retain all rights over their use. She 'fervently believed' in Hague and his policies, and although by week two of the campaign the Tory party's 'initial elation had given way to the realisation that no one was listening . . . Amanda remained amazingly upbeat.' Rogers said that by week three it became clear that some in the party were preparing for life after the defeat. 'Amanda is a romantic. She wanted to fight the fight; she couldn't stand the idea of disloyalty. One day she simply broke down in tears.'

Another flattering preview of the programme was written for the *Daily Telegraph* by the political columnist Peter Oborne, who worked for Ms Platell when she edited the *Sunday Express*. He said she was a 'good tabloid editor' who recruited some 'brilliant' staff, and he believed she had been just as effective in running the media department at Conservative Central Office. 'She can take some credit for mending relations with the *Sun*, which had gone disastrously wrong, and for making the broadcasting operation more professional.' Oborne's most significant insight was that Hague was 'more relaxed' about her 'confessional' than appeared to be the case, and was not unhappy that 'Portillo's duplicity' was about to be exposed. 'One admirer who knows her very well says that "Amanda had two motives for doing it. First, she wanted to show that William Hague was fighting with one hand tied behind his back because of Michael Portillo, and what he was up to. Second she is eager to build up a career for herself as a television star and a big name columnist." She will probably succeed.'

Enticing previews of Ms Platell's programme were eclipsed in tactical terms by another far more serious setback for Portillo. The day after Michael Ancram's elimination from the contest, David Davis withdrew and advised his supporters to back Iain Duncan Smith. If, as seemed highly likely, most of his eighteen votes went the way he suggested, Duncan Smith had every chance of topping the poll on Tuesday 17 July. Portillo had to prepare for the worst, and he told *Today* on Saturday 14 July that he accepted Duncan Smith would definitely qualify for a place on the shortlist and realised he had a fight on his hands with Kenneth Clarke over who would finish second. Being the favourite had always been a difficult position, but he was no longer the front-runner and it was going to be 'a matter of chance' which of them joined Duncan Smith on the ballot paper for the vote by the membership. Although his prospects of becoming leader had taken a severe knock, Portillo believed he had maintained an honourable position in setting out the 'enormous' policy shift which would be needed if the Conservatives were to return to the middle ground of politics. 'I would not have wished to win this election unless people believed that in many respects the party needed to change and that I must have a mandate for change.'

Portillo acknowledged that Ms Platell's video diary would do him no favours. 'From what I know of all this, I am pretty sure this is going to be a pretty spiteful effort . . . If there were an accurate account of this election campaign, that account would be one of how I supported William Hague every day. Not only politically and not only up to the hilt, but how I supported him emotionally. Of how every day, although he was very, very robust and very, very strong, how every day I was there encouraging him, saying: "Go on, one more try today, more effort, be cheerful, go out there, make the most of this, enjoy the election."' Portillo's defence of himself, and his reflective assessment of his own prospects, had little effect on the headlines in the Sunday newspapers. 'How the assassin in stilettos put the knife into Portillo' was the headline over Kamal Ahmed's report in the *Observer* predicting how Ms Platell's diary could 'end her greatest enemy's career'. She wrote her own account of her experiences for the *Mail on Sunday* and claimed the disloyalty shown by people around Portillo amounted to 'treachery'. When she was asked on *Breakfast with Frost* to substantiate this she declined and instead urged viewers to watch her programme. 'Anyone who knows me knows that I've been fiercely loyal to William Hague and to the Conservative Party and I'll go on being loyal to them . . . that loyalty was the secret weapon of the Conservative Party. I'm afraid in the last two and a half years I've discovered that they have lost that weapon.'

In terms of its dramatic impact I found Miss Platell's programme arresting and compelling, because of the way she had been framed by Zad Rogers looking straight to camera, giving viewers the impression they were watching her through a peephole as she sat in her small hotel room, often with her three-legged cat Ronnie on her lap, delivering a nightly account of life at Central Office. To begin with her diary entries were upbeat, reflecting the early advances in the Conservatives' campaign; then her mood slowly changed, becoming increasingly downcast, as the opinion polls continued to show that Hague was going to be heavily defeated. She revealed that she had been responsible for advising the party's Treasury spokesman Oliver Letwin on how he should extricate himself from the confusion which he had created on Monday 14 May by suggesting in an off-the-record interview for the *Financial Times* that the Conservatives aspired to make tax cuts of not just £8 billion but £20 billion. Letwin was ordered by Central Office not to speak for two days, giving Labour the opportunity to exploit the situation by putting up 'Wanted!' posters and hiring bloodhounds to sniff round Smith Square. Ms Platell did not refer to the tactical mistake made by the party in not coming clean about who was responsible for the story straight away, but she acknowledged that it was difficult to know what to do when something jeopardised the whole campaign – and she was precise about her own role when Letwin finally confirmed his involvement on Wednesday 16 May: 'I briefed him on what he should say.'

Her diary entries for the final week seemed to indicate that she was spending most of the day gossiping on the telephone to a small group of friendly newspaper journalists who were feeding her information about what was being said by various unidentified aides of Michael Portillo and Francis Maude. Although she gave her own commentary on various news conferences, speeches and publicity launches, she did not imply that there was much of a connection among these events or that she was pursuing an overall media policy which she had mapped out in advance. Her lack of any assessment of the direction of the campaign or her own effectiveness as head of media confirmed my conclusion, reached early on in the election, that she did not have much understanding of, or interest in, how it might be possible to influence or change the course of the news coverage which Hague was getting. In her diary entries recounting conversations with journalists she did not once refer to having spoken to a broadcaster; yet output on television and radio was of vital importance to the party, and the absence of any apparent feedback from the electronic media highlighted her limitations.

Many of the stories about alleged backbiting involving Portillo, Maude and Hague appeared in tabloid newspapers. Although they were occasionally picked up in newspaper reviews or discussed in current affairs programmes, they were rarely covered in the mainstream news bulletins, which tended to stick closely to the big political events of the day. Unsourced stories about infighting between politicians are difficult to report on television and radio, particularly during an election campaign, when we have a responsibility to maintain fair and balanced coverage. Second-hand information which few broadcasters would have relied on or dared to use became the main component of Ms Platell's account of the closing stages of the campaign. Initially she made only passing references to Portillo. On one occasion he ended up being filmed in front of a van carrying a Labour poster; then, much to her irritation, he kept getting in the way during a combined photo-call for William and Ffion Hague and John and Norma Major. Television pictures were used to illustrate her diary entry explaining how Portillo kept sidling up to the Hagues and Majors on a flight of stairs, and she mimicked what she thought he was thinking: 'Michael had a bit of a bad hair day . . . that should be "h-e-i-r" as in heir to the throne . . . There was this photo-op and there was this guy at the back bobbing in, trying to get into all the photos, and the photographers were saying "Portillo, get out" . . . "Hi, do I look good in this? Does my quiff look big in this?"'

One of Ms Platell's most revealing disclosures was her account of the panic inside Central Office over Lady Thatcher's interview in the *Daily Mail* on Monday 21 May, when she said she wanted Britain to be 'a society of opportunity' and not 'a multicultural society'. Hague was due to appear with Lady Thatcher at a rally in Plymouth the next day, and Central Office wanted to establish 'a form of words' to respond in case he was challenged by reporters. 'Michael Portillo said he thought that William should stand on the platform and say, "I don't agree with what she says . . . Thank you Margaret, I just don't agree" . . . Then I think we would have had the end of the 2001 Conservative campaign. Yes, today I felt was meltdown.'

Her diary entries for the final seven days of the campaign concentrated on the behind-the-scenes briefings which she claimed were being given to newspaper journalists by aides and supporters of Portillo and Maude. 'You begin to find out the people who are really behind you in what you are doing . . . the ones who start saying "I have to be supportive up front, but I never agreed with us going hard on the euro" . . . The only people I've been told about, that I have been called up about from my sources and contacts, is that Francis is doing it and Michael's people are doing it.'

Ms Platell said certain journalists 'owed' her a favour and kept her informed. 'There are a few people out there who want to make sure I am looked after and they will phone me and say "I got a call last night from Francis Maude and he was saying that the strategy is wrong" . . . or they will say "I got a phone call last night from Portillo's people saying that Hague is wrong and we should be campaigning on public services but we don't want to rock the boat."' Ms Platell's entry for Monday 4 June suggested that Portillo was positioning himself to challenge Hague once the election was over. 'I am getting endless calls from people saying, "I have just had a phone call from Portillo's people who have given me all their mobile numbers for polling night." . . . I suppose I still find it slightly shocking that we are fighting so hard at the moment and to find all they're concentrating on is how they will pull it down . . . yes, that is a bit shocking.'

What struck me when Ms Platell referred to her 'sources' and 'contacts' was that she appeared to have been actively enquiring about the activities of Portillo and Maude, suggesting that the acquisition of such information was probably of help in strengthening her own position with Hague. All political correspondents were having to prepare themselves for the possibility of a leadership contest, should the Conservatives be defeated, and it was obvious that newsrooms would have to plan for such an eventuality. Stories about Tory splits had been a staple component of the news agenda since the final years of Lady Thatcher's government, and yet at no point in her diary did Ms Platell suggest she had given any thought as to how the party might try to counter this with alternative media strategies. She also seemed to be unaware, or unconcerned, about another factor in the equation: namely, that the media staff at Millbank Tower were doing all they could to feed the storyline that Hague was being undermined by Portillo and Maude, and that the journalists who were ringing Ms Platell because they owed her a favour would have been making precisely the same calls to their Labour contacts. Every time Ms Platell spoke to a journalist and acknowledged a possible leadership crisis she was helping to feed the very storyline which Labour was trying to promote.

Portillo's woes in the wake of the damage inflicted by the Channel Four programme only compounded those occasioned by another botched attempt to boost his flagging fortunes. 'Thatcher says Portillo is the right leader' was the *Sunday Telegraph*'s front-page headline over a report claiming that the paper had 'learnt authoritatively' from a member of the former Prime Minister's inner coterie that she was supporting his campaign and thought he was a stronger candidate than Iain Duncan Smith. The source was quoted as giving what was supposed to be Lady Thatcher's endorsement: 'I don't think Iain's got sufficient experience. Michael is the best candidate. He's the man with the charisma, the cabinet level experience, and he was very loyal to me.' But when the story broke late on Saturday evening, the former Prime Minister issued a statement through the Press Association denying that she had intervened in the contest: 'I do not want to make any comments about any of the candidates. I like all three. It is for the party to make their decision.' In a second highly unusual public pronouncement, issued mid-morning, she branded the report untrue and implied she was giving her backing to Iain Duncan Smith. 'The story is plain wrong. I do not hold the views which it attributes to me and I am not backing Michael Portillo against Iain Duncan Smith.'

Lady Thatcher's forthright denunciation was a significant boost to the burgeoning 'Stop Portillo' campaign and was greeted with delight by Duncan Smith's supporters. David Davis said Lady Thatcher's reaction spoke for itself and he was confident the shadow Chancellor would get none of his eighteen votes nor any of the seventeen which had gone to Michael Ancram. Sir Teddy Taylor, another Duncan Smith supporter, described the *Sunday Telegraph*'s story as a 'shameful attempt' to influence votes. 'Lady Thatcher is saying it is a fabrication . . . It is the most shameful thing I have seen in the contest.'

Tuesday 17 July

Michael Portillo's elimination by one vote from the race to become the new leader of the Conservative Party was eclipsed by an astonishing about-turn in the fortunes of Kenneth Clarke, who went from last place to first to win the MPs' ballot. Political journalists were as surprised as everyone else in the Westminster village by so sensational an end to a contest which had rekindled long-standing animosities in a much reduced parliamentary party. Portillo's bid to succeed William Hague had been faltering for some days as support grew for Iain Duncan Smith, but Clarke's success in pulling ahead of both of them meant the former Tory Chancellor, who had spent the previous four years languishing on the back benches, was well placed to pull off a remarkable political comeback when the party's 300,000 members had their chance to start voting in mid-August.

The third-round score line confirmed Portillo's failure, despite having started out as the favourite, to make any real headway during the latter stages of the contest. His final vote of fifty-three was only three more than he secured in the second round, when he had added just one vote to his initial tally of forty-nine. Duncan Smith gained twelve extra votes on his second round total of forty-two to finish on fifty-four; Clarke, who took twenty of the votes which had previously gone to David Davis and Michael Ancram, finished well in front on fifty-nine votes.

Once Sir Michael Spicer had announced the result at 5.23 p.m. in a House of Commons committee room the action moved across the road to College Green, where the candidates and their supporters had to shelter under umbrellas as they gave their reaction to the television and radio programmes which were providing live coverage of the declaration. Clarke emerged through St Stephen's entrance with a broad grin on his face and his arms raised like a boxer who has just won a bout with a knockout punch. As the rain got heavier he donned a trilby hat and a Barbour jacket which he kept for birdwatching. Clarke savoured every moment of his triumph as he went from interview to interview expressing surprise at having come first, saying he was convinced he had drawn support from across a wide range of the 166 Conservative MPs. 'The party is held together by above all a desire to win elections and the desire to replace the Blair government, which is a fairly lightweight, unsuccessful administration.' Portillo, sheltering under a large dark blue umbrella, told the waiting journalists that he intended to give up front-line politics. 'Now has come the time for me to look for other things to do. I don't intend ever again to seek office on the Conservative front bench. I really don't think it is an option for me to serve in a shadow administration. Apart from anything else, if I was in somebody's shadow cabinet there are so many people to make trouble I would just get in the way of Ken or Iain and make their life more complicated . . . I don't intend to be on the front bench ever again and, for the avoidance of doubt, I am not interested in the leadership . . . It was perfectly clear from the scores I was getting from the earliest rounds onwards that I was not going to have the sort of mandate that was going to be necessary for me to make the sort of change that I thought was needed. I think it would have been a miserable prospect to have scraped in by a vote or two and then try to do what I thought had to be done without a really vigorous and definitive mandate from the party . . . My main interests now are in the arts, media and perhaps some business.'

Duncan Smith was delighted to have finished in second place and 'relieved and pleased' to be going forward to the one member one vote ballot of the party membership. 'I am getting a lot of warm responses and a lot of local associations writing to me to urge me to keep going, so it is all to play for.'

Portillo's dejected supporters, who included a majority of the shadow cabinet, still believed he was the most capable of the three candidates and would have gone furthest in modernising the party and making it more inclusive by abandoning the right-wing stance which William Hague had adopted. His elimination was blamed on the damaging publicity which resulted from his support for reviewing both the law on cannabis and the Conservatives' continuing support for the Section 28 ban on the promotion of homosexuality in schools. Andrew Mackay, one of Portillo's campaign managers, thought some of the MPs who might have voted for the shadow Chancellor were put off by fears that he would continue to be dogged by the controversies which his message of 'adapt or die' had attracted. There was no suggestion that his campaign team tried to persuade him to continue on the Conservative front bench, and the word was that he was privately 'relieved' to have lost because he had been upset by the renewed criticism of his having admitted to homosexual experiences in his youth and by the unpleasantness of Lord Tebbit's pointed remarks about Duncan Smith being 'remarkably normal' and married with children.

Alan Duncan told *Channel Four News* he thought Portillo's defeat was a tragedy because although what he said about social policy frightened the party, the social agenda was influencing people's voting intentions more than ever before. 'At the end of the day there was an aura of suspicion behind Michael and that was why enough MPs didn't want to take a risk and vote for him . . . He is a good man, he is a capable man. But he gives a lot of people the shivers.' Another Portillo backer, Nicholas Soames, feared a contest between Clarke and Duncan Smith would polarise the split in the party over Europe and be a recipe for disaster. He told *Newsnight* the outlook was not good. 'The only candidate who could have unified the party is Michael and it is a tragedy he is no longer taking part. In the last three days of the campaign there was an astonishing attempt to derail him. It was a nauseating campaign by the *Daily Mail* and *Sun* but Portillo fought a principled and honest campaign.'

In a statement issued to his supporters after being declared winner of the MPs' ballot, Clarke urged Portillo to think again about letting one vote drive him out of politics. 'We are going to need Michael in govern-

336 • *Campaign 2001*

ment, so if he is feeling a bit crushed at the moment – and I understand that – I hope he gets a good rest, goes away and comes back refreshed having rethought his decision.' Clarke gave an assurance that he would not spend the summer arguing about Europe. 'I hold my own firm opinions and I respect those who stick to their own opinions.'

As for Duncan Smith, while he promised to continue carrying the banner for opponents of British membership of the euro, he said there were many things which Conservatives shared in common and he was sure they could unite as a party despite being divided on Europe. He hoped a leader would emerge in September who had 'honesty and integrity', and he appealed to the supporters of the two camps to run a campaign which avoided personalities. 'Keep it clean. Keep it on the issues and unite round whoever is leader at the end. Ken knows that if he was to win I would back him, and he has told me that if I won he would do the same.'

Sunday 22 July

To meet my publisher's deadline I had to finish my diary in late July, just as Conservative Central Office was making final preparations for its first-ever ballot by one member one vote to elect a new party leader. I chose for my final entry a day which brought home to me the true magnitude of the challenge facing William Hague's successor. Having spent eight and a half years running the Labour Party, eight and a half years which ended in his failure to make it into government, Neil Kinnock could speak with greater authority than any other politician of his generation about the awesome task of trying to gather together a dispirited and recalcitrant party to take on a powerful government. In an interview for *Broadcasting House*, Kinnock reflected on the gruelling time he spent in the 1980s rebuilding Labour when he was up against the dominance of

Margaret Thatcher's administration. He believed the mission to be undertaken by Kenneth Clarke or Iain Duncan Smith was far more daunting than his own because the Conservative Party had fallen into a much deeper pit than the one from which Labour had had to climb after its 1983 defeat. He agreed that there were many similarities between the current plight of the Tories and the civil war between the left and the right of the Labour Party which had led to the formation of the break-away Social Democratic Party, but he thought the Tories' ideological split over Europe was far graver than anything he had had to tackle and that the animosity between the leading personalities was visceral by comparison.

Having followed Kinnock's fortunes from the moment the big trade unions moved to support him after Michael Foot lost in 1983, through to his own wounded retreat after the 1992 election, I thought his reflections were a timely reminder of the immense burden to be taken on by either Clarke or Duncan Smith once the Conservatives announced the result of their ballot on Wednesday 12 September, just a month before the start of the party's 2001 annual conference. Kinnock began his long and weary journey as leader of the opposition in a far more commanding position within his party than Hague's replacement seemed likely to enjoy within his. In the 1983 Labour leadership election he topped every section of the party's electoral college, beating Roy Hattersley by a margin of almost four to one and leaving the two other candidates, Eric Heffer and Peter Shore, trailing in his wake. Moreover, although Kinnock commanded the support of only half his parliamentary party, he had the overwhelming backing of the union and constituency sections, and his authority over the party could not be questioned. His real power lay in the loyalty he was shown by the leaders of the biggest unions, who provided the money he needed to rebuild the party and who delivered the votes he needed at party conference to keep the left at bay. His tactical strengths were tested often and severely – almost to destruction – during the struggles he faced when jettisoning dearly held policies or rooting out hard left infiltration by groups like the Militant Tendency. Abandoning support for the closed shop, after all the setbacks which the unions had faced during the major industrial disputes of the Thatcher years, was another traumatic episode which he had to be endured.

One of the toughest personal U-turns which Kinnock accomplished came in the mid-1980s when he dropped his commitment to unilateral disarmament and backed the use of nuclear weapons. I remember the guidance we were given at the time by Peter Mandelson, then Labour's director of communications, who told us that Kinnock had finally gone the last lap and promised that if he became Prime Minister he was ready to press the nuclear button. Mandelson briefed journalists after emerging from a party meeting in Transport House where Kinnock had outlined the latest shift in his position during a discussion on the reshaping of Labour's defence policy. I had been reminded of the depth of Labour's split on nuclear disarmament when returning to Bevin Hall, in the renamed Local Government House, to attend the Liberal Democrats' election news conferences. Charles Kennedy's much strengthened position was another factor which could not be ignored in any assessment of the future prospects of a newly elected Conservative leader. The total of fifty-two seats won by the Liberal Democrats was well over twice what the Liberal and Social Democratic Alliance had achieved at the height of their success in the 1983 and 1987 elections, and it left Kennedy better placed than any previous Liberal Democrat leader to open up a new chapter in third party politics. Unlike his predecessor Paddy Ashdown, Kennedy rarely overstated his potential influence in the House of Commons, and when reflecting on his party's success for *The Westminster Hour* on Sunday 8 July he said the 2001 election had proved to be a watershed in one important respect. He had gone through the entire campaign without once being asked by a journalist whether people thought voting Liberal Democrat was a wasted vote. 'I think that was a real achievement, but it's another question entirely to ask whether we can replace the Conservatives as the main opposition party. What we do know is that the Tories will be off the field of play for a considerable time.'

The final run-off between Clarke and Duncan Smith presented the Tory membership with the starkest possible choice. They had either to opt for Clarke, a devout pro-European, in the knowledge they might have to execute a huge U-turn and abandon their opposition to the euro, or alternatively to back Duncan Smith's Euro-scepticism and maintain a Thatcherite outlook. The day after he came top in the MPs' ballot, Clarke held a news conference to launch his national campaign and issued an uncompromising warning about the danger of allowing the contest to become a battle between the pro-euro and anti-euro wings of the party. 'We have wrecked our party over Europe in the last ten years and headbangers on either side will wreck it again if we allow them to. I don't accept that the campaign need be divisive. With a few exceptions, most people out there in the party at large are going to agree that Europe has got to be resolved, calmed down and put in perspective.'

Duncan Smith spent the first day of his campaign embarking on a tour of constituency parties, beginning at Romford in Essex where the fervent Euro-sceptic Andrew Rosindell had taken the seat from Labour with the election's biggest swing to the Conservatives. He repeated his promise to refrain from personal attacks during the leadership campaign and, although he was sure they would remain 'good friends', he disagreed with Clarke's suggestion that the contest might be dominated by Europe. Under his leadership, Conservative MPs who wanted to campaign for the euro would be allowed 'utter tolerance' and his aim was to 'park' the whole question of the single currency and talk about matters like health and education. 'I don't think the issue is about headbangers turning this contest into a referendum on the euro.'

When asked to give his assessment of the opening skirmishes in the run-up to the Conservatives' ballot, Neil Kinnock said he doubted whether the Conservatives were ready to call a truce on their ideological split over Europe; nor did he think they had any real understanding of the loyalty and unity which would be needed to mount a sustained fightback against Labour. 'I am sure whoever becomes leader would love to be able to think that after a few months it would be possible with one speech to cauterise the wounds in the Conservative Party. But it'll never be done in one single dramatic blow because it's going to be a very long, arduous and completely unrewarding passage of years and the leader has to take the enemy citadels street by street.' Kinnock felt that Clarke had gone some way towards recognising the problem by talking about 'headbangers' having inflicted appalling damage on the Tory party, and he agreed the former Chancellor probably stood a chance of turning the party round. However, it would take a decade for the Conservatives to come together again – which meant Clarke would be too old to continue standing for election as Prime Minister; and if Duncan Smith won the leadership, he would be unlikely to outlast the next general election. Kinnock paused for a moment before delivering the abiding lesson of the 2001 election: 'You know, the electorate do punish you if you don't change, and I think the Conservatives will demonstrate at the next general election that they haven't learned a damn thing from the last four years.'